A WILD LIFE

Adventures of an Accidental
Conservationist in Africa

DICK PITMAN

summer

A WILD LIFE

Summersdale Publishers Ltd
46 West Street
Chichester
West Sussex
PO19 1RP
UK

www.summersdale.com

Printed and bound in Great Britain

ISBN: 1-84024-571-9
ISBN 13: 978-1-84024-571-4

About the Author

Dick Pitman was born in Kent and, after emigrating to Rhodesia (later Zimbabwe), worked variously as a magazine editor, national parks officer and wildlife guide before becoming founder-chairman and then director of the Zambezi Society, an NGO working on conservation issues. He has written three books on Zimbabwe and has published feature articles in magazines in the UK and USA such as *BBC Wildlife*, *Washington Post Magazine*, *International Wildlife*, *Yachting Monthly* and *Pilot Magazine*.

Contents

ACKNOWLEDGMENTS

Wildlife and wilderness may be the subject of this book, but its true genesis lies in the people who inspired it. I met many of them when I first travelled through the great wildlife parks of Rhodesia – now Zimbabwe – 30 years ago. They were of a breed I'd never encountered before. They were fiercely independent and self-sufficient, their minds sharp and intelligent, but their creed was simple: wilderness and wildlife are priceless, there's a job to be done, so let's get on with it. Any difficulties along the way were met with an equally simple proposition: we'll make a plan.

Some of these people – Rob and Paddy Francis in the Gonarezhou, Nick Tredger in Chizarira, Ronnie van Heerden, John Stevens – are mentioned in these pages. And special mention must go to the people in Mana Pools and the Matusadona who inspired my love for these very special places. In Mana Pools, Dolf Sasseen cut through all the complexities with a single phrase – 'it's all so beautiful'.

In Matusadona, Rob and Sandy Fynn, who built their dream on Fothergill Island, shared it with me for almost two years and so gave me the freedom to think, absorb, and begin to understand my own most profound enigma – myself.

Kevin and Fay Dunham and Russell Taylor put some of the complexities back by showing me the biological truths that underlie the Zambezi Valley's fragile beauty. They may feel they wasted their time when they see how I've dealt with some controversial wildlife issues, but they possess two important – and sometimes rare – scientific traits: a lack of dogmatism and a sense of humour.

There were many others, and if I tried to list them I'd be in grave danger of giving offence by omission. But, to all those who gave so freely of their hospitality, knowledge and friendship to a would-be writer all those years ago (and, by example, diverted him into wildlife conservation for the next quarter-century), I have to say: thank you.

Then, years later – when the make-a-plan breed was in danger of dying out – Mike Cock and Mark Atkinson saved what was left of Zimbabwe's fast-disappearing black rhinos with a magnificent disregard for bureaucratic obstruction. Andy Searle, persecuted in other contexts by the same bureaucrats, lived and died in pursuit of his ideals.

And the flame still burns – in Loki Osborne and Richard Hoare, for instance, dedicated to the survival of Africa's elephants. In the late Zeph Mukatiwa, a recent Matusadona warden and in Duncan Purchase, now director of the Zambezi Society, who bore many of my administrative burdens while I was writing this book.

If I have misquoted them, I apologise; but I like to think that I have preserved the general tenor of their inspiring lives, actions and words. They led me to make my own plan – to write this book.

But putting the plan into effect is, it goes without saying, the most important part of the tradition. This was deceptively easy – until I sent the resulting manuscript to Jennifer Barclay at Summersdale Publishers. That's when the hard work really began. Jennifer's given me constant

Acknowledgements

encouragement through three drafts in as many years, gently but firmly pointing out my literary sins, from the superfluous and pretentious to the misplaced apostrophe. Lucy York, who knows and loves many of the places I've mentioned, has put me right on many points of detail in the course of her painstaking copy-edit. But a book's useless if nobody buys it. Elly Donovan and Nicky Douglas, Summersdale's publicity and sales managers respectively, have worked very hard to make sure that they do. I can't thank Jennifer and the Summersdale team enough for their endless patience and help.

Lee Durrell is a very special person, who deserves an equally special mention. I sent her an early manuscript, on the strength of a brief but deeply inspiring acquaintance with herself and Gerald almost twenty years ago. That Lee – who has walked with literary giants – should agree to write the foreword is, I think, more of a tribute to her generosity of spirit than to my own talents.

And that brings me, above all, to Sal, my friend, bush-companion, colleague, fellow writer and wife. Those who can read between the lines of this book will gather that I spent many years in an emotional wilderness, as well as a literal one, before Sal came into my life. Without Sal, nothing would have been written at all, because it wouldn't have been worth the effort. Nor would anything else in life.

FOREWORD

It was a pleasant surprise to hear from Dick Pitman, a genial voice from the past, asking if I would write a foreword to his book and attaching an early draft. It was clear the book would bring together a number of threads for me – memories of the fabulous visit Gerry and I made to Zimbabwe in the 1980s and certain home truths in the conservation world that need airing – and so I said yes.

Little did I know that the finished version would affect me so deeply. Dick's style is very similar to Gerry's in that it intersperses good old-fashioned storytelling with lyrical prose, and it ranges from hilariously funny to profoundly moving. His purpose in setting pen to paper is also like Gerry's. To paraphrase them both, 'one of the duties of privilege is to share it', and their privileged experiences with wildlife and wild places are generously bestowed in their writings.

A Wild Life is no simple string of anecdotes from the notebook of a wildlife enthusiast, but the unfolding of a grander story, told with wit and affection. There are elephants addicted to oranges, a friendly hippo who frequents a swimming pool, a schoolboy know-it-all who pops in and out of the story at the most unlikely moments. But some episodes are unnerving, as when slogan-chanting political heavies detain his elephant survey teams, or tragic, as when he witnesses the aftermath of war in Mozambique. Dick treats each situation with the sensitivity it merits.

He lampoons political correctness in conservation, and while doing so he deals with an issue that is dear to my own heart: that of 'single species conservation', which has become unfashionable these days. It is the defining characteristic of much of the work of my own organisation and is clearly Dick's preferred focus. The problem is the current perception that working with particular species – rhinos, elephants and cheetahs in Dick's case – deflects attention from the more important matter of whole ecosystems and their processes. What an oversimplified view! Good species conservationists do their utmost to bring attention to the factors which threaten their target species, to create an understanding of the context which explains the species' parlous state.

Having spent twenty-five years at the sharp end (and the dull) in wildlife conservation, Dick potters among Lake Kariba's secluded, blissful bays and inlets and hopes for eternal truths to be revealed. What is wilderness? What is the real price of human arrogance? Have I in fact achieved anything? The answers come and go, elusively, but he firmly appreciates that he has been able to live his life to the full, a special privilege in these modern times when so many people, so incomprehensibly, seek only virtual reality.

A final word about the incident on a dilapidated raft surrounded by hippos in the middle of the Zambezi, as described in Chapter Five. Gerry and I were having a ball, and living life to the full!

Lee Durrell
Honorary Director, Durrell Wildlife Conservation Trust
February 2007

PROLOGUE

Not long ago, Sal and I were camping at Mana Pools, on the Zambezi River. Sal shook me awake, in the middle of the night.

'A hyaena is stealing our cooler-box,' she whispered urgently.

The sound of a cooler-box being dragged away by a hyaena is unmistakable if you've heard it before, which I had. There's a lot of determined grunting and snuffling, mingled with a muffled *thump-clunketty-thump* and the tinkling of bottles.

I also recognised the tone of voice that implied it was my job to do something about it. However, the cooler-box contained most of our food for the following week, so it was a matter of more importance than the crickets trapped in the sleeping bag that I'm usually woken up about.

I disentangled myself from the mosquito-net, grabbed the pepper spray we carry in case of such events, and climbed down from our bed on the roof-rack of our old Land Rover.

The hyaena had obviously done this sort of thing before. It had knocked the top off the cooler-box, got a good grip on its rim and lifted the whole thing off the ground. I saw its dim outline loping across the sand, and gave chase. The hyaena paused briefly to inspect its loot, in the middle of the campsite under one of Mana's splendid acacias, but ran off again as I caught up with it, and disappeared into the bush.

At this point Sal arrived with the powerful flashlight I had forgotten to take with me, and turned it on. I found myself stark naked, holding a pepper spray aloft, floodlit like a malnourished Statue of Liberty, and the focus of attention of a crowd of fellow campers awoken by the disturbance.

I now feel similarly exposed. Any work with an autobiographical element involves some baring of the soul, and makes the preposterous assumption that the soul thus revealed is likely to be of interest to others. My indecent exposure at Mana Pools can at least be excused as accidental. Writing about it can't.

So why do it?

Because I've been privileged; and one of the duties of privilege is to share. I've spent half my life fossicking around some of the most beautiful places in Africa, and still do. I got into wildlife conservation by happy accident, and stayed there mostly through luck.

It's been a roller coaster ride of gloom and elation, catastrophe and profound satisfaction, all mixed up together. Whether it's actually achieved anything is another matter altogether. But at least I feel I've lived, to the full (and intend to go on doing so for some time yet). This, too, is a privilege in a world of increasingly plastic experiences and virtual reality.

It isn't all rhinos, cheetahs and elephants, much as I would like it to be. They're inseparable from people, money, aeroplane crashes, homicidal pigs, flying, fishing, and falling off boats into creeks full of crocodiles. They're all threads in my personal tapestry of experiences. If I pulled them out, the picture wouldn't make much sense.

The book is set almost exclusively in Zimbabwe. Whatever sins it may have committed in the eyes of the world – and I'm not blind to these – Zimbabwe took me in, dusted me down, and gave me the life I've enjoyed. I'm not about to kick it in the teeth. I've mostly refrained from political comment and merely described those events that have impacted on my own activities.

Saving wildlife and wilderness is a serious business. One of the reasons why it is so serious is because we're not all that good at it, myself included. So – if you can't be good in bed, be funny. Whoever said that didn't offer much help if your audience doesn't think you're funny, either. But I've at least tried to be a little light-hearted about it.

Chapter One

WALKING IN STRANGE WAYS

There's a flash and a loud bang somewhere behind our house as the illicit panel-beating business down the road fires up its welding machine. The lights go out and my computer dies, along with a thousand unsaved words of immortal prose.

'Bugger it,' I hear Sal say in the kitchen as she is plunged into darkness, 'not again'. The pasta, which had been simmering nicely, subsides into a glutinous mass inside its saucepan.

The telephone is working for once, but it takes me an hour to get through to the Zimbabwean Electricity Supply Authority (ZESA), possibly because half of Harare is trying to do the same thing. When I finally do so…

'Your fault number,' a pleasant voice says in a Shona accent, 'is five-seven-nine-four-five.' My fault? Nicely worded, guys. Shifts the blame squarely onto my shoulders.

'And when can you attend to it?' I ask, with studied courtesy. There's a long silence.

'Aaaah,' the voice finally says. 'We don't have fuel.'

It being my fault, I suppose I'm responsible for giving them the fuel to come out and fix it. I grab a can from my little stockpile of diesel, drive to the ZESA depot, watch the cheerful, blue-overalled truck driver pouring it into his tank, and go home before I can watch him siphoning half of it out again.

The electricity – the ZESA, as everyone calls it here – comes back on at two in the morning and sets the burglar alarm off. Its siren wails and shrieks through the house, and starts the dogs howling in chorus. A car screeches to a halt in the road outside and three sinister-looking men in black with big boots come leaping over the wall. I go out to meet them, and am instantly transfixed by a blinding spotlight.

'Stand steel and put your hands up!' a voice yells at me. 'What is your cod number?'

We haven't got any cod, but there are a couple of goldfish in the pond right beside you, why don't you ask them? I'm not sure why this sort of smart-arse retort should come to mind when someone's pointing a pistol at me. They're not the sort of last words I'd want to be remembered for.

'FIVE, SEVEN,' I bellow, 'um… er…' There's a slight but menacing movement of the spotlight, and the click of a safety catch.

'That's the ZESA fault number, idiot,' Sal mutters, materialising beside me. 'Code number two-five-four-one, guys,' she says sweetly, turning to the spotlight. It goes out.

'Ah, Madam, it is you,' the biggest and most intimidating man says, with the relieved air of a man who's finally found someone who talks sense. 'Your husband must learn the cod number. Otherwise we might shoot him.'

'Don't bother, I'll do it myself one of these days,' Sal says. The dogs are still howling away. 'Shut up, Crash, quiet, Ember. And for God's sakes, love,' – she addresses me, without any detectable change in tone, 'turn that bloody siren off.'

16

I give the security guys a handsome tip for their trouble
– it's not often you pay someone to stick a gun in your ear
in your own front garden – and let them out, noting that
similar scenes are being played out up and down the road.

When we get back inside, a column of black smoke is rising
from the pasta on the stove, which has accidentally been left
on. Pity we noticed; we could have had a visit from the fire
brigade as well.

'At least,' I say to Sal, whose feathers are distinctly ruffled,
'we can have a nice hot bath in the morning.'

Fat chance. When I wake up in the morning the ZESA's still
on, but I turn the bath tap and a miserable trickle soon dries
up altogether, with a gloomy gurgling of pipes and geysers.
Sometimes the water comes back in an hour. Sometimes it
takes three days.

'Time,' I say to Sal over the breakfast cornflakes – twice the
price they were last week, Sal tells me – 'to go to the bush.'

The bush. That strange, mysterious and infinitely alluring
entity, out there, far from the city; where these things don't
happen, because you know you've got to cook on gas, or wood,
and camp near a spring or carry your water with you. Where
such people as you do meet don't instantly produce a 9 mm
pistol and demand your cod number or, worse, your money
and your mobile phone. Where a mobile is useless, in fact.

Mental images: quiet Matusadona bays, the water turning
to shot-silk against a mountain backdrop, the hippos
nosing up to the banks before coming out to graze and
the first hyaena calling. Mana Pools, and herds of impala
leaping like shards of sunlight in the cool, enchanted
mahogany woodlands. Sometimes lions, dozing on the
sandy tracks; maybe a leopard, slinking silently through
the tall, dry, whispering grasses. Maybe even a rhino, or
a cheetah; and elephants. Always elephants. Herds of
females and their tiny calves, slipping silently from the

edge of the woodlands to drink at dusk; stolid old bulls, ripping up the grass on the Kariba lake-shore or reaching up for acacia-pods at Mana Pools. Dry leaves crackling underfoot, the red sands of the Zambezi Valley trickling between my toes and, over it all, the warm, brown scent of buffalo dung.

That's why we put up with it all. That's why we are here. The bush. These visions arise in my mind, like fragments of fantastic dreams.

'Let's go,' Sal says.

'I'll have to find some more diesel first,' I say. 'Bloody ZESA.' By the time I've spent half the day in a fuel queue I'm out of my mind with the kind of rage and frustration that only Africa can cause – and which, oddly, only Africa can cure. The rage starts to ebb away when we begin the long descent down the lonely, winding road into the Zambezi Valley, lying vast and golden in the afternoon sun.

I'm still unreasonably irritated when we're held up by an elephant plumb in the middle of the road, plodding slowly along the white line and sturdily refusing to move aside; but it takes time to adjust to different worlds.

My first encounter with Africa's wildlife took place in a hotel bedroom in Salisbury, Rhodesia on 23 November 1977, while I was unpacking my suitcase after a long and exhausting flight from Heathrow.

An enormous, brownish-black millipede emerged from behind the curtains and undulated purposefully towards me. It looked capable of leaping across the room and chewing half my face off.

'Aaaargh!' I screamed. A porter arrived at the double.

'Ah,' he said. '*Chongololo*.'

The *chongololo's* idea of aggression, it turned out, is to curl itself into a little ball and pretend it isn't there. The porter picked it up and threw it out of the window. Since my room was on the eighth floor, this possibly wasn't the best start to a career in conservation. But then again, I hadn't planned to start one. I hadn't even planned to end up in Rhodesia. Technically, I was supposed to be emigrating to South Africa. It was all arranged: immigration, sponsors, the lot.

However, I'd met a Rhodesian émigré in England, just before I was due to depart.

'Wonderful country,' he'd said. 'Sunshine, scenery…' His voice tailed off and a dreamy, faraway look crept into his eyes as he glanced out of the window at the London drizzle.

The big question, of course – which I failed to ask – was: what are you doing in London, then? I'd still bought myself a ticket to Johannesburg, but decided to stop over in Salisbury, just to check it out.

I liked the place, once I'd discovered the truth about *chongololos*. The scenery wasn't too inspiring, as it consisted largely of 1960s concrete office blocks rising from a sea of corrugated-iron roofs. My migrant friend hadn't been entirely accurate about the sunshine, either. I'd arrived at the start of a rainy season that continued on and off – but mostly on – for the next four months.

But the sun did shine warmly in between the thunderstorms, the immigration people were friendly and there was a warm, sociable air about the place. By the evening of day two I was comfortably ensconced in the local press club. By lunchtime on day three I'd got a job with a local newspaper on the strength of a few freelance specimens from the English media.

I was granted residence a couple of weeks later, and a retrospective 'assisted passage' into the bargain. It all seemed too good to be true, and it was.

Rhodesia was embroiled in a nasty little civil war with a lot of its own citizens, who believed that they should be permitted a few basic freedoms, such as the right to vote. A few months later, an ominous-looking brown envelope pitched up in my mailbox.

'You will,' said the letter inside, 'report to Cranborne Barracks at 08.00 hours on the...' etc etc. Oh, I will, will I? Yes, you will, it went on to say, or very nasty things involving military policemen will happen to you.

My colleagues, most of whom were exempt from the regular part-time call-ups because of age, infirmity and simulated or real insanity, regarded me with pity.

'Well,' one of them said at last. 'Maybe they won't send you into the bush.'

They did. I felt reasonably upbeat about this at first. It would be a 'new experience', which was what I'd come to Africa for. I could, I told myself, adopt a lofty attitude of academic interest, but reality soon put paid to that little idea.

For starters, the army tried to kill me before I got anywhere near the bush, by putting me into the back of a five-ton truck and rolling it down a twenty-foot embankment. Several other innocents, with whom I was sharing the back of the truck, were crippled for life by broken spines and pelvises. I was lucky to escape with a badly-sprained ankle.

Then, when I finally made it to the bush, it was full of low-ranking people who didn't want to be there, commanded by a few howling lunatics who'd been promoted because they did. They yapped like demented Dobermanns as they ordered the rest of us to go out and get shot at. Mostly, they looked as if they'd like to shoot us themselves and save the guerillas the bother.

The bush was also full of things that bit, scratched and stung you, and there wasn't a wild animal to be seen, since most of the waterholes had been poisoned by one side or another.

Worst of all, though, people got killed. I am still haunted by the memory of bullet-riddled corpses, and of the black African soldiers who fought alongside us Europeans, singing soft and low through the velvet lowland night as they mourned their losses.

I ended up in a small country hospital, with legs like purple hot air balloons cratered with abscesses that wept blood and pus all over the bedclothes. A little white-haired old lady came visiting, and clucked sympathetically.

'Dear, oh dear,' she said, 'you poor thing. Shrapnel?'

Several thoughts flashed through my mind. Maybe she was handing out big fat disability cheques to wounded soldiers. A nice little smallholding, even. On the other hand, two doctors, six nurses and ten fellow patients with real shrapnel injuries would know I was lying.

'Tick bites,' I said lamely, and got a bag of boiled sweets instead.

It was, in short, horrible – so horrible that it inspired a heartfelt desire to go somewhere extraordinarily lovely, preferably with lots of wild animals around, and forget the whole thing. Mysterious names like Mana Pools had popped up regularly in conversations with my cannon-fodder colleagues, with a dreamy wistfulness, a yearning for what sounded like paradise lost. Most such places were closed to visitors because of the war. So that ruled that idea out. Or did it?

'Hold on. Let me get this straight,' said one of the powers-that-then-were within Rhodesia's Department of National Parks and Wildlife Management, staring at me incredulously from behind a desk cluttered with wire baskets full of buff government-issue files.

'You want to go down to Mana Pools, with a war going on, and write an article about it?'

Well, yes, more or less, although it'd be nice to omit the article bit, if I could get away with it.

He went on: 'We've got enough problems as it is, wouldn't you say, without chauffering' – I could almost hear the words 'stupid bloody Poms' forming in his mind, but he thought better of it – 'reporters all over the place. And feeding them. Besides,' he added, more as an afterthought than anything, 'what if you get killed? Be all over the newspapers, won't it? Be our fault, won't it?'

God knows what made me say it, because I had a nice regular job, but he was irritating me. 'Actually,' I said, 'I'd like to go to all the big parks. Maybe do a whole book, as well as an article. I'll get myself there. And feed myself. And I'll sign an indemnity, if you like.'

And, I almost added, this place could do with some coverage about something other than peasants getting killed in 'crossfire'. I'd heard some nasty stories in the army.

The same thought possibly occurred to him, because my outburst of barefaced bravado stunned him into silence for several seconds. He fiddled with one of the folders. 'Well, I'll forward your request, if you like. But don't get your hopes up.'

The authorities chewed things over for a while, then became cautiously supportive, possibly hoping that charging elephants or man-eating lions would succeed where the army had failed. I was called back for another interview.

'Will you,' an authority-in-chief asked, 'let us read what you've written before you send it off to anyone?'

Journalistic integrity demanded a firm refusal. Integrity be buggered, however; by now my newspaper had been taken over and the new owners had fired the entire newsroom, including me. I signed on the line. All I needed now was some form of transport, in a country where cars advertised as being in 'showroom condition' looked as if they'd got there by crashing through the window.

The second-hand car salesman knew a sucker when he saw one. 'Got just the thing,' he said. He led me out of the showroom full of battered Peugeots, through the workshops, and into the backyard. He indicated something that turned out to be an early Series II Diesel Land Rover, once its covering of tattered black plastic and dead leaves had been cleared away.

'Tendai!' he yelled.

'Baas?' came a voice from somewhere in the yard.

'Jump leads! Battery!'

Tendai materialised in a tattered blue overall. He gave me a pitying glance, connected the battery and pressed the starter. After a good deal of fruitless churning, the engine staggered into life and blanketed us in clouds of black exhaust smoke. "Asn't been started for a while,' the salesman said unnecessarily. "Ark at that. Sweet like a nut. Tendai, git some air in them tyres, hey?'

I bought it for an outrageous sum, christened it the White Elephant, packed it with everything I owned – which left a lot of room for food, fuel cans and other extras – and set off before the inherent absurdity of the exercise could sink in too far. What I'd wanted to do was to go to the Zambezi and Mana Pools. Mana, I was finding, was almost iconic among Rhodesia's white population, redolent of long, lazy, pre-war days among the elephants, before the Dreams of Empire turned into a nightmare of bullets, bombs and bodies.

However, I'd let myself in for some geographically extensive research instead of just a cosy little trip to the Zambezi. The White Elephant and I had to explore the remote reaches of a war-torn country almost twice the size of the UK. I decided to visit the other wildlife parks first and leave Mana and Lake Kariba until last, like the strawberries in the fruit salad. A lot of people were convinced I wouldn't make it as far as the city limits, let alone Mana Pools.

'Do what?' was the general tenor of things. 'Lunacy. You're bloody mad. Insane. *Penga*.'

Producing a vehicle as slow as the Series II Diesel Land Rover must have been a major design triumph. Rover's chief engineer probably burst into the boardroom shouting, 'We've done it! We've got its top speed down to less than forty miles an hour!'

It seemed wise to join the armed convoy that escorted travellers for much of the journey from Salisbury to the Gonarezhou National Park, in the south-eastern corner of the country. As soon as we set off, the rest of the convoy accelerated to warp speed and galloped off over the horizon, while two enormous police trucks positioned themselves fore and aft of the White Elephant and idled along at snail's pace. Their drivers looked up occasionally from their novels to check their navigation.

Their patience didn't extend to escorting me down the 50 miles of the horrendously corrugated excuse-for-a-road that represented the last stage of the journey to the Gonarezhou. The White Elephant split a radiator hose halfway, and I arrived at the park headquarters in a cloud of hissing steam, like a lost railway engine.

I quickly got an inkling of the kind of beauty I was looking for. The park wardens had been warned of my proposed visits and – to their eternal credit – none of them applied for urgent leave. On the contrary: they went far out of their way to be hospitable and helpful. Within an hour of my arrival, Rob Francis, the then warden, bundled me into his aeroplane and we took off for a bird's eye tour of the Gonarezhou.

In the army, my view had been restricted to a few yards of rather menacing bush. Now, though, cloud-dappled woodlands stretched from horizon to horizon, broken by winding, blue and gold sandy rivers. We followed one of them – the Runde – eastwards for 30 miles, down to the Mozambique border. Elephant bulls with enormous tusks – the Gonarezhou is renowned for its tuskers – dozed under riverine trees; and huge herds of buffalo flowed like black rivers through the woodlands.

Then we flew southwards for 70 miles, across the Gonarezhou's vast interior, where herds of sable and impala clustered round the fast-drying pans, until we came to another great river, the Mwenezi; and thence back to the park headquarters.

It was a vast wilderness, so far removed from the patchwork fields and woods of my native England as to lie utterly beyond my previous experience. Its physical features were easy enough to describe, I thought, as I made my notes that evening; the mental impact, almost impossible: an overwhelming sense of size, spaciousness, and sheer wonder at the fact that such places still existed in a crowded world.

Other than being closed to tourists, business at the national park seemed to be going on as usual. There was even a buffalo capture taking place, on a cattle ranch just outside the park.

Cape buffalo – great black bulls with sweeping spreads of horn, the cows more lightly built – are thought to carry foot-and-mouth disease. Often, they are shot wherever they may come into contact with cattle. A fortunate few are captured and moved elsewhere, as in this case. A herd had been located on the ranch, and been driven into a 'boma', made of plastic sheeting, that enclosed several hectares of bush.

Young calves were in particular demand, as they don't carry the virus and can form the nuclei of foot-and-mouth-free buffalo herds. Inside the boma, game rangers from the parks department's capture units were periodically launching themselves off the back of a careering Land Rover and into a dust cloud that hid a melee of whirling hooves and horns. When the herd moved on and the dust cleared they'd be nonchalantly pinning a protesting buffalo-calf to the ground.

It looked easy enough. I volunteered to help, found a place on the back of the Land Rover, and threw myself enthusiastically on top of a small buffalo-calf, about the size of a black Labrador. When I came to, I was lying on the ground doubled up in agony with an anxious-looking ranger standing over me. The calf was nowhere to be seen.

'Doesn't matter,' I squeaked, between spasms. 'No, really. I'll be fine.' It was probably cheaper than a vasectomy anyway. Besides, the small country hospital wasn't far away, and I wasn't about to explain this one to the little old lady.

I'd brought a tent and provisions, but Rob and Paddy Francis would have none of it, accommodating me in their spare bedroom instead. I abused their hospitality shamelessly, I'm sorry to say, because I stayed for almost a month.

By the time I left I'd filled several notebooks with a riot of new experiences: footslogging through miles of hot, dusty bush as we tried to find Kabakwe, a legendary old elephant bull whose tusks swept almost to the ground (we didn't); fishing in the turquoise pools of the Runde with the towering red sandstone cliffs of the Chilojo Cliffs glowing in the setting sun; climbing Nyamtongwe, the mysterious flat-topped hill beneath which, according to legend, an ancient Arab city lies buried; becoming lame and footsore as

I walked yet more miles of bush with park patrols following up reports of elephants killed by poachers.

And that was the amazing thing about the national parks' wardens and rangers, in the Gonarezhou and in every park I was to visit. Their budgets had been cut to vanishing point because of the civil war. Their lives were at perpetual risk, whether from guerillas or armed poachers. But they went about their work as if nothing untoward was happening. They were utterly dedicated to their jobs, and determined to pass on the incredible legacy of wilderness and wildlife they themselves had inherited.

The police declined to accompany me when I left Gonarezhou for the Matopos National Park, south of Bulawayo, a couple of hundred miles away. Maybe stories of the awesome performance of Series II Diesel Land Rovers had got around. Instead, they offered me a thin and fidgety pastor who wanted to get to South Africa rather faster than his little legs would carry him. He leapt eagerly into the passenger seat, and discovered his mistake when the White Elephant slowed to walking-speed up a gentle hill lined with superb ambush sites. He peered anxiously out of the window.

'Won't it, ah, go any faster?'

'Sure it will,' I said lightly. 'Downhill, anyway.' The ambush sites being too menacing to contemplate, his gaze shifted to the dashboard shelf and zoomed in on my last packet of biscuits. 'Mind if I have one?' he asked as he reached for them.

'The Lord provides,' he said, as he finished the packet. Funny: I thought I had. 'And now I shall pray for our safety' – which he did, interminably, until I hove him out at the junction with the South Africa road. Nobody shot at us, so maybe it worked, but I'd have preferred a police truck with a machine gun.

The Matopos consists largely of unvegetated granite domes. They also shelter the world's largest concentration of black eagles and Khoisan cave paintings. I am sure they can be beautiful. But I arrived on a grey May afternoon, with a cold wind sending tatters of cloud scudding off the hilltops.

I settled into one of the lodges at the park's headquarters, then I drove into the hills, alone, on a wild and windy evening, with the indigo clouds racing across the sky. Now and again a shaft of weak sun merely deepened the gloom of the long, misty valleys. After a few miles I stopped, and switched off the White Elephant's engine, in a narrow, grassy valley between two rearing ridges of tumbled granite.

Neither cicada nor birdsong relieved the loneliness of this wild, grey evening. There are buffalo, sable, eland, even white rhinos in the Matopos, but it's not one of Africa's great wildlife parks. Most of them had been reintroduced, at some time in the early twentieth century; and none were visible.

I strolled across the valley floor, through the dry brown grass, and tried to climb one of the ridges, but it turned into a nightmare of yawning crevices, clutching thornbushes, impenetrable shrubs and tangled roots, and I soon gave up.

Maybe it was the weather; maybe the – temporary, no doubt – absence of wildlife. Maybe it was the Matopos's human history, because it has seen much slaughter and blood: of Khoisan bushmen, of Ndebele warriors, of protagonists on both sides of the Rhodesian Civil War. Whatever it was, I felt a sense of alien menace in those grey granite hills. I retreated to the White Elephant and drove back to my lodge.

In the morning, the warden allocated me to a group of game-scouts who, he said, would show me around. I asked them if we were likely to bump into guerillas.

'Ahhh, no,' their leader said cryptically. 'We walk in strange ways, in the bush.'

I was still walking in a fairly strange way myself, after the buffalo-calf had done its worst. As it turned out, though, all he meant was the business of walking in well-spaced arrow-head formations and Indian files, so that the guerrillas could only shoot one or two of you at a time, that I'd learnt in the army.

This made it all the more surprising when he marched six game-scouts and myself up an exposed granite slab on which a well-aimed burst from an AK-47 could have wiped out the lot of us; brewed tea on its summit; and walked back down again. Very strange ways, indeed.

I didn't stay long in the Matopos hills. I found them claustrophobic after the vastness of the Gonarezhou. So I drove northwards through Bulawayo and up the long, lonely and well-surfaced tar road (on which the White Elephant blew two tyres and broke a rear spring) to the world-famous Hwange National Park.

Here, low granite hills fall away into endless Kalahari scrub, where water is scarce and seasonal, and would dry up altogether were it not for the boreholes and diesel pumps that fill many of the park's waterholes during the dry season.

I went with an engineer to fix the water pump at Mpafa Pan, deep in the Kalahari sands. By sunset, the water was flowing into the long-dry pan, and we relaxed against an anthill as the twilight faded and a near-full moon rose. Suddenly, the bush at our backs erupted with a tremendous trumpeting and crackling of branches underfoot. A herd of elephants stampeded past us, almost close enough to touch, and flung themselves into the pan. Huge backs gleamed silver in the moonlight; mud and water flew high in the air. Calves writhed and wriggled in the mud and sprayed water at each other. Water, in a waterless wilderness; the elephants summoned from the depths of the bush by the *thump-thump* of the diesel pump.

Hwange was still open to visitors, so I was able to pick up some hints on dealing with disgruntled tourists – a useful skill, as things turned out later.

'I've been in this park all day,' a German visitor complained, 'and all I've seen is a couple of tortoises.'

'Hey, man, you're lucky. That's really unusual,' the ranger said. 'You usually see them on their own.'

The tourist was also possibly lucky because several kinds of mongoose are also common in Hwange. The plural can be troublesome even for native English speakers and is best resolved by saying: 'I saw a mongoose. Then I saw another one…'

It was now June: the height of the southern winter. The nights were cold, but the days pleasantly warm by noon. It hadn't rained for three months, and wouldn't for another four. The sun swung across a cloudless sky, becoming hazy with dust and the smoke from bush-fires. I'd bash the White Elephant down the corrugated track to Ngweshla Pan, where white sand and the sun-washed stumps of long-dead trees surrounded a shrinking pool of grey water and tall, bleached grasses whispered in the wind, and park in such shade as I could find. Then I'd walk out onto the sand and sit at the base of an anthill in these distant reaches of a wide wilderness.

Great piles of elephant dung lay at the water's edge, and there was a giraffe on the woodland fringes, sniffing the air before walking hesitantly to the water: he splayed his legs, lowered his head and took a few brave sips before retreating purposefully across the sand and back into the bush.

This evidence of life relieved an otherwise desolate scene of leafless trees, fallen branches half-buried beneath drifts of scorching sand, and low, monotonous scrub. I was beginning to learn that the enjoyment of wilderness is a very personal thing. Some love the Matopos hills; some love Hwange's dry desert sands. I cannot live for long away from water. It was time to go to the Zambezi.

To get there, though, I had to drive back to Bulawayo, through Salisbury, and northwards again to Kariba town.

From there, I hoped to get into Mana Pools, 60 miles or so downstream. It was almost 1,000 miles from Hwange to Kariba by road – ones without landmines in them, anyway – and survivors of the Series II Land Rover Diesel design team will be excited to note that this took five days of solid driving.

Kariba town, which sprawls over the hills and the lake-shore near the dam wall, is uninteresting except for the dam itself. The dam could become very interesting indeed, if it ever collapsed. Streaked with algae and rust, its slender concrete arc is periodically shaken by small earthquakes. As it holds back several cubic miles of water, you don't want to dwell on this too much, especially if you're going somewhere further down the Zambezi, like Mana Pools.

The lake, on the other hand, is stunning – and utterly incongruous: an inland sea, blue and windruffled, extending to an unbroken, misty horizon, and plonked down half a century ago in the midst of some of southern Africa's most arid landscapes. I booked myself into a hotel with a magnificent view across to the mountains of the Matusadona National Park – where, I promised myself, I'd go after Mana Pools. But first I had to get to Mana. I hadn't given much thought as to how I was going to do this. I sought the advice of the girl at the hotel's reception desk.

'Meno Pause,' she said, as if addressing a small child, 'is shit.' Southern African accents produce some strange truths at times. 'Closed. Unavailable. Didn't your travel agency tell you? Shame, hey?' she went on soothingly. 'They are naughty. Why don't you go to the Matusadona instead, or Fothergill Island; lovely place.' She reached for the telephone.

'Not shut to me, it isn't,' I said, producing my laisser-aller from the parks department. 'Can I drive there?

'Drive there? Over ninety kays of landmines? There's a war on, you know,' she added.

'Well, what about a boat, then? Down the Zambezi?'

She gave me the stupid-bloody-Pom look I was getting used to. 'Well,' she said at last, 'you could always try Pete. He's got a floatplane.' She paused. 'He's crazy enough to try it.'

Pete Anderson, a genial Aussie who was subsisting by flying the occasional tourist around Lake Kariba, jumped at the chance.

'Mana?' he said. 'Love to go there. Yeah, we can land on the Zambezi alright, used 'ta go there a lot. Haven't been for a long time.'

There was only one fly in all this ointment: my budget didn't run to floatplanes. It didn't even crawl within miles of them. Pete balanced the attractions of Mana Pools against the drawback of my empty wallet for a few moments.

'There's a coupla Pommy tourists around, bumped into 'em in the pub last night. Mebbe they'd like to go for the ride, pay for the trip.'

Sure enough, Pete had a couple of young sheilas in tow when I rendezvoused with him the next day. He packed them into the back seats, put me in the front, and we took off from a small inlet and headed over the hills that flank the Kariba dam, north-eastwards towards Mana.

The Zambezi Valley was thick with smoke and haze. An endless carpet of leafless mopanes – the tall, slender trees that characterise the low-lying valley – unrolled beneath us. Gusty thermals slammed us against our seat belts. The two sheilas beat me to the sick bags, but only by a minute or so. And then the Zambezi came into view: a broad ribbon of windruffled water, over a mile wide, bigger – vastly bigger – than any river I'd seen before and, like Lake Kariba, stunningly incongruous: millions of gallons of sparkling water in the arid harshness of a wilderness that hadn't known rain for half a year.

I absorbed the view, awe-stricken. The great river divided and reunited as it flowed past long, grassy islands dotted with trees and speckled with herds of buffalo, impala, elephants in ones and twos and family groups with calves, grazing on the fringes of lush, green grass beside the water.

Pete descended to treetop height and then down into the river channels themselves, weaving and jinking like a Messerschmidt with Douglas Bader on its tail. 'To confuse the SAM-7s,' he said, in the cheerful sort of voice Boeing captains use when they're telling you the undercarriage won't come down. SAM-7s are portable anti-aircraft missiles, and the guerrillas had already shot down a couple of airliners. We all started reaching for the sick bags again.

The huge evergreen mahoganies and grey acacia trees that line the Zambezi at Mana Pools flashed past the wingtip. 'Lion!' Pete exclaimed suddenly, and pulled the Cessna round into a tight turn. A great, black-maned male lion lay under one of the acacias, on a small promontory, and watched us idly as we roared past.

More elephants, and yet more, out on the midstream islands, swimming across the channels, trunks to tails like strings of grey pearls; hippo, lying like fat brown sausages in tiny bays and inlets, and sharing them with immense crocodiles, uncountable hundreds of crocodiles, hauled out onto the sandbanks, basking in the sun. And herds of impala – the most common, yet loveliest of antelopes – flowing like golden rivers through the trees.

Pete suddenly throttled back, landed the floatplane in a narrow channel and taxied into the riverbank. After a minute or two a strange figure emerged from the trees and strolled across the glaring sand to meet us.

Some of him, it turned out as the apparition got closer, was clothed in what might once have been a national parks uniform. He seemed to have a ragged oval of dense black hair instead of a face, topped off with the battered remains of a wide-brimmed, Boer-style hat. Pete opened his window and leant out.

'Dolf,' he said. 'Howzit?'

The oval of black hair suddenly parted to reveal a pair of twinkling, deep-set eyes and a broad grin.

'*Lekker,*' it said. 'Welcome to Hotel Mana. 'Tea's made.'

This, it turned out, was the legendary South African-born parks warden, Dolf Sasseen. Dolf, it was rumoured, would vanish into the bush for months at a time with nothing more than a couple of sticks of dried meat and a camera whenever some bureaucrat tried to post him away from Mana Pools.

Pete passed out a coil of rope and a picket, and Dolf pulled the floatplane in until the floats nudged the sandy bank, and tied it up. I climbed out onto one of the floats and stepped ashore. The two girls followed. Dolf led us across the sand, up a steep bank and into the shade of one of the Mana acacias – great, gnarled trees, with delicately-fronded leaves that bud in the southern autumn, fruit in the depths of winter and drop their leaves in the spring, before the summer rains begin. Apple-ring acacias, they are sometimes called, because of the shape of their pods. They taste like newly-baked bread, and elephants love them.

A concrete table was set into a circle of paving stones and surrounded by canvas chairs in varying states of disrepair. It was flanked, rather ominously, by a machine gun and a couple of belts of ammunition.

A game-scout, who seemed to have retained more of his uniform than Dolf had, appeared with a chequered tablecloth and a tin tray with a large, blackened teapot and some cracked cups.

'Heard ya comin', miles away,' Dolf said cheerfully, by way of explanation. 'Good flight, no problems?'

'Nope. Some technicolor yawnin',' said Pete. 'Bit rough over the hills. Otherwise, no prob.'

'It was amazing,' one of the girls said, bravely. 'Never seen so many animals.'

'This is Mana,' Dolf said, 'they're all coming down to the river now, gettin' dry up in the mopane. Sugar? Milk? Powdered, I'm afraid.' He poured the tea carefully, and handed the cups round. 'OK, who's stayin' here, who's goin'? Head office was a bit vague.'

'Only me staying, I'm afraid,' I said. If a shadow of disappointment fleetingly crossed Dolf's face, it was well hidden under the hair.

'You're the one that's writin' the book, then,' Dolf said cheerfully. 'Where else've ya been?'

I told him.

'Ah, rubbish places. This place is unbelievable, man. We'll show you.' He paused. 'Can't get around as much as we used to. A bunch of guerrillas came across the river and gave us a good stonkin' a coupla weeks ago, we stopped goin' on patrols and we're all sleepin' in the fort now, but it doesn't matter, there's still plenty to see…' He looked up, stopped abruptly, raised a finger to his lips. 'Shhh…' We followed his gaze.

A venerable old bull elephant had silently materialised on the sandbank. His wrinkled grey hide was splashed with sand and mud, his long, thick tusks streaked with brown. He paused, one foreleg swinging idly to and fro, felt around in the sand with his trunk, and picked up a fallen acacia pod. Then he turned and ambled up the bank towards us.

'Sit very still,' Dolf murmured. The elephant paused again to pick up another acacia pod, then kept coming until he towered over us. He studied us carefully with gentle, liquid eyes beneath long, silky lashes. His hide was pocked and pitted with the scars of ancient battles. His trunk, curled up at the end, swung loosely as he chewed the pod with a sound like a wooden ship grinding on a reef. His huge ears swung idly to and fro; then he slowly extended his trunk, its tip searching the ground, until it came across another pod under Dolf's chair.

Nobody moved. Nobody breathed. We sat, frozen and stiff, like a *tableau vivant*. The elephant chewed thoughtfully while its trunk went off on a mission of its own, feeling for more pods under each of our chairs in turn.

I'd been close to elephants before, but not this close. I'd like to say it inspired wonder, humility, a sense of immense privilege and a lifelong determination to protect these gentle, intelligent creatures against the ravages of mankind, and in fact it did. But at that precise moment, I simply thought: 'oh, shit'.

Possibly mistaking this for an instruction, the elephant raised its tail and a volley of huge turds the size of footballs thudded damply onto the ground. Then it turned and ambled leisurely away. There was a collective explosion of pent-up breath.

'Ker-ristmas,' one of the girls said shakily, staring at the vast pile of steaming dung. 'Does that happen often?'

'All the time,' Dolf said, grinning hugely. 'This is Mana.'

Later in the day, Pete and the girls took off to fly back to Kariba. The roar of the Cessna's engine slowly died away in the distance. Dolf and I chatted.

'Excuse me,' he said after a while. 'I gotta go and sort out my truck. Be back in a bit.' Then, as if reading my thoughts…

'You know what to do if he comes back. Just sit quiet, an' he'll go away again in the end. Just likes to check things out now and then. I'll get Cephas to bring some fresh tea.'

I slowly became aware of the tiny sounds of Mana going about its business: the gentle calls of doves in the acacias, the harsh squawk of Egyptian geese on the sandbank, the faint cry of a fish eagle thermalling high over the river, a hippo grunting in a distant creek and, underneath it all, the near-subliminal hum of millions of insects – bees, hornets, crickets – that pervades the African bush.

Late afternoon, in August; winter was almost gone, but it would be another three months before the rains came. Across the river, the Zambian hills were almost invisible in the haze, their outlines dimly seen; and over them the sun turned to a flaming orange ball. Ahead of me, across a narrow river-channel, lay a sandy island with steep, silty cliffs topped with green grasses and dotted with grazing buffalo. Downstream, the Zambezi slowly curved away in a broad sweep of billowing, grey-green acacias. A distant group of elephants waded across a bay, belly-deep, clambered up the bank and disappeared into the woodlands.

It was a far cry from my fourth-floor flat in Eastbourne and the 7.10 to London, now no more than dim memories. But it felt more like a homecoming than an excursion. The Zambezi Valley and Mana Pools itself seemed somehow friendly. Familiar, even: as if I'd known it all my life, but been away for a long time.

The sun disappeared behind the Zambian hills. Dolf returned, covered in oil and grease.

'Flippin' Land Rovers,' he said. 'If it's not one thing, it's another.' I knew how he felt. He settled back in his chair and studied the view.

'Yup, they're all coming down to the river now,' he said. 'You should see this place in October. Full of animals. This is just the start of it. Then the rains come, and pfft! Everything gone, back up towards the hills. You wouldn't believe it now, but you can't even walk down here, grass gets so thick. Anyway,' he sighed, 'better head back to the fort, I suppose. The guerillas hit us at sunset, last time.'

He stood up, hefted the machine gun, and we strolled

off into the woodlands. A few minutes later we arrived at a clearing in which a collection of shacks with corrugated-iron roofs was sealed off behind low concrete walls and a security fence. Dolf led me through a gate in the fence, then through a steel door set in the concrete walls.

'Game-scouts live here,' Dolf said, indicating a couple of the shacks. 'Got a couple of army guys in this one, they're out on a patrol at the moment, be back soon. You can park off in mine, got plenty of room.'

The aroma that hung over the fort was already familiar to me: a compound of rifle-oil, sweaty webbing, and the delightful scent of a bunch of males living in close proximity. The fort slowly filled up with game-scouts, with labourers, with the young army guys back from patrol. Dolf, the two young national servicemen and I sat round a makeshift table.

Everyone longed for peace, but worried about the possible consequences of an independent Zimbabwe.

'Lose our farm, that's for sure,' Andy, one of the servicemen, said. He was 19, and had been conscripted into the army straight out of school. 'What then? No way I can work in town, man.' He turned to Dolf. 'Have to join the zookeepers, like you.'

'Don't count on that,' Dolf said, scraping the last of the baked beans off a battered enamel plate. 'I'll be out of a job as well. And as for this place,' he gestured vaguely 'well…'

'Be turned into mealie fields,' put in Vicus, the other serviceman.

'Never mind mealie fields,' Dolf said. 'The dam.'

'Dam?' I asked. 'What dam?'

Dolf turned to me, with a look of incredulity. 'Haven't you heard about the dam? Goin' to turn Mana into another Kariba.'

The dam, he said, would be built in the Mupata Gorge, 50 miles or so downstream. It would create a lake almost as big as Kariba, and drown the whole of Mana Pools, with its magnificent acacias and mahoganies and dry-season grazing and browsing for thousands of animals, leaving only the arid mopane country towards the hills to the south. The Rhodesian government had planned it several years ago, but couldn't afford to build it.

'It's not the war we gotta worry about,' Vicus sighed. 'It's peace.'

Dolf shook me awake at four o'clock the following morning, while it was still pitch dark. 'Coffee's up,' he said cheerfully.

I dragged myself out of my sleeping bag, pulled on my shorts and a shirt, and staggered through to the makeshift table, where a candle was burning brightly. He handed me a large tin mug. I put it to my lips, took a swig, and almost choked. I like my coffee strong, but there are limits. I didn't know if I should drink it slowly, to soften the impact on my digestion, or get it down quickly before it ate through the bottom of the mug and got to work on the table.

'Best time of the day,' he said. 'Get out there while it's cool.' In better times, he added apologetically, we could have gone out for a few days, walked down the river and camped on its banks, looped back through the mopane hinterland and back down to Mana. 'But we can still do a few kays,' he said, 'and get back before it's too hot.'

We strung water-bottles onto our belts. Dolf jammed his ancient hat onto his head, picked up a military rifle and inspected it carefully.

'Know how to use it?'

'More or less,' I said. He handed it to me, with a spare magazine. 'Just in case.' As we left, we bumped into one of the army guys, coming off guard duty.

'Bloody 'ell,' he said, in the half-light, 'Sparrows 'aven't even farted yet.'

'Due any second,' Dolf said. We struck off from the fort, away from the Zambezi, into the woodlands that extend across the Mana floodplains. In the east, the sky was brightening by the second, turning from indigo to turquoise, then to flaming orange. The air was cool and still, and scented with the blossoms of early spring.

At Mana the Zambezi has slowly shifted northwards, creating a mile-wide floodplain of fertile silt. Here and there, groves of immense mahoganies mark the remains of ancient islands. Often, these islands lie on the edge of long-abandoned river-channels, which fill with water during the rains – the pools from which Mana takes its name.

The wide spaces between these channels and islands are scattered with apple-ring acacias, growing in ones and twos and occasional clusters, their light grey traceries and delicately-fronded foliage contrasting with the dark green, heavy canopies of the mahoganies. During the rains, Dolf said, the floodplain had been covered with tall, impenetrable grass. Now, though, only a few unpalatable stems remained, the rest eaten by termites and the tidal wave of wildlife forced back to Mana from the dry pans to the south.

As we walked, the long vistas beneath the acacias slowly filled with the slanting, golden rays of the rising sun. A waterbuck ram, with grey, shaggy coat and long, curving horns, lay beneath one of the acacias, chewing the cud and watching us warily. Behind him, several females foraged in the dusty soil; still further on, a herd of zebra.

'Over there,' Dolf said. 'Eland. And there. And there.' He pointed. The shafts of sun, the dark bars of the acacia tree-trunks and the deep shade between created a riotously dappled background that confused my eyes at first: then, slowly, came into focus. The eland – great antelopes, the size of domestic cows – materialised out of the landscape: grey bulls, golden females, wandering slowly between the acacias.

We walked on. The trees thinned and the view slowly widened and filled with animals. There was an elephant family in the far distance, with tiny calves at foot, throwing up dust that glowed red in the sun; more zebra; kudu, reaching up to browse on the mahoganies; a troop of baboons squabbling in the dust over a scrap of food. And impala – impala everywhere, in tens and hundreds, great golden explosions of impala, snorting with alarm as we approached.

After a while we came to a long, towering wall of immense figs and mahoganies. Beneath them lay a long, glittering pool, with steep grey banks pitted by the hoof-prints of buffalo and impala. A pod of hippo dozed against the far bank; and a crocodile had already hauled out onto a small patch of sand, warming itself in the early morning sun.

There was a faint crackling of branches, off somewhere to our right, and an elephant bull emerged onto the bank of the pool and started browsing idly on a small shrub.

'Ah-ha!' Dolf said. He took a small cloth bag from his pocket and tapped it. A tiny cloud of fine ash puffed from the bag and drifted away. 'We're downwind of him', he said. 'He can't scent us.' He shrugged off his pack, rooted around inside, and pulled out a battered camera. 'Come. Try not to tread on twigs and things.'

We picked our way along the bank until we crouched in the undergrowth a few yards from the elephant. 'Wait here,' he whispered. 'Be back in a minute.' He evaporated into the shrubbery.

Dolf had very few failings, apart from serving up coffee-flavoured sulphuric acid in the middle of the night. However, he also had a burning ambition to publish photographs of elephants in *National Geographic*. There was nothing wrong with this per se, but he apparently laboured under the twin delusions that the magazine was only interested in close-up portraits, and that telephoto lenses were for wimps.

He suddenly reappeared, crouching beside the very shrub on which the elephant was browsing. I watched in frozen amazement as he slowly stood up, raised his camera, stuck it more or less in the elephant's face, and let fly.

Cameras were less sophisticated then than they are now, and Dolf's went off with the sound of a hundredweight of tin cans being dropped down a garbage chute. The elephant went rigid with surprise, eyes wide and ears spread, while Dolf fired off a couple more frames. Then it spun round and took to its heels.

Dolf strolled back to where I was still crouching under my bush. He was grinning gleefully.

'Nice shots,' he said. '*National Geographic*, here I come.'

Nobody would have dreamt of doing anything like this to the Gonarezhou's notoriously tetchy elephants.

'But what if he, uh, got stroppy?' I asked.

'Eeesy,' Dolf said. 'No problem. Just shout at 'im. If that doesn't work, fling your hat at 'im. And if that don't work… 'he paused for effect, 'then run like heck. Crosswind, of course,' he added as an afterthought. So that was all right, then. Nothing to worry about.

'C'mon,' he said. 'Let's walk along the pool, see if we can find some more. Then we'll go back before it gets too hot.'

The first of the carmine bee-eaters were arriving, beautiful migrant birds that nest in burrows in the Zambezi's steep, sandy banks and return each year to the same spot to breed.

'There's a colony on the island,' Dolf said. 'Let's go and have a look.'

We launched a canoe and paddled strenuously across the fast-flowing channel until we reached the slower water beside the island. We watched the bee-eaters for a while, flashing crimson overhead and hovering almost motionless outside their burrows before disappearing inside: then we beached the canoe on a tiny shelf of sand and scrambled up a low cliff and onto the island.

An elephant bull, hitherto hidden from our sight, was grazing a few yards away between the tall, spiky clumps of *Vetiveria nigritana* – sometimes known as 'adrenalin grass' because it often conceals animals likely to prove hazardous to the unwary. The elephant heard us coming as we scrabbled over the top of the bank, and instantly charged us. Maybe it was getting fed up with having wide-angle lenses shoved in its face.

'*Voetsak!*' Dolf yelled and, in case it didn't understand Afrikaans, added, 'Bugger off!'

This only made matters worse. The elephant accelerated, and came at us like a turbo-charged block of flats. Dolf wrenched the hat from his head and flung it at the animal. The hat vanished under the elephant's feet in a cloud of dust.

'Ach, man,' Dolf sighed, in a tone of resigned exasperation. There was nowhere to run, crosswind or otherwise, and in any case I was paralysed with terror. Dolf turned and shoved me squarely in the chest. I fell backwards over the bank and into the river, six feet below. While I was still submerged I heard another resounding splash, which I hoped was Dolf and not the elephant.

'Big flatties in here,' Dolf spluttered helpfully as we both surfaced. This wasn't reassuring. Flatty is short for flat-dog, a term of unknown derivation – to me, at any rate – meaning crocodile. They're also called mobile handbags, which is of more self-evident origin, but you still don't want to go swimming with them if you can help it.

We edged back to the canoe, picked the bits of weed out of our hair and peered furtively over the top of the bank. The elephant was nowhere to be seen. We snuck back onto the island and found Dolf's hat. It didn't look hugely different after being run over by five tons of elephant, which led me to wonder if this sort of thing happened more often than Dolf let on. Then we paddled back to camp for tea.

The days passed in a strangely surreal combination of wartime constraint and glimpses of extraordinary beauty. Overnight patrols – which would have meant camping in the bush – had been temporarily halted because of the recent guerrilla attack. By sunset, we'd be walled up inside the fort. But Dolf and I made up for this by going walking at first light, to shake off the claustrophobia.

We'd stroll along the Zambezi in the sunrise, or head inland through the acacia and mahogany woodlands to one of the Mana pools. Busy little mopane squirrels scurried up the tree-trunks as we approached, then peered at us through the leaves, their tails twitching with irritation. Sometimes we'd glimpse a nocturnal civet, or a hyaena belatedly hurrying back to its den. Sometimes, too, we found the tracks of black rhino beside the pools – 500 of them scattered throughout the park, Dolf said, one of the biggest populations in Africa – and followed the spoor until it led us off the floodplains and petered out in the mopane hinterland.

In the evenings the breeze died away and the Zambezi fell glassy-smooth, with long orange sun-pillars reaching across the water from the Zambian hills. The call of hippos in distant bays would be taken up by others, up and down the river, the air reverberating with grunting laughter. Sometimes the tranquillity would be shattered by the army youths, who'd let off a burst or two of tracer across the river – 'to see if anyone wants to play', Vicus said – before retreating into the fort.

I took my turn at guard duty among the grey concrete and machine guns. I paced slowly round the parapet and listened to the whoop of hyaenas and the grunt of hunting lions; and watched the measured tread of elephants, transformed by moonlight as they materialised out of the black woodlands and ambled over the grass towards the river.

In the army, the bush had made me ill. At Mana, in the Zambezi Valley – which had claimed thousands of European lives from malaria, dysentery, blackwater fever – I felt not only well, but fit, fitter than I'd ever been in England. Bits of me – the ones I could see in the scraps of mirror in the fort's rudimentary shower – were even beginning to look like a Real Bushman: tanned a deep brown, where they weren't hidden under a beard that was getting as unruly as Dolf's.

Also, like Dolf, I was learning to leave my watch behind, live by the sun and forget the calendar. Until Dolf casually remarked, 'Resupply convoy comin' tomorrow.'

'Bugger. I could stay here for ever.'

'Then stay, man. Stay as long as you want. I didn't mean you'd have to go with it.'

I'd already been at Mana for almost three weeks. Such supplies as I'd been able to cram into the luggage compartment of Pete's floatplane were almost exhausted, the tins of beans thrown into the evening stew, the biscuits eaten to absorb the worst impacts of Dolf's four o'clock coffee.

'Better go.'

Next morning I left Mana Pools, via 60 miles of barely discernible track, in an armoured truck preceded by a 'pookie' – a locally-made mine-detecting vehicle that looked like an early prototype of a Mars rover.

The pookie skidded to a halt from time to time, its bright orange warning lights flashing. The occupants got out wearing fatalistic expressions and poked the ground with long sticks, unearthing wheelnuts, bottletops and fragments of exhaust pipe left behind by tourists in happier times.

We finally reached the tarred road that led to Salisbury and Kariba, ground up the hairpin bends of the Zambezi Escarpment, and stopped in a lay-by overlooking the Zambezi Valley. In the far distance I could just see the dim outline of the Zambian hills, the thin silver thread of the Zambezi at their feet, across miles of undulating forest and woodland. Dolf's last words, as I threw my pack into the dusty truck, echoed in my mind:

'Are you goin' to write about the dam? Look at it all.' He gestured at the panorama before us: the hazy mountains, the sweep of misty acacias, the hippos lying sleepily in the Zambezi and the elephant and buffalo grazing on the islands.

'How can they even think of it? It's all so' – he groped for words – 'so *lekker*, man. So beautiful.'

Dolf had summed up a simple truth that would – eventually – guide me for the years that followed. There is much ugliness in the world, and I'd seen some of it since I'd come to Rhodesia. But there is overwhelming beauty as well.

The huge, luxuriant trees that grow on Mana's floodplains and the secluded pools shrouded with mahoganies and fig-trees; the splendour of the wildlife panoramas I'd witnessed; above all the majesty of the Zambezi itself, all combined to create the sudden realisation: this is what I've been searching for.

There didn't seem to be much I could do about dams at the time, though, except to go and have a close look at one. Which I did.

Chapter Two

THE FATHEAD'S
HAUNTING CALL

Back in Kariba, the White Elephant was covered in dust and sulking badly. Spiders had been hard at work inside, two tyres had gone flat, and when I pressed the starter there was a faint '*clunk*' followed by a stony silence.

Not that it mattered. I was only trying to be nice to it, as I'd already organised a hired launch to take me across Lake Kariba to Fothergill Island, on the north-eastern tip of the Matusadona National Park, and wouldn't be back for some time. I lectured the White Elephant on the likely rewards of ingratitude, left it to think things over, and hopped onto the motorboat.

Fothergill Island consists of a couple of square miles of mopane scrub, and is named after one of the heroes of Operation Noah, the animal rescue operation that took place when Lake Kariba began to fill. Elephant and buffalo swim across to the island, often followed by lions; there are resident herds of impala, and hippo in most of the bays. It was an obvious place to put a tourist camp – or would have been, in normal times.

However, these weren't normal times (I'm not sure what are, in Zimbabwe). Rob Fynn built his camp on Fothergill Island in 1977, when tourism hit a record low that has only recently been beaten. Fynn transported hundreds of eucalyptus poles, tons of bricks and cement, thousands of bundles of thatching grass, and boatloads of washbasins and lavatory pans across Lake Kariba in the middle of a guerrilla war, and assembled it all into a dozen tourist chalets, an immense open-sided dining room and upstairs bar, and several communal toilet and shower blocks.

All it needed was tourists, and there weren't any – except me, it turned out, as Fynn greeted me on the jetty and the hired boat sped away across the lake. I had, I told Fynn, enough money to spend six weeks on his island, while I tried to bash out some words on the ancient typewriter I'd left stowed in the White Elephant while I was in Mana Pools.

'Also,' I said, 'I'd like to hire a boat if possible, go around to Tashinga' – Tashinga being the Matusadona Park headquarters. I could afford this, since I'd saved fairly heavily on the floatplane.

'No problem,' he said. He indicated a row of small outboard launches tied to the jetty. 'Bit short of drivers, though. Take it yourself, if you like.'

Who, me? Oh all right, then, I know how to drive one of those things – I'm an old English Channel hand, and Kariba's only a lake.

It was too late to go anywhere. Fynn and his wife, Sandy, allocated me one of their chalets. I emptied my pack onto the bed, threw most of its contents into the washbasket, enjoyed the first decent shower I'd had in some weeks, and headed for the bar.

The Fathead's Haunting Call

I woke up in the small hours with a bursting bladder and headed for one of the toilets. Beside its doorway was something that looked curiously like a sleeping hippopotamus, but was probably only a largish rock. When I got there I found it was a sleeping hippopotamus. Hippos are one of Africa's most dangerous animals. They kill a lot of people in Africa, usually on land. I froze. The hippo gave a great sigh, and wriggled itself deeper into its sandy hollow. I abandoned the toilet block idea, tiptoed away and used a tree instead, glancing anxiously over my shoulder.

I mentioned the hippopotamus episode to Fynn in the morning, as I heaved my pack into the boat.

'Ah,' he said, 'Should've warned you. That's Esmeralda.' He looked around the harbour. 'There she is. Over there.'

Esmeralda had apparently been hand-reared by persons unknown and later released into Lake Kariba. She'd attached herself to Fothergill Island while the Fynns were building their camp, and spent her days in the harbour and her nights tearing up the lawns Sandy had carefully planted around the dining room. As I was settling myself into the boat Esmeralda submerged with a faint plop. A few seconds later the boat rocked alarmingly as she scratched her back vigorously on the bottom of the hull. Then she surfaced beside the motor, raised her immense head out of the water and rested it on the transom. Water slopped into the engine-well as the boat settled a few inches.

'Scratch her nose,' Fynn said. 'She loves it.' I did. It was like scratching a wire brush. A dreamy look came into Esmeralda's eyes. Finally she exhaled, a long, hissing, satisfied sigh, slid gently off the boat and vanished.

'Um. Tashinga,' I said to Fynn. 'Couple of headlands or so west, right?'

'Thereabouts,' Fynn said. 'Nice deep harbour. You can see the buildings and watertanks for miles. Can't miss it.'

'Watch out for the trees,' he added, rather puzzlingly, as I set off. Trees? What do they do? I was learning not to take things for granted in Africa.

The stiffish breeze, blowing down from the mountains, didn't register until I emerged from the shelter of Fothergill's harbour. Yesterday, the lake had been a deep, calm blue, riffled here and there by tiny cats' paws. Now, a hazy sun was rising over a grey wilderness of tumbling waves, topped with off-white horses.

The boat instantly buried its bow in a wave. Water slopped into the boat, and sloshed around in the bottom. I was drenched by icy spray, and my teeth began to chatter as water trickled down my back. I slowed down, and pitched and tossed and shivered out into the lake until I could turn and head in the general direction of Tashinga.

It might only be a lake but, I suddenly realised, it's a bloody big one. Fothergill had almost disappeared behind me in the haze. A long, thin strip of barely visible coastline curved away from me. Otherwise, there was nothing to be seen.

The waves got bigger. They'd stopped coming in over the bow since I'd slowed down, but started coming in over the stern instead. Rather belatedly, I inspected my safety equipment. It consisted of a tatty life jacket with kapok oozing out of the seams, a ducky little paddle, and half a plastic milk-bottle. They were all floating around in several inches of water in the bottom of the boat, along with my pack.

The coastline began to curve back towards me, speckled with the tiny dots of elephant and buffalo grazing along the shore. A headland loomed out of the haze, but it didn't have any buildings and watertanks on it, so I headed offshore again across another wide bay, the shore falling away until the elephants and buffalo were lost in the haze.

Another headland appeared. I edged the boat slowly shorewards. Must be Tashinga, I'd been going for ages.

I still couldn't see anything remotely resembling a park headquarters, though. Probably hidden in the bush. Unfortunately I couldn't see any nice deep harbours, either.

But I could see trees. Dead ones – the millions of mopanes, terminalias, acacias, majestic tamarinds and leadwoods that died when Kariba filled. They had been cleared around Fothergill, but not here. Densely packed, grey and forbidding, their skeletons extended far into the lake, hiding the shore behind them. A-ha, I thought, must be what Fynn meant.

They looked harmless enough, but I kept an eye on them all the same. The boat surged forward on the waves, then sank back into the troughs. There seemed to be a small gap through the trees in more or less the right place. Cormorants, drying their extended wings like ragged crucifixes, watched warily as I approached, then dived off the branches into the lake as I passed.

The boat suddenly ramped upwards and stopped dead with a jarring crash that hurled me off my seat and into the bilges along with the paddle, life jacket and about forty gallons of water. It slid sideways and down, off whatever it was I'd hit, with a terrible rending sound punctuated by ominous thumps as the waves passed under us. More water slopped in over the stern. I heaved myself up to the gunwale and peered over the side.

People ought to be more specific. Stumps are what you have to worry about – huge, jagged stumps, blackened with algae and hard as steel, lying in ambush a few inches under the water and suddenly popping up in the wave-troughs all round the boat.

I glanced at the water in the bilges, but there was so much there already it was hard to tell if more was coming in. I edged the boat towards a tree a few yards away, until I could rush forward to the bow and tie the painter round it; then cut the engine and subsided onto the thwart, soaked to the skin and shivering with cold. Nice way to end a 'great adventure', I thought, dying of hypothermia in the middle of a dead subtropical forest.

I set about emptying the boat with the plastic milk-bottle, more to warm myself up than anything. I'm not going back through those stumps, I reflected as I chucked half of Lake Kariba back where it belonged, even if I have to sit here for a week. I could see a few stretches of sandy beach through the trees. Maybe I could swim ashore, and live on nuts and berries until somebody found me. Maybe I could catch fish with the milk-bottle, or brain them with the paddle. Or maybe not. With impeccable timing, a largish crocodile hauled itself out onto one of the beaches.

The sun grew warmer. I seemed to be winning with the milk-bottle. I stopped shivering as my clothes dried, and the wind was slackening. The white horses were disappearing; and, from being grey and uninviting, the water was turning a dark Mediterranean blue.

I looked at my surroundings with more interest. They weren't as hostile and unlovely as they had seemed at first. A small group of impala rams, not yet old and strong enough to claim a herd of females, wandered slowly across one of the beaches. A trio of hippo lay in some calm water behind a small promontory, ears waggling, eyes fixed unwaveringly on me. They vanished underwater, then bobbed up again.

But it was the dead trees that fascinated me. Stripped of their smaller branches, bleached steely-grey by wind and sun, they were reduced to their essential shapes: fan-like mopanes, spreading ebonies and tamarinds. Some were topped with the great, untidy nests of herons and fish eagles. Brilliant blurs of crimson and sapphire streaked between the trunks, and condensed into tiny malachite kingfishers as they perched on the stumps. Pied kingfishers hovered overhead with whirring wings, peered down into the water, then plummeted down with a tiny splash and re-emerged with small fish in their beaks. The mass death of countless trees should have been ugly: instead, it was hauntingly beautiful.

The wind died altogether, and the blue water lay calm except for a long, easy swell. I'd got most of the water out of the boat, and it didn't seem to be coming back in. Well, come on laddie, I said to myself sternly, man or mouse? Squeak up. You won't die of hypothermia, you'll die of heatstroke if you sit around here all day. I untied the painter and paddled the boat back down the inlet until the stumps were safely behind me.

I started the engine and cruised cautiously into the open lake. The haze was clearing a little. I rounded another headland and a mile or two ahead, across one more bay, I saw the rooftops, green-painted watertanks and radio masts of Tashinga. The harbour entrance was easy to find, and deep and wide when I got there. I clambered off the boat and discovered, from a game-scout named Jackson, that I was a silly-arse skipper.

Like many Shonas, water made Jackson uneasy, especially with a stranger at the wheel as we motored into the tiny Chura River. I'd been telling him about my excursion into the tree-stumps. Also like many Shonas, he'd picked up a colourful colonial vocabulary, which he thought was the norm for polite social chit-chat.

'Eeeeh, this fuckin' lake,' he said. 'I went with one big silly-arse skipper one time. I say to him, we go twelve o'clock, too early now, too dangerous, but he say no, we go now. And the boat, it come down whack on this stump,' – he plunged his hand downwards with dramatic finality

– 'and next second, zup! The boat gone, sunk, finish. Me, I can't swim, he pull me to this tree and we sit there all day until the boss come looking for us. What a bugger-up. Silly-arse skipper. You go careful.'

Kenny, another scout, sat on the bow and watched for stumps. We were following a narrow, winding channel between gentle grassy banks that rose to meet tall riverine forest, dark and mysterious. By the banks, the water was blanketed with bright green carpets of *Salvinia* – a floating water fern accidentally introduced into Kariba.

The Matusadona didn't then have the huge concentrations of animals that make Mana Pools or Hwange so spectacular. Instead, it had a blend of beautiful scenery with enough wildlife to bring it vibrantly alive. We rounded a bend, and quietly glided past an elephant standing stolidly in the shallows, thrashing the mud off a trunkful of grass; round another, and a couple of old bull buffalo – *dagga* boys – heaved themselves wearily onto their feet and eyed us reproachfully from the bank. Ageing male buffalo retreat from the hurly-burly of herd life to lie around in the *dagga* (mud) by day and get themselves eaten by lions at night.

A few moments after we'd passed the buffalo, the carpet of *Salvinia* suddenly erupted like a small submarine volcano and a boiling tornado of mud and bubbles headed straight for the boat. 'Eh! Eh!' Jackson cried, clutching the gunwale. Just when a cataclysmic collision seemed inevitable, the underwater tornado changed course and shot across the bows in a bubbling rush. It vanished under the weed along the far bank. The weed heaved violently up and down for a few seconds, then calmed down.

'Hippo,' Kenny said placidly from the bows.

'Too fucking close,' Jackson said. 'You go careful.'

John Stevens, the Matusadona warden, had seconded Kenny and Jackson to me for the day. As I was keen to look for rhinos – which, so far, had eluded me, even at Mana – he'd suggested we head for some of the patches of *machesa*, a form of dense bush unique to the Zambezi Valley, favoured by black rhinos and usually known simply as '*jesse*'.

We pushed on as far as possible up the river, beached the boat, and waded ashore onto a wide plain of red sand, pocked by the muddy wallows of elephant and buffalo. The bleached trunks of giant trees lay strewn across the sand. Those still standing were battered and torn, the bark peeled off in long strips.

'Elephants,' Kenny said, fingering the bark. 'Too many elephants.' Spoor everywhere, in the sand: elephant, buffalo, kudu, impala, crocodile slithers and clawed prints on the riverbank.

'Ah.' He pointed to a large, three-lobed print beside one of the wallows. 'Rhino.' He followed the tracks until they vanished into a dense thicket. Kenny plunged in, and Jackson and I followed.

The best – often the only – way to move through *jesse* thickets is to follow the game-paths. These paths are lined with unbroken walls of vegetation, and they meander and wind so that it's impossible to see more than a few yards ahead. There's a good chance of bumping into a rhino or buffalo coming the other way, a situation akin to a Fiat Uno meeting an articulated truck in a narrow country lane. Something has to give way, and it's not going to be the truck.

The rhino spoor we were following was sharp-edged and new, Kenny said. This did nothing for my nerves, or Jackson's if his expression was anything to go by. We stepped slowly and carefully.

Suddenly, the bush exploded as Kenny almost trod on a *dagga* boy that had abandoned the heat of the lake-shore for the relative cool of the *jesse*. It took off with a snorting rush. Jackson and I leapt about ten feet into the air and came down gibbering with fright. Kenny merely peered calmly down the path, as the snorting and crashing dwindled in the distance and eventually stopped. We explored his resting-place: a few feet of bare earth, along a narrow side-tunnel in the *jesse*.

There was a renewed crashing-about in the bush, somewhere ahead of us. 'Eh! He's coming! He's coming back!' Jackson exclaimed.

We threw ourselves headlong into the tangled stems beside the path. There was a thundering of hooves and the buffalo came tearing back, puffing and snorting and tossing his huge, grizzled head with its flabby dewlaps and glinting black horns. We tried to make ourselves as tiny and inconspicuous as possible and, happily, the buffalo passed by harmlessly. Buffalo are also one of Africa's most dangerous animals. Actually, I was beginning to think, just about everything was one of Africa's most dangerous animals. People have been killed by bushbuck, for God's sake. We held our breath while, once again, the crashing and snorting died away in the distance.

'Too damn cheeky,' Kenny said.

'Big bugger-up,' Jackson said, with feeling. It wasn't his day. It wasn't mine, either, for rhino anyway: he'd probably be miles away, after all the mayhem created by the bull buffalo. We made our way back out of the *jesse*. Kenny reminisced.

'I got hit by a buff, once, at Mana. I couldn't run fast enough, he hit me here.' He slapped at his backside.

'Right up the bum!' Jackson chipped in. He and Kenny dissolved into helpless laughter. We made our way back to Tashinga, where I had a final chat with John Stevens before I went back to Fothergill.

I'd been deeply impressed by what I'd seen of the Matusadona and – as in all the other parks I'd visited – even more so by the men and women who remained at their posts in spite of difficult circumstances and an uncertain future. I said as much to John. He thought for a moment.

'What,' he said, 'would future generations think of us if they knew we had all this, and threw it away?' More articulate than Dolf, maybe, but it came to the same thing in the end.

Back on Fothergill – I'd taken a hint from Jackson, and set off in the late afternoon, by which time the lake was flat, calm and looking as if butter wouldn't melt in its mouth – I was no longer the one and only tourist. I made a beeline for the bar, and found it already occupied by a bunch of tobacco-farmers and their wives.

'We're here for the fishing,' one of them revealed, a mountainous fellow with a beer gut like a pregnant whale. He eased it aside and leant over the bar. 'Never…? NEVER!' he called out. 'S'why he's called Never,' he opined to the world at large. 'Never around when he's needed. NEVER!'

Never appeared, tottering up the stairs beneath three crates of lager. ''Bout time, too. Set 'em up.' Never deftly knocked the caps off a row of bottles and passed them round as if he was dealing cards.

'I'm Frikkie, by the way,' the mountain went on, 'And you? You fishing?'

I explained myself.

'Hah! You work for national parks, then?' said a woman in tight jeans, who'd tried to hide her sell-by date under layers of peroxide and nail varnish.

''Course he doesn't,' one of the company put in. 'He's a Pom,' he went on, as if it accounted for everything.

'Shame.' She stubbed her cigarette out on the bare wooden window ledge. Sparks drifted down onto the thatch below.

'Just as well,' Frikkie said to her. 'Get one o' them uniforms in your sights, you're after it like a long-dog. Khaki fever, that's your trouble.'

It was my week for learning colourful local English. Long-dogs have nothing to do with flat-dogs. They don't even seem to exist, except as metaphors for things that run very fast.

Frikkie turned back to me. 'Come with tomorrow, why don't you?' he said. 'Have a bash at the tigerfish.'

The little I already knew about fishing came from a book titled Mr Crabtree Goes Fishing. My schoolfriends and I had had a brief love affair with fishing before we discovered girls, and held Mr Crabtree in almost mystic awe.

Mr Crabtree went fishing with his son Peter. He described his adventures in hand-drawn pictures with speech bubbles, and could infallibly predict the sort of fish he was going to catch.

'Let's go after roach today, Peter,' he would say – or bream, or carp, or whatever he hadn't caught in the previous chapter – and that's what he got, and usually a whopper, too. You never caught Mr Crabtree saying 'oh bugger it, not another bloody gudgeon.'

Whenever he got a bite, the single word 'STRIKE!' erupted over his head in bold black pen-strokes in a particularly spectacular bubble. The multiple exclamation marks may have given our own exploits an over-emphasis that Mr Crabtree never intended. Yells of 'STRIKE!' echoed across the water as one or the other of us whipped our rods backwards over our heads. Occasionally, a small fish of random species rocketed from the water like a baby Polaris missile, hurtled overhead and made an impact crater on the bank behind.

Fishing with Frikkie could only broaden my experience. 'Love to,' I said.

His boat was a far cry from the tiny motorlaunch I'd taken to Tashinga. The best part of 30 feet long, it had a flying bridge covered by a gaily-striped awning, two immense engines on the back, and *Costa Fortuna* written down each side in technicolor script adorned with flourishes and curlicues. It skipped over the early morning waves and white horses as if it was on a paddling pool.

We headed into the Sanyati River, which runs into Lake Kariba through a deep, flooded gorge. The open lake disappeared behind us and was replaced by towering granite cliffs and steep slopes covered with sparse grass, dotted with sprawling figs and slender, ghostly white star chestnuts. Dassies – rock-rabbits – scuttled over the boulders, and the sharp bark of baboons echoed between the granite cliffs. Sometimes, elephants were silhouetted in single file along the razor-backed ridge-tops.

Frikkie steered us a mile or two into the gorge, then stopped the boat midstream. We drifted slowly in the wind. 'First things first,' he said. 'Grab us some coolies, Margs!' His wife Margs appeared from the bowels of the cabin and handed us each a beer.

Frikkie selected a rod from the holder on the stern and carefully threaded a fillet of fish onto an immense hook.

'Right,' he said, handing me the rod. 'There you go.'

He and his mates busied himself with their own rods, while I watched the fillet of fish slowly disappear into the depths. A minute or two later, I felt a slight tug. Well-schooled by Mr Crabtree, I walloped my rod upwards as hard as I could, and hooked something that felt as solid as the Rock of Ages.

The Rock of Ages thought about things for a moment or two, then tore off downstream. Line fizzed off the reel.

'Bleddy 'ell, that was quick!' Frikkie stopped what he was doing. 'Watch it, it'll try to jump and…'

It did. Something that really did look like a Polaris missile came jetting out of the water. It hung in mid-air for a moment, glistening silver and shedding clouds of spray as it shook itself violently. The rod leapt and shuddered in my hands, then went slack. The Polaris missile aborted its launch, fell back into the river with a mighty splash, and vanished.

'Ohhhh,' Frikkie groaned. 'Ach, shame, hey. Lovely tiger. Threw the hook. Don't hit 'im so quick next time, give 'im a chance to get it in 'is mouth properly.'

So much for you, Mister Bloody Crabtree, I thought. Unfortunately, there wasn't a next time for me. Frikkie and his buddies caught a couple of tigerfish between them, and I had a chance to study them more closely: beautiful creatures, shaped like flattened torpedoes, with olive-green backs giving way to steel-hard scales that flashed like newly-minted coins and shone with a rainbow fire; ruddy fins; and teeth like razorblades. The rainbow colours dulled to grey as the tigerfish died.

Mr Crabtree never tried to catch tigerfish in Kent. If he had, though, he'd never have let it die slowly in the bottom of his boat. He might have whacked it smartly over the head and eaten it. Otherwise, he'd have weighed it and put it back.

'Sis, man. Can't eat them,' Frikkie said, as we headed back to Fothergill for lunch. 'Oily things. Full o' bones. Use 'em as bait. Or give 'em to the…' He used one of about a hundred derogatory terms for local people I'd heard since coming to Rhodesia. 'They'll eat 'em.'

The farmer-fishermen were kind, hospitable and generous to a fault, and – strangely, because they were a lot brighter than they sometimes sounded – utterly bewildered as to why several million people failed to appreciate it.

I arrived at the dining room for breakfast a few days later to find Fynn moodily contemplating the swimming pool in which, he said, Esmeralda had spent the night. It was full of hippo dung and half-chewed grass, and generally unsuited to luxury tourism.

'Bloody hippo!' he said with feeling. Due to cash-flow problems, Fynn hadn't got round to fitting the pool with refinements such as pumps and filters. Instead, he'd employed a small shoal of bream, which were supposed to swim around and eat up the algae. This usually worked quite well, he said. The water stayed fairly clean, if a little cloudy, but you don't always want to see what's on the bottom of a swimming pool in the middle of the African bush. Lizards, frogs and scorpions fall in at night and drown.

Esmeralda's visit imposed a heavy workload on the bream, and it took them a long time to clean up the pool. As soon as they had done so, Esmeralda visited it again, but this time she was still in it when Fynn got up. The spectacle that followed is possibly unique in wildlife history. Fynn found a shovel, crept up on Esmeralda and whacked her on the backside. She shot out of the pool, with Fynn following her, whacking her rump with the shovel and bellowing – 'Get out! Bad hippo! Naughty hippo! And don't come back!'

Six weeks might have been long enough to get something written, if it hadn't been for the farmers. They seemed to spend half their lives fishing and the other half in the bar, and I was only too happy to join them. It beat the hell out of bashing a typewriter in creative solitude, but I was fast running out of time and cash. I resigned myself to the prospect of leaving Fothergill and getting a job, and mentioned this to Fynn. He thought for a moment or two.

'Why don't you write for half the day,' he suggested, 'and pay for your keep by being a guide for the other half?'

This seemed improbable. I couldn't even spell *Phalacrocoracidae* – the family that includes some of Kariba's most common birds – let alone recognise them. 'No problem,' Fynn said. 'The guests can't either. Anyway, you'll pick it up as you go along.'

In my new identity as 'great white hunter', I spent a great deal of time poring over books imaginatively titled The Mammals of, Birds of, Reptiles of, and innumerable other animate entities of, Southern Africa. But Fynn was right. The tourists of the time not only knew less than I did; most of them didn't want to know. They wanted to see lions or, if that was not possible, elephants. A small and disoriented minority wanted to see manatees and tigers. And one or two irritating know-alls were only too eager to help me pick it up as I went along.

October had been scorchingly hot. Day after day, towering thunderclouds built on the Matusadona hills, then slowly melted away in the evenings. The night before though, the storms had swept down from the hills, heralded by a roaring gale that set the boats tossing in the harbour and tore the few remaining leaves from the mopanes. The rain had come stair-rodding down, sending torrents of red, muddy water over the lawns and between the chalets, while thunder crashed and roared overhead.

First light revealed a wet and dripping world, with a sullen grey sky from which a light drizzle was still falling. I dressed myself carefully in Real Bushman grunge, starting with an ancient khaki shirt with the sleeves torn off and a few remaining threads casually draped around the biceps. Then came beaten-up shorts, sandals and an anti-elephant floppy hat, which I'd had to buy new and stomp around in the dust for an hour or two. I shivered my way to the dining room, trying to look rugged.

There, awaiting my pleasure, were a farming couple and their spotty teenage son, taking a break from tigerfishing while the weather sorted itself out. There were also two genuine tourists kitted out in regulation Vogue Africa gear: khaki jackets with imitation cartridge-loops and hundreds of tiny pockets, long trousers tucked into boots that could have stomped the life out of an elephant, and floppy hats with imitation leopard-skin bands. Finally, there was a – then mercifully rare – example of a strange and humourless European migrant species known throughout Africa as the third world groupie.

Females, as in this case, wear artificial dreadlocks, granny-glasses, and shapelessly drab long dresses. They start off by living in mud huts to show solidarity with the starving masses, and end up scrounging food off them. Now and then they visit places like Fothergill to reinforce their prejudices against white farmers, unreconstructed colonials and bourgeois reactionary neo-imperialists, and spend their time inciting the waiters to go on strike.

'Gosh no,' the spotty youth was saying to the boutique tourists as I arrived. 'Manatees can live in fresh water habitats, but they certainly aren't found in Lake Kariba,' he continued.

I swung Rob's hunting rifle onto my shoulder with the easy, casual movement I'd learnt in the army, dealing one of the tourists a glancing blow with its butt as I did so. 'OK. Let's go.'

We trudged through the squelching red mud, down to the lake-shore. Grey waves broke listlessly on the sand, washing up a mess of tangled weed. A bitter wind raised goosepimples on my exposed arms, the tourists huddled into their jackets, and the groupie's dress became even more shapeless, as it began to stick to her body. The hills were hidden behind curtains of drizzle.

'Stuff-all here,' boomed the farmer, Hansie – another absurd Afrikaans diminutive for someone who looked like a mountain on the move. 'Not even a buck.'

'Antelope,' I corrected, as I scanned the bleak lake-shore grasslands with my binos. Hansie was right. Not even a mouse to be seen, let alone a buck. Just one little brownish bird, huddled in the grass. I flicked mentally through the pages of *Roberts' Birds of Southern Africa*.

'Ah. A buffy pipit,' I said. 'Not very common. Aren't we lucky!'

'What's that, some sort of buck?' Hansie said.

'No, a bird. See there. On the ground.'

'Actually,' the spotty youth said, 'it isn't a buffy pipit. Buffy pipits don't have streaks on their backs. It's a Richard's pipit. They're quite common, actually.'

Thank you for that, I thought.

'And over there,' the youth went on, indicating an almost microscopically tiny bird among the grass stems, 'is a rattling cisticola. You can distinguish it from the tinkling, croaking and chirping cisticolas by...'

There are twenty-odd kinds of cisticola, almost all identical. Mercifully, one of the tourists interrupted.

'Where are all the lions, then?' he asked, indignantly.

'Miles away,' I said. 'Over on the mainland. They don't come here all that often.'

'That's not what your leaflet says. Well, what about elephants? Your leaflet says...'

'Somewhere in the bush, probably.' I know what the leaflet says. For starters, those photographs weren't taken in a howling gale and driving grey drizzle at six in the morning.

'Well,' the other tourist said, 'can't we go and look for them?'

This was something I'd hoped to avoid. Watching elephants across a couple of hundred yards of open lake-shore would have been one thing, if there'd been any to watch. Deliberately seeking them out in Fothergill's mopane scrub, with half a dozen people in tow, was another thing altogether. The scrub was almost as thick as the *jesse* at Tashinga.

"Course we can,' Hansie said. 'Can't we, Dicko?' Dicko?

We plunged into the mopane. Cascades of rainwater fell from the branches and down our necks. The groupie tore her dress on a branch. I went into Macho Hunter mode, rifle held across my body, and instantly got the barrel stuck in the fork of a small tree. We crept under low branches and stumbled round the bases of huge anthills. Behind me I heard Hansie holding forth on elephant dung.

'… pack it round your chicken,' he was booming, 'stick it in the oven, cook it for an hour or two, 's'*lekker*.'

'Shhh,' I hissed.

'Yes, shut up, pops,' the youth said. 'You'll scare it away.'

Scare what away, I thought. Then my eyes followed his until they came to rest on a large grey mass, about thirty yards away, that slowly resolved itself into the shape of an elephant, almost invisible among the mopanes. I pointed it out for the benefit of the tourists.

'Need to get closer than this,' one of them said truculently. OK, have it your own way. I reached for some sand to test the wind, and came up with a handful of sticky mud instead. Oh, so that's why Dolf carried that little bag of ash. We crept closer to the elephant until we had a more-or-less clear view, except for some stray branches. The elephant reached for a mopane branch, twisted it off and chewed on it. 'There,' I whispered. 'Lovely pic. Go for it.'

The tourists and the groupie had cameras like Dolf's. All three went off serially, with the sound of a goods train hitting the buffers. The elephant paused in mid-munch, wheeled round, spread its ears and peered at us intently. All three cameras went off again. The elephant took a step in our direction. I fingered the brim of my hat.

'PISS OFF, Dumbo!' Hansie bellowed from behind me. Dumbo? I had one of those oddly mistimed flashes of irrelevant thought. I didn't know Dumbo had penetrated the Afrikaaner culture.

'Hansie! Language!' his wife said mildly. The elephant turned and crashed off through the bush.

'Bloody things,' Hansie said. 'You wanna see what they can do to a field o' mealies.' He raised an imaginary rifle. 'Pow!'

'You shoot them?' the groupie asked, incredulously.

'Blow 'em away' Hansie said cheerfully.

'How could you?'

'Easily,' Hansie said. He offered her what looked like a handful of hairy brown snakes. 'Some of those plait thingies of yours got caught on a twig.'

'They're not plaits. They're dreadlocks,' she said fiercely, and snatched them from him.

'And now can we go back, for Chrissakes, an' have a bloody beer,' Hansie concluded.

As we trudged out of the mopanes and back along the lakeshore, I heard the spotty youth monologuing as we went.

'... members of the *Phalacrocoracidae* family,' he was saying, indicating a cormorant sitting on a tree-stump.

'The what?' one of the tourists said. 'How d' you spell that?'

'... R-A-C-I-D-A-E,' the youth finally finished, as we reached the camp. Somebody's little darling could be destined for a nasty accident, preferably involving crocodiles.

I'd still planned to return to Salisbury when I'd finished writing, but life on Fothergill was easy and undemanding, except for having to shepherd the occasional group of better-informed visitors into eyeball-to-eyeball contact with elephants. I still did occasional call-ups with a rinky-dink little outfit called the Boat Squadron, sometimes known as the Rhodesian Navy, but since there wasn't very much war going on around Lake Kariba there wasn't much to do except learn new ways of catching tigerfish.

'Bugger that,' one of my colleagues said, watching me assemble my rod and reel. He produced a hand grenade, pulled the pin and dropped it over the side. There was a muffled underwater explosion, and a miscellany of dead barbel, bream and small tigerfish floated to the surface in a boil of muddy foam. Mr Crabtree wouldn't have done that.

I built myself a small thatched hut out of mud bricks and mopane poles, where I could wake up and look out over the foreshore and its impala and elephants, without getting out of bed. Zizi, an orphaned eagle owl, took up residence in my hut. At night, when she went hunting, I could call her if she was close by – *hooo-hu, hooo-hu* – and she would sweep down out of the night, with the barest swish of air over her wings. By morning she would be asleep on her perch, occasionally opening one eye if I disturbed her and regarding me with faint distaste.

Time passed in a slow, measured way, interrupted only by incidents such as that of Rob's mum and the lion. Viv Fynn is one of the dying breed of make-a-plan, get-it-done women who kept the British empire going when their menfolk were prostrate with fever, yet managed to remain unmistakably and magnetically feminine. She had been pressed into service as camp cook during one of Rob and Sandy's periodic absences. Around three o'clock one morning I was woken by a distant bellow:

'Come quickly, Dick, and bring your rifle!' I stumbled blearily out into the darkness and down to the camp.

'Lion got into number eight,' Viv said, with the exasperated tone of a London commuter complaining about a late train.

'A what?'

'A lion. Wake up, Dick.'

We marched off to number eight. One of its occupants, a slightly dazed-looking middle-aged man, was nursing a heavily punctured shoulder. His wife dabbed at it with a towel.

'Damn thing sneaked in while I was asleep,' he said, 'and dragged me out of bed.'

The lion, he continued, was trying to heave him through the narrow doorway when his wife shouted 'Drop!', or words to that effect. Lions aren't used to being shouted at like naughty Labrador puppies. It obeyed, and vanished into the night.

Fothergill was having a good run of business that week. A small crowd of curious pyjama-clad onlookers had gathered. They clustered round the door of the hut and goggled at the blood dripping from the victim's shoulder. Viv turned to them.

'There's nothing to worry about,' she announced. 'He's just been eaten by a lion, that's all. Now go back to bed, all of you. Tea will be round in an hour or two.'

On the debit side, I began to realise why – far from deploring the lack of tourists induced by the bush war – most of the park wardens I'd met were positively revelling in their absence.

'Yes,' I'd say, wearily, 'I'm afraid it is blocked again. Terrible smell.' And we'd asked you, very politely, not to use the bloody thing until we'd got the waterpump sorted out. What was that about the swimming pool, incidentally?

'No, not water-snakes, we don't get those here, get them in Panama, places like that, probably a baby cobra or something, must have fallen in during the night. But you're right about the fish. Well, we put them there, actually. They keep it clean. Well, yes, I suppose they do, er, poo in it.'

But I stayed, all the same. This hadn't been the way I'd foreseen things going, when I'd put my proposition to the authorities. Write up the national parks thing had been the general idea, then move on to something else, like 'How to Fix Your Land Rover with a Bent Spoon and a Bootlace'.

But some kind of sea change had set in amid the beauty of Mana Pools, and was slowly being consolidated by the Matusadona. I went to Kariba, exhumed the White Elephant from its burial-mound of dust, mud and dead leaves, and shipped it to Fothergill on one of the ferries that deliver vegetables, coal and defunct vehicles up and down Lake Kariba. Fynn and I floated it across to the Matusadona mainland on a raft made out of oil drums, steel girders and odd bits of timber.

'Hmm,' Fynn said thoughtfully, as waves began to break over the deck. 'Should've checked those drums more carefully…'

He gunned the engine. An angler in a small boat, fishing near our selected landing spot, froze in horrified disbelief at the sight of two tons of outboard-powered Land Rover tearing across the lake, throwing up a large bow wave and apparently bent on running him down. We swerved around him, hit the bank and drove the White Elephant off as the raft sank under us.

The White Elephant gave me more freedom to explore, but I often found myself driving through miles of waterless mopane woodlands and scrub, with few animals to be seen. The Matusadona's loveliest feature of all, I discovered, is its shoreline.

I'd borrow one of Fothergill's motorboats and ease it carefully through the drowned forests and into secret creeks that ran far inland, past low sandy spits where Goliath herons and black egrets stood motionless in the shallows; past red sandstone cliffs topped with tamarinds, figs and leadwoods; and into secluded lagoons in the heart of the Matusadona.

Families of hippo grunted and snorted as I approached, sending up little puffs of spray from their nostrils; and crocodiles – many small, some large and a few monsters – slid silently into the water. Once, I was sitting quietly in one of these lagoons when one of the monsters surfaced alongside the boat. I could have reached out and touched it.

The boat was 12 feet long and the crocodile overlapped it by another six. It could have overturned the boat with a mere flick of its olive-green, wickedly serrated tail. Its jaws could have engulfed three spotty youths and a whole library of bird books. The spotty youth wasn't around, but I was. I sat very still. Eventually the crocodile didn't so much disappear as dematerialise, slowly melting into the water as it sank without a ripple.

I'd watch impala and zebra grazing on the lush grasses that grow on the shores of the lagoons. Sometimes there would be lion, single males or family prides, lying up in the shade, close to the remains of one of the old *dagga* boys. I'd almost always see an elephant bull or two, drinking in the shallows or browsing along the wall of bush beyond the high-water mark; and sometimes they'd be joined by a family group, led by a cautious old matriarch. She'd lift her trunk and sniff the air before leading the calves out of the bush and down to the water.

The babies would roll in the mud and try to spray each other with water, but they hadn't yet learnt how to control their tiny trunks; they flailed around like unrestrained garden hoses. Then they'd go and chase the cattle egrets, lovely snowy-white birds that follow the elephant herds around and feed on insects disturbed by their footsteps.

There were Egyptian geese and white-faced duck; storks and plovers, and the brilliant flash of malachite kingfishers. There were heronries in some of the bays, untidy nests of sticks perched in the dead trees. Bigger and even untidier nests marked the territories of fish eagles: they swooped low over the water and snatched up small fish in their talons; and they circled in thermals high overhead in the heat of the day, their duetting cry '*I'm-over-here*, *Where-are-you*?' filtering down from an eggshell-blue sky.

The Fathead's Haunting Call

'The haunting cry of the fish eagle' is a stock phrase in every tourism brochure ever written about Lake Kariba, and so it is: harshly, eerily haunting. For me, though, the essence of these secret creeks is a shy, brown bird about the size of a bantam that hides away in the day and emerges furtively at dusk, creeping around the litter of jumbled rocks below the sandstone cliffs. As the sun vanishes behind the fringing bush and the windruffled water falls calm and turns to shot-silk, these birds call, long and mournful, *tieeeeu-tieeeeu-TIEEU-TIEEU-tieeuuuu*, dying away in a long diminuendo cadence to silence before the first hunting lion grunts, far across the bush.

Sadly, my iconic little brown bird is called a dikkop, an Afrikaans word that sounds like a bad attack of hiccups. It's even worse in English: loosely translated, it means 'fathead.'

The haunting cry of the fathead. Doesn't have quite the same ring, and it's never caught on.

The Matusadona's secret bays, the slow roll of the seasons – from the summer thunderheads rearing tall into a deep blue sky over the green hills, to the far end of the dry season when the dry leaves crackle underfoot and the mountain backdrop dissolves into the haze – held me captive and entranced for almost two years, in the end. But the arrival of Zimbabwean independence and the associated elections in 1980 felt rather like the full stop at the end of a chapter.

'Well, that's it, then,' Frikkie said, as the news of Robert Mugabe's landslide victory came in over the portable radio perched on the bar. 'There goes the farm. South Africa, here we come.' He'd recovered enough to go tigerfishing in the morning, though.

All I had to lose was a beaten-up Land Rover with bald tyres, a dwindling income from a book that went on at tedious length about dams and Mana Pools, and a collection of wildlife photographs of varying degrees of incompetence.

'Time to stop playing on Fothergill and do something with your life,' said a faint but insistent voice somewhere in my head.

'What?' I asked it.

'Dunno,' it said, and refused to answer any further questions.

Once again, I packed my belongings into the White Elephant. I drove out of the Matusadona, past the now familiar landmarks, over the sandy beds of the lovely Jenje and Mukadzapela rivers, and through the Matusadona hills to Salisbury, now about to morph into Harare. When I got there, of course, I wished I hadn't. The folded mountain backdrop, the dusky bays and the sentinel trees all seemed immensely desirable, once again.

Drink from the Zambezi, they say, and you'll always return. Well, I'd drunk from it fairly copiously, what with being chased into it by elephants and with gallons of it arriving uninvited into small boats. It must be true, because I've returned time and time again to my own special places: the magical Mana woodlands, and the tranquil Matusadona bays.

Chapter Three

IT'S ALWAYS THE ELEPHANT'S FAULT

I rented a bed-sit and survived by selling photographs of back-lit elephants to tourism companies. Meanwhile, a faintly preposterous idea began to take root: maybe I could 'help save Africa's wildlife'.

It would have startled the hell out of my parents, a score of desperate schoolteachers, and a hundred other teenage truants in winklepickers and stovies if I'd shown any signs of such an ambition back in my far-off youth, which I didn't. Scratch a lot of conservationists and you'll find a spotty youth who collected butterflies when he was ten and could spell *Phalacrocoracidae* by the time he was fourteen. Scratch me, and you'll find a spotty youth who could spell M-O-T-O-R-B-I-K-E by the time he was fourteen and C-R-A-S-H a week or two later, but got L-I-S-E-N-C-E wrong, since he'd never seen one.

Not that early education had been much help. A prehistoric old crone known to me and my fellow primary school pupils as Ole Ma Rossiter used to teach us a subject I still think of as 'naycher study.' This occasionally involved walks in the Kentish hills, where Ole Ma Rossiter discussed owl pellets with a tiny band of earnest disciples while the rest of us slipped away into the undergrowth and traded glimpses of bums and belly buttons.

Mostly, though, naycher studies were confined to the classroom, where we learnt even less from the dessicated bits of plant and animal matter Ole Ma Rossiter presented for our inspection and wonder.

I'd learnt more from Mr Crabtree, who slotted in somewhere between Ole Ma Rossiter, girls and motorbikes. Once, when my friends and I were furtively poaching fish from a small lake in the grounds of an old and deserted manor house, I hooked something big enough to resist the Polaris missile treatment. After a titanic battle I landed a four-pound tench, one of the loveliest fish in British waters. Unmistakably golden-scaled and red-eyed, it lay gasping on the bank.

We gazed at it in awe. Usually, anything we caught that was more than four inches long got bashed over the head and taken triumphantly home where it ended up in the dustbin after successive mothers refused point-blank to cook it. But by unspoken agreement we decided to let the beautiful tench live. As none of us owned a portable spring balance – they were unnecessary at our usual level of piscatorial achievement – I wrapped it in a wet cloth, cycled home, weighed it on my mother's kitchen scales and tore back to the lake, leaving her to clean up the mess.

We slipped it gently – reverently, even – back into the water and held our breath as we watched it recover, right itself, and swim back into the mysterious darkness. Something hard-wired into our minds, some sense of wonder at real nature, had survived Ole Ma Rossiter.

This same something began to operate at full throttle after spending almost three years in places like Mana Pools and the Matusadona. Maybe it was just the typical reaction of a suburban Brit who's discovered that not everyone, everywhere, has chopped down all their forests and killed off anything bigger than a badger, and wants to stop them doing it before it's too late. I wouldn't be the first though – Africa's full of us.

But I'd undergone a life-changing experience and a fundamental shift in perception as a result. The dull, solid world I'd known in England – of train timetables, business suits and occasional glimpses of tamed and sanitised landscapes – had been replaced by a wild and endlessly fascinating entity, of incredible loveliness and terrifying fragility. It wasn't just animals or forests, wild rivers or breathtaking scenery. It was all these things, and more. Call it the green chaos, call it wilderness, call it what you like: after a lot of fruitless efforts at analysis, I realised that Dolf had got it right. Just call it beauty.

I was ignoring several fundamental questions, of course: save Africa's wildlife from whom, for example, or what? Did it even need saving at all, since I had spent a couple of years witnessing – and publicising – its blatantly rude health? And, if it did indeed need saving, how? Certainly not by selling photos of back-lit elephants to postcard manufacturers. I wasn't making enough money to save myself, let alone Africa.

I was rescued from impending starvation and handed a unique opportunity to achieve my mission by a surprising turn of events. My book may not have made a huge impact on the local buying public, possibly because they had other things besides dams on their minds, like how to get into Australia. However, it had certainly impressed the powers-that-were, possibly because it said a lot of nice things about

Zimbabwe's national parks and their management. The parks department offered me a job – not, sadly, as director, or even chief warden – they weren't that impressed – but as a rather lowly form of office-bound life known as an interpretive officer.

'Sort of PR job, really,' said the officer who interviewed me. 'You know, get us in the newspapers without having to pay for it, all that sort of thing.'

Well, better than nothing, I thought, not realising that the department was perfectly capable of getting itself into the newspapers without any help from me. On the flip side, I'd have to stop looking like a Real Bushman and start looking like a civil servant instead. Bang went most of my hair, and a lot of the beard. On the other hand, I'd get to wear epaulettes on my shoulder and a natty green beret. I was unattached at the time, and khaki fever seemed to be widespread. No need to tell them I'd be armwrestling a typewriter in head office rather than lions in the bush.

My world imploded from the broad horizons of the Matusadona, to a plasterboard-walled box in the collection of temporary huts which, in those days, passed for the department's head office. Someone knocked on the door, on the morning I took up residence. 'Come in!'

The door flew open with a crash that echoed up and down the corridor outside, and the plasterboard walls shook violently. A game-scout marched in, came to attention in front of my desk with a thunder of boots on concrete, and saluted vigorously. His upraised hand quivered like a tuning fork.

He stood there expectantly, slowly vibrating to a standstill. I'd learnt about giving salutes in the army, but the need to return them hadn't arisen. I tried to stand up, got my knees stuck under the desk, fell heavily into my chair and almost tipped over backwards, my hand half-raised to my forehead.

I made a grab for the edge of the desk, dragged myself upright again, and decided against having another go. A look of pained disappointment passed across the scout's face.

'Sah! Come to take the inventory, sah!' he shouted, in a voice that sounded as if someone had rammed a very large stone halfway down his throat.

'OK, well, take it then,' I said. Must be something the last occupant left behind. The scout reached up behind the door for a clipboard, which I hadn't noticed until then. Instead of taking it away, he turned back to me with another crash of boots and stared at my desk.

'Desks, kneehole, six-drawer, one!' he bellowed. The desk had the sense not to try to return the salute. The penny began to drop.

'Yup, well, er, gosh. So it is.'

We worked our way down from chairs, swivelling, one, to waste bin, metal, one. Baskets, wire, two had either migrated or gone extinct. The scout frowned, and sucked his pencil thoughtfully.

'I will report the wire baskets. Sah,' he said portentously, with a look that implied I'd joined the department with the sole intention of stealing the furniture. 'Otherwise all in order. Sah.' He threw another salute, spent a couple of seconds in tuning fork mode, and marched out before he had to witness another humiliating fiasco.

I soon found that, apart from the possible destruction of the entire Mana Pools National Park, Zimbabwe's wildlife didn't seem to need saving at all. On the contrary: there seemed to be far too much of it about, mostly in the wrong place. Another truth, which I also discovered almost instantly, was that the department had a talent for extraordinarily bad PR. My telephone rang on the second morning.

'You're the fourth person I've spoken to,' a voice said wearily. 'I've got a monkey in my garden.'

Well, lucky old you, I thought, I haven't even got a garden at this stage, let alone monkeys.

'How interesting,' I said. 'What sort?'

I think maybe I'd missed the point. 'I don't know what bloody sort,' the voice said, 'but I want it taken away.'

Something in his tone stopped me asking why. 'Give me your name and address and I'll see what I can do,' I said.

'Thank you.' The tone warmed a little. 'Nice to speak to someone who'll actually do something.' He hung up.

It transpired that I needed the services of an entity known as Problem Animal Control . I relayed the gist to one of its representatives, titled the Warden (PAC).

'Not another one,' he said. 'OK, give me the details, leave it with me.'

My caller was back on the line on the following afternoon. 'Your blokes've just been about the monkey,' he began, without preamble.

'Good-oh,' I said. 'All sorted, then. Glad we could help.'

'Sorted? Help? I expected them to catch it and take it away,' he said, working up into a frenzy of rage, 'and do you know what they did? They shot it!'

'Oh.' It wasn't much of an answer, but it was all I could think of.

'I thought you blokes were supposed to save animals, not go around shooting them in people's back gardens!'

So did I, but I was soon disabused of this notion. 'Well, what did he expect us to do?' said Warden (PAC). 'Spend a week trying to trap it? Dart it? D'you know what drugs cost? Only a bloody vervet, for Gawd's sake, millions of them around.'

There were indeed, as I was to find in the months to follow, and most of them were apparently hanging around in Harare's suburbs. I began to see why I'd been appointed. It wasn't so much to improve the image as to take the flak, which reached the intensity of an artillery barrage when some irredeemably gun-happy lunatic controlled a leopard that had moved into a Harare suburb and was wreaking havoc among the local cats, dogs and domestic rabbits. All hell broke loose. Children, already tearful from the loss of the family tabby, became hysterical and had to go into trauma therapy, if the telephone calls from outraged citizens were to be believed.

The local press got in on the act. 'PARKS MEN BLAST RARE LEOPARD' the headline read, and noted in passing that a 'spokesman was unavailable to comment.' Bloody right I was. I'd grabbed some leave and gapped it back to Fothergill for a few days. Tourists might be a pain in the butt, but they weren't about to lynch me, not with a .458 in my hands.

I welcomed the idea of accompanying a 'darting safari' to Mana Pools, when it was put to me by one of the department's senior biologists.

For one thing, I'd succeeded in enraging the entire research branch within a fortnight of taking up my post. An article about some project or other, written for the department's internal newsletter by a senior warden, had arrived on my desk. It said, inter alia, that the project 'would be managed by practical people – not by biologists.' Being unaware of the merciless warfare that raged between the department's biologists and its field wardens, I took this as a harmless bit of joshing between friends and published it as it stood.

Bad move. On the day the newsletter appeared, my office door was flung open to reveal an apoplectic chief ecologist. 'Biologists,' he enunciated carefully, as if addressing a mentally-challenged chimpanzee, 'are the most practical people within this department.' He turned and left, closing the door carefully behind him. My own image needed a bit of polishing, where the scientists were concerned.

For another thing, the darting safari might provide a welcome relief from the unrelenting carnage that seemed to be characterising my foray into professional conservation. The department wanted to put radio-collars on some elephants to find out where they went and what they did.

An elephant radio-collar is made from a strip of tough material such as conveyor-belting, and incorporates a radio transmitter embedded in plastic. It's a heavy, cumbersome device, which has to be wrapped round the elephant's neck and bolted together at the ends – a process involving large spanners and hammers and a fair bit of swearing and cursing.

Elephants are liable to resent this procedure, so they are tranquillised beforehand by shooting them with a 'dart' filled with a narcotic drug. The elephant falls down; the radio-collar is fitted; an antidote is injected; and the elephant gets up again and walks away, a bit unsteadily but none the worse for the experience. In theory, anyway.

The darting safari would also get me back out of my plasterboard cage and into the bush, which I'd begun to miss badly, and furthermore to Mana, which I hadn't seen for two years. So far, so good. However, things soon began to go downhill.

The department had decided it would be novel and – more to the point – profitable to allow foreign hunters to do the darting for them, and had sold the idea to an American hunter and his wife, whom I shall call Arthur ('Art' for short) and Martha, in return for a significant sum in American dollars.

'What they want,' the senior biologist said, 'is for someone to film the whole thing. With a film camera,' he added, rather superfluously. I thought this over for a moment or two. I can get some sense out of a 35 mm still camera – indeed, this was one of the rather tenuous grounds on which I was recruited into the department – but I'd never shot a single foot of movie film in my life. I pointed this out. Maybe, I said, I ought to get some practice first.

'We don't actually have a film camera,' the biologist said. 'They're bringing it with them. Anyway, I'm sure it's not very difficult,' he went on, rather patronisingly, I felt. 'Just point the thing and press the button.' Ideal job for a mentally-challenged chimpanzee.

As a mere button-pusher, I wasn't allowed anywhere near Art and Martha until I made my own way down to Mana Pools along roads that had, I was glad to note, been carefully graded and cleared of landmines after the end of the war.

The abundant rains, which had persisted until 1980 or thereabouts, had given way to a series of droughts. Mana was dry and dusty, and such shrubs as hadn't been eaten were wilted and drooping in the heat. The great herds of buffalo and impala had broken up into groups of twos and threes, their ribs and hip bones prominent under coats dulled by dust and hunger. I drove slowly past the carcase of a dead elephant hide streaked with vulture-droppings.

Art and Martha were being installed in a small tented city that was springing up in a riverside grove of mahoganies well away from the hoi polloi of the officially designated campsites. A small army of game-scouts was busily erecting vast government-issue canvas tents. Kitchens and toilets were being built from mopane-poles and thatching-grass trucked in from the Mana hinterland. Crystal glassware and bottles of imported Scotch – God only knows where the department got all that from, I made a mental note to examine my miniscule PR budget carefully when I got back – were being laid out on a trestle table.

Art and Martha themselves were perched on canvas-backed chairs a little aside from the general mayhem, glasses in hand, holding court with a gaggle of senior biologists and wardens who, it seemed, had declared a temporary ceasefire.

'... best goddam shot Ah've ever taken,' Art was saying, 'that goddam buff went down like he'd bin sandbagged, more 'n forty-five inches round the horns...'

I approached cautiously, and cleared my throat.

'Ah,' said one of the moguls. 'Ranger Pitman.' He turned to Art and Martha. 'The cameraman, sir.' Art stood up. He was fifty-ish, short and overweight – characteristics I've since come to associate with a lot of hunters.

'Very important man,' he said, shaking my hand. 'Wanna get this all on film. Mostly when Ah shoot sump'n, it don't get up again. Martha, where's that goddam camera?'

'In our tent, hon.' Martha was also overweight, bottle-blonde, with a sunlamp tan. One of the moguls hurried off and returned a few seconds later, carrying what looked like an enormous suitcase. Art opened it carefully. Inside was the biggest camera I'd ever seen in my life. It dripped with knobs, buttons and levers. 'Bought it specially,' Art said cheerfully. 'I dunno nuthin' 'bout cameras, but it's a good 'un, cost a heap. Anyway, you're the expert. Guess you'll figger it out. Jes' film everything, got miles of film.'

He handed me the suitcase. The departmental moguls gave me the sort of dismissive smile that says you're not important enough to be offered a Scotch, whatever Art might say. I retreated, put up my own little one-man tent on the outer fringes of the camp, and removed the camera gingerly from its case. An hour or so later I'd mastered some of its more basic functions, like where to put the film in and which button actually produced the clatter of film through shutter instead of the whine of a huge telephoto lens extruding itself from its sheath like the penis of a randy elephant bull. This was just as well, because a game-scout materialised outside the tent. He couldn't crash his boots on the silty sand of the Mana floodplain, but he did the tuning fork trick all the same.

'Mister Art wants you, sah. He says to bring the camera, sah.'

'Hey, uh, what's your name?' Art greeted me. 'Well, Dick, you jes' call me Art. Now, Martha here's jes' goin' for a reel bush shower, ain't that so, babe? Great background stuff. Now, babe, you jes' walk up to that cute lil' shower, nice an' slow.'

Martha set off towards the thatched walls of the shower at a glacial pace. 'Dick, you gettin' this?' Art said.

I was, except I kept hitting the telephoto lens button by accident. The elephant's penis whined in and out, and Martha ballooned until she overflowed the viewfinder, then shrank to the proportions of an ant in the Kalahari.

'Turn round now, babe,' Art yelled as Martha reached the doorway. 'Give us a beeg smile.' She did. I overshot, capturing the smile and a bit of her nose as well. Then she vanished into the shower. I wondered if I was supposed to follow her.

Art was revelling in his new-found role as film producer and director. 'Turn it on, babe,' he shouted, then turned back to me.

'See that shower-rose there, stickin' out over the top? Get in nice an' tight on that, get the water comin' out of it. There! Now, babe,' he addressed the thatched shower, 'you jes' stand on tiptoe an' wave the soap up real high, where we can see it.'

Martha's hand appeared above the thatch, holding a bar of soap. It slipped out of her hand and fell in the sand beside the shower. I panned down five feet of thatch and caught up with the soap a couple of seconds after it hit.

'Gosh-durn it,' Art said. He retrieved the soap and tossed it back over the thatch. 'Do it again, babe,' he said. 'Hang on to it, this time. Dick, you ready? OK, there it is… you gettin' this, Dick?'

Yeah, sort of.

''Kay, babe, you ready to come out now?'

'No ways, Art,' Martha squawked from inside the shower, 'ain't even started yet, goddam soap's all covered in dirt.'

Art sighed. ''Kay, babe. Hurry it up. We'll git some other stuff while we're waitin'.' We panned slowly across the river, left to right. Then back the other way. Now the camp. Then a game-scout struggling across the sand with a bundle of tent poles on his shoulder. The scout noticed us in mid-shot, froze on one leg, tried to salute and dropped the poles. 'Great shot,' Art said enthusiastically.

'Ah've finished, hon,' Martha called from the shower.

'Jes' a minute, babe,' Art said, turning back to the scout. 'Pick 'em up, son. Nice an' slow. Dick, you gettin' this? 'Kay, babe. Come out now.'

Martha had aspirations for stardom all of her own. A single foot with glaring red toenails appeared in the shower's doorway, slowly followed by a scrawny calf, then a terrifying expanse of thigh covered in sunburnt cellulite as Martha slowly raised her leg as high as she could and waved it around like a cancan dancer.

'Hoo, boy!' Art said. 'Lookit that! Ain't that something! 'Kay, babe, let's have the rest of you.' Martha sashayed out of the shower in a pink bathwrap, like a mobile blancmange, a sight Art seemed to find transcendently erotic. ''Kay, Dick, that's jes' fahn,' he said . 'Time for a rest. C'mon, babe.' He gave me a huge wink, took Martha by the arm and disappeared into their tent.

Soap, Sand'n Sex. Ought to go over big at Cannes.

This excitement apart, the going was slow. The Mana elephants, usually plentiful, largely vanished when they were most needed, possibly alerted by the sudden presence of lots of game-scouts carrying guns.

'Bloody desert,' one of the biologists announced, during an evening campfire chat. 'Look at the place.' This wasn't easy since it was dark, but I knew what he meant. Mana always looks like a desert at the far end of the dry season.

'Ecological slum,' he went on. 'Far too much of everything. 'Specially elephants. Look what they're doing to the albidas. Too many elephants. Need managing.'

Animals only get 'controlled' in ones and twos. Management implies a more comprehensive approach to things. Either way, you can lay odds that something's going to get shot.

One of the parks department's articles of faith was that there was far too much wildlife in most of the country's national parks, as well as in Harare's suburbs. This *embarras de richesses*, they thought, was eating itself out of house and home and damaging the country's bush and woodlands beyond repair in the process. In particular, the department wanted to shoot about half the country's 40,000 elephants.

Not everyone agreed with this, in Zimbabwe or elsewhere in the world, and I'd already been required to write a spirited defence of 'elephant population management' in the course of my duties.

Other animals weren't about to get away with it, though. 'And the bush-goats,' another biological guru chipped in. 'Impala,' he added, for Art and Martha's benefit. 'Need to manage them, too, never mind elephants.'

Someone else caught the enthusiastic mood. 'What about the hippos? Nobody ever even thinks about the hippos. River's packed with them.'

'Hippos?' Art said. 'Ah never even thought of shootin' a hippo. Whyn'cha sell 'em to us hunners?'

'We do,' I said. You could pay to shoot just about anything in Zimbabwe, down to field mice. I'd got a copy of the price lists in my office.

'But we gotta manage all of them, males, females, calves, the lot,' said the Save the Hippo representative. 'You guys only want to shoot the big ones.'

'Oh, I dunno,' Art said, thoughtfully.

While the game-scouts beat the bushes for dartable elephants, Art whiled the time away by filming more background. We graduated from bush showers, cellulite and startled game-scouts to impala, crocodiles, baboons and buffalo. Art casually mentioned over supper that he particularly wanted some footage of lion – which, like the elephants, are usually abundant at Mana, but had vanished the moment we arrived.

'Sorting the lion thing,' a junior warden announced, early next morning. 'Shot a kudu, we'll use it for bait.'

'Goddammit, when did'ya do that?' Art asked, disappointedly. He had to be content with a whole spool of film of the ensuing butchery, which involved dragging the carcase for several miles to lay a scent trail, hacking it into pieces and hoisting them up trees.

The Mana lions obstinately refused to come to the baits that night, or the next, however, and the bits of kudu slowly putrified. A small expedition went out and shot a buffalo, cut a brand-new mile-long track through the *jesse* to get the carcase out, took down the remains of the kudu and hung bits of buffalo in the trees instead. The lions turned their noses up at that, too.

Elephants came at night, when they came at all. I was asleep in my tent and having, as I thought, a strange dream.

'Arnwood Christian soo-oldiers,' someone was bellowing, with a bad ear for pitch and an American accent, accompanied by the sound of breaking branches. There was a burst of hysterical laughter, and a renewed crashing of branches. I suddenly realised I wasn't dreaming at all, and poked my head out between the tent flaps.

Art and Martha's tent was heaving and tossing like a tarpaulin in a gale. So was the tree under which it stood. Someone turned on a flashlight, revealing one of Mana's larger elephant bulls, tugging at the tree and giving the tent a good working-over in the process.

The elephant temporarily abandoned the tree, focused its attention on the flashlight-wielder, and screamed with irritation. The flashlight went out abruptly, and there was the sound of someone beating a quick retreat.

'Maaarchin' as to waaar...' came Art and Martha's voices in duet, from the tent. The elephant gave a final tug at whatever it was after. A large branch fell from the tree onto the tent, which began to show signs of imminent collapse, and the elephant fled.

'With the crarss of Jeee-sus... whoa there, Martha, shush. Cain't hear nuthin', now.' There was a long and pregnant silence; then the tent-flap was slowly unzipped from inside, and Art's head appeared.

A bevy of parks department officers emerged from the shadows. A pyjama-clad Art stepped cautiously out of the tent, followed by Martha, looking even more like a blancmange in her frilly chiffon nightdress.

'Goddammit,' Art said, 'thought we wuz goin' to die in there.'

'Think he's gone now,' one of the parks contingent said, casting the beam of his flashlight cautiously into the bushes. Art borrowed the flashlight and surveyed the ruins of the tent.

'Darn,' Martha said. 'Shine it in the tree, hon.' Art complied. 'Where's those oranges?'

'Oranges?' the parks officer said in a slightly strangled tone.

'Whole bag full of 'em. Hung 'em in the tree, thought they'd keep better up there. Goddam ele's stole 'em.'

Art and Martha's tent was temporarily repaired and they went back to bed. One of the rangers and I went and sat on the river bank, enjoying a bit of peace and quiet. A Scops owl – tiny little things, no bigger than a dove – called in the woodlands behind us, *prrrup! prrrup!* Hippos grunted in the backwaters, and the saxophonal call of a distant hyaena echoed down the river.

The ranger explained. It turned out that some bright tourist who'd left his telephoto lens at home had recently rolled a couple of oranges at a passing elephant, to see if it could be tempted within range for a close-up portrait. It could indeed. The elephant sniffed at the oranges, picked them up, sucked at them tentatively and liked what it tasted.

After hanging around a while to see if any more oranges were forthcoming, this particular elephant went on its way harmlessly enough. Unfortunately, the idea caught on, with both elephants and tourists. Every wannabe wildlife photographer had started doing it. The Mana campsite had begun to look like a psychedelic bowling green in a thunderstorm, with oranges rolling all over the place, elephants chasing them like kittens after balls of wool, and a constant flicker of flashbulbs.

Now, the inevitable was happening. Oranges emerge from tents and trucks: there must be more where those came from, the elephants had begun to reason, correctly. Instead of waiting meekly for handouts, they'd gone on the offensive. Good thing Martha hadn't stowed the oranges under her bed, the ranger said.

It's difficult to construct a dramatic piece of cinematic art out of a broken branch, a re-erected tent and a bag of oranges that isn't there, but Art had a good go at it. Once we'd exhausted these possibilities, though, there wasn't much left to film that hadn't already been filmed several times before, from varying angles and in different lighting. Even Art got tired of filming game-scouts scouting and rangers ranging, and we all sat around in increasing boredom.

A suitable candidate for darting finally turned up, close to one of the Mana pools. We set off in a kind of presidential cavalcade headed by Ronnie van Heerden, then one of the department's most experienced field officers. Ronnie was carrying a hunting rifle, and Art had the dart gun. A second rank consisted of Martha, a couple of junior wardens, a gaggle of game-scouts, and myself plus camera. Behind us came the hangers-on: a phalanx of eighteen (I counted them) friends of the various participants, friends of friends, and other assorted freeloaders who hung around grousing about the lack of action but hadn't bothered to bring their own food and drink.

Almost as soon as we set foot outside camp, a lioness suddenly emerged from a stand of Vetiveria grass, a few yards away from Art and Ronnie, spitting and snarling. Ronnie motioned at the rest of us to stop, and slowly raised his rifle.

Suddenly the grass all around us erupted with two more lionesses and a riot of young, golden cubs. The game-scouts raised their rifles as well. The rest of us held our breath and tried to pretend we weren't there. The three lionesses stood their ground, all growling, deep in their throats, covering the retreat of the cubs: then they backed off slowly, still snarling, and vanished into the grass. Ronnie lowered his rifle. Art tiptoed back to me.

'Did ya get that?' he whispered. Well, no, actually. The whole episode was over in about ten seconds flat, and I'd barely got as far as turning the camera on. 'Goddammit' he said, and went back to Ronnie.

Surprisingly, Ronnie managed to manoeuvre his army of participants and hangers-on into darting distance of the unsuspecting female elephant that was browsing peacefully on what was left of the Mana Pools vegetation. He positioned the peanut gallery among the surrounding shrubbery and gave Art a quick briefing.

'We'll take her from behind that anthill,' he said quietly. 'Nicely positioned if she stays that way. Hit her in the backside, Art, in the muscle, like we've talked about.'

He glanced round. 'You guys,' – Martha, the junior wardens and me – 'park behind that tree.' He pointed at an acacia a few yards from the anthill. He and Art made their way carefully to the anthill. I leant against my tree, had the usual contretemps with the telephoto lens, and began filming.

Art slowly raised the dart gun and sighted carefully. Then, just as he was about to fire, one of the spectators hidden in the bush tried to stifle a sneeze. The elephant stopped browsing and half-turned towards us, swinging her head to and fro, ears spread and trunk raised, ready to make off at the slightest hint of human sound or scent.

It had taken Ronnie several days to get Art within range of an elephant, and now even this opportunity seemed about to evaporate. Ronnie turned and silently mouthed something at us, his face creased with frustration. The whirring of the camera, I suddenly realised, sounded thunderous in the silence. I switched it off.

After what felt like an age, the elephant finally turned back to the shrub she'd been browsing on. A few seconds later Art raised the gun again, and there was a faint 'phut' as he fired the dart. It thwacked neatly into the elephant's backside, its flight looking like a small white butterfly.

Things happened very fast after that. The elephant spun round, trumpeted shrilly, and charged straight at Art and Ronnie.

Ronnie stepped out from behind the anthill, into the path of the oncoming elephant. '*VOETSAK*!' he yelled, as Dolf had done at the elephant bull on the sandbank, and with the same disconcerting lack of impact.

'Oh, my Gawd!' I heard Martha say, behind me.

Ronnie couldn't push Art into the river, because there wasn't one. He shoved him up the anthill instead, then turned back to the elephant, which was almost on top of him. He fired from the hip and shot the elephant straight through the brain, skipped backwards as she fell at his feet, and put another round into her to make sure.

The echoing boom of the heavy rifle faded across the Mana floodplains. The elephant twitched, and lay still. Blood oozed from the bullet-wounds, and pooled in the sand. Slowly, hesitantly, people emerged from the bushes and gathered beside the corpse, bewildered and quiet.

Art broke the silence. 'Whoooeee! he whooped, sliding down the anthill like a kid on a playground slide. 'Fahn shootin'! D'ya see that, babe?'

He picked Martha up, whirled her around a time or two, then put her down again, puffing with the effort. 'Gawd's sakes, hon,' Martha said, half-tearfully, 'Ah thought you was goin' to die.'

'Not with ole Ronnie here. Fahn shootin'' he cried again. He turned to Ronnie, who was studying the elephant thoughtfully, and shook his hand with the joyful energy of a foundering sailor who has finally located the bilge-pump handle.

'You save that cartridge case, Ronnie, Ah'll have it gold-plated. Hey, lookit ma trousers! Got mud on 'em, she came that close! Hey, Dick, film ma trousers! C'n ya get the mud?'

Then he clambered up onto the bleeding corpse. He reached down to Martha.

'Babe, c'mon, git up heah!' He pulled her up beside him. 'C'n ya get us all in, Dick? Us 'n' the ellie?' He got Ronnie up there as well and they all balanced there, wobbling slightly as if perched on a vast grey jelly. After I'd panned and zoomed to Art's satisfaction they all climbed down again.

'Whoo, babe, lookit them tail hairs! Gotta have some o' them! Make great bracelets!' Art cried. He and Martha set about wrenching the hairs out of the poor beast's tail.

Ronnie was sad and subdued that evening, and sat apart from the others. The really bad bit, he told me, was that she'd had a calf, young enough for her still to be in milk.

As for me: I was secretly glad I'd switched the camera off before the elephant charged and died. Art may not have been too happy about it, though.

Back in the office, I discovered that Mana's orange-eating elephants had acquired the status of Problem Animals, along with the urbanised monkeys and leopards, and were about to get themselves controlled.

'Look at this lot,' the chief warden said to me, brandishing a file of complaints. The tiniest whiff of an orange buried deep in someone's camping stores was sparking orgies of violence. Orange-crazed elephants were ripping tents to shreds, battering tin trunks to pieces, and bouncing up and down on campervans until orange squash came oozing out of the wreckage. Sometimes they'd get through half a bag of lemons before they realised their mistake, which only made matters worse. They'd pucker up – one ranger swore he'd seen this happen – and go berserk until they found some oranges to take the taste away.

Several visitors, either stuck inside the targeted tents and campervans or rash enough to try and defend their property, almost got themselves classified as collateral damage. The complaints described these incidents in lurid detail, and ended with demands for compensation.

The chief warden wasn't much of a one for euphemisms. 'Those elephants,' he said with an air of finality, 'will have to be shot.'

This seemed unfair to me, even if it did conform to what, I was beginning to learn, was a guiding principle in southern African elephant conservation: it's always the elephant's fault. Nobody ever talks about controlling a few tourists instead. I said as much, and left. A few minutes later I was fiddling miserably with some paperwork in my own office when the chief warden appeared.

'You've got two weeks to save those elephants,' he said, rather more gently. 'Get on the radio, get onto the newspapers, say something about bloody tourists who feed oranges to elephants.'

Tourists were banned from taking oranges to Mana Pools, on pain of heavy fines. I sent out a press release and did some radio and television interviews. I believe a couple of elephants got shot all the same, but it felt good to redress the balance, just a tiny bit.

The Art and Martha episode at my beloved Mana Pools had come as something of a shock. Once again, I took refuge by escaping. I went to Fothergill, but the Matusadona landscape was changing. The lake was slowly falling, to expose immense, gently-shelving shorelines, and leaving thousands of the dead trees high and dry. They lost their beauty and the shorelines looked like old photographs of Flanders after a particularly nasty bombardment.

My favourite creeks and bays had dried up altogether and become mere grassy depressions, lying beyond dense barricades of trees, unreachable by boat. So I went back to Mana Pools instead, and discovered another 'great truth' in the process: khaki fever's all very well, but you have to be very careful about who you infect.

Sophie was a radiographer who claimed to be able to say 'drop your trousers' in ten different languages. She hadn't said it to me yet, though, in English or any other language. I thought a trip to Mana Pools might do the trick.

I should have known better. She'd had an encouragingly licentious gleam in her eyes when I'd met her, but it had begun to fade when I took her to the sort of restaurant I could afford on a parks department pay cheque. And it faded even further during the hot and dusty eight-hour drive from Harare to Mcheni, one of Mana's so-called 'exclusive campsites'. Something to do with the White Elephant's speed, comfort and air conditioning, or rather the absence thereof.

When we finally got to Mcheni I climbed stiffly out of the White Elephant, strolled to the riverbank and studied the view. Upstream, the riverbank curved round in an immense sweep of dusty floodplain, broken by tiny gullies, isolated clusters of apple-ring acacias, and tall stands of Vetiveria grass. A herd of buffalo meandered slowly across the floodplain, sending up clouds of grey dust.

Downstream, a long, lovely vista of grey-green acacias in full dry-season leaf, like a huge, billowing wave breaking over the riverbank; an island, covered in dark mahoganies; and a string of elephant-pearls between bank and island, grey against sparkling blue. Ahead, hippos in a tiny backwater and the dark olive-green backs of basking crocodiles. Fantastic, I thought to myself.

Sophie, however, had other things on her mind. 'Where,' she enquired, 'are the toilets?'

I directed her to a small, thatched, termite-eaten structure which housed a toilet pan perched over a deep and rather smelly hole in the ground. She wandered across to it and peered inside.

'No ways,' she said, truculently. 'I'm not using that for four days.'

'Well, then…' I waved vaguely at the surrounding bush.

'What!? With all those snakes and spiders around? You've got to be joking. Where's the nearest proper loo?'

'At Nyamepi,' I sighed – this being the assortment of shacks, derelict tractors and jam-packed campsites that had replaced the fort at Mana's headquarters. 'They've got flush toilets at Nyamepi. They don't always work, though.'

Sophie got back into the Land Rover. 'Let's go.'

Nyamepi was predictably dreadful. Beatboxes boomed beside immense tents that made my puny little two-man effort look like a pocket handkerchief strung between two hatpins. Datsuns – the Mana access road had been over-improved, in my opinion – tore through the campsite, throwing up choking clouds of dust.

The flush loos weren't working. I tried to knock up an omelette for supper, but the dustclouds kicked up by the Datsuns came billowing over the tent on a fresh breeze, then fell in deep drifts in the calmer air behind. Most of it went into the frying pan, plus a lot of insect biodiversity attracted by the flickering light of the gas stove.

The omelette might look as if it had been sprinkled with currants, raisins and pepper, but it tasted like beetles fried in dust, as Sophie took care to point out. The ambient temperature was in the high thirties, but the atmosphere between Sophie and myself dropped to near-freezing during supper, and neared absolute zero during the night that followed.

To cut a long and painful story short, Sophie's khaki fever went into remission and she hitched a ride back to Harare in the morning. I drove back to Mcheni as fast as the White Elephant could carry me. I watched the moon rise over the woodlands; left the tent in its bag and erected my stretcher-bed beside the riverbank, with a nice view of the river on one side and the White Elephant's buckled bumper on the other; and fell deeply asleep.

I woke up during the night to find that four good-sized trees had sprung up in the three-yard gap between me and the White Elephant. The trees had grubby toenails and were attached to a very large elephant. There's no such thing as a small elephant, seen from ground zero. It was running its trunk over the White Elephant, pausing now and then at the gaps between the battered doors and their frames.

Like the Queen of England, storybook elephants don't fart, burp and suffer from perpetual borborygmus – an up-market term for rumbling guts, which I'd learnt from Sophie while we were at Nyamepi. Something to do with beetle omelettes, maybe. Real elephants do all these things, often simultaneously. Its internal cellulose processing-plant was generating a deafening symphony of rumbles, gurgles and slabbering farts that echoed eerily off the White Elephant's door-panels. It's an endearing characteristic, making them seem fallible and more human than ever, but not when it's happening six feet away.

Luckily, I'd obeyed my own instructions to the public at large, and left the oranges at home. Instead of wandering off in disappointment, though, the elephant turned its attention to the apple-ring acacia tree under which I had been dumb enough to sleep.

It's Always the Elephant's Fault

It planted its forefeet squarely about a yard from my stretcher, reached up and heaved enthusiastically at a branch, high overhead. Leaves, twigs, a lot of miscellaneous arboreal detritus and a few ripe pods showered down around me. Then it set about hoovering up the pods, including those that had come to rest on my abdomen – a sensation like being tickled with a very large hosepipe. It chewed them up with the sound of woodchips being fed to a pulping-machine, and splinters rained down on my face.

There is little to be done in these circumstances. One has already set oneself up as a hostage to fortune or, more concisely, as a silly twit. I began to realise how Art and Martha must have felt, but I couldn't remember more than the first line of 'Onward Christian Soldiers.' Besides which, I can't sing. I decided against it.

I could always leap to my feet, shout '*VOETSAK*!' and jump into a river full of crocodiles, but this needed split-second co-ordination which, I thought, the elephant could probably match or surpass. You'd be surprised how fast they can move, especially if they think you might be running away with the oranges. You'd be surprised how fast crocodiles can move, too.

Better, I thought, to lie very still, quiet as a little mouse. No, not a mouse, you hear nasty stories about elephants and mice. Quiet as a termite-eaten tree-trunk, then. I'd never seen elephants pinning termite-eaten tree-trunks to the ground. Maybe it'll go away.

And after a minute or two, during which it investigated the underside of my stretcher-bed for errant pods, it did. I spent the rest of the night curled up uncomfortably inside the White Elephant, and slung the pocket handkerchief between its hatpins in the morning.

I took advantage of my unplanned freedom by going for a long, luxurious stroll in the morning, unpunctuated by complaints about thorns in sandals, itchy mosquito-bites and cornflakes soaked in sour milk. Not far from Mcheni, behind an old, dry river-channel, I discovered one of the most magnificent woodlands I've ever seen.

It wasn't very large – half a mile square, maybe – but it consisted almost entirely of huge mahoganies, with immense trunks and dark, leafy canopies. Occasional shafts of sun penetrated the dense foliage and suffused the woodlands with a golden glow. Here and there, pools of blinding light marked tiny open glades where ancient trees had died, their massive trunks slowly being eaten away by termites and providing perches for troops of baboons.

Impala herds stood almost motionless: then, as I approached, erupted in a blaze of amber hide and flashing hooves. There were eland and zebra; and kudu browsing on the mahoganies. I picked my way carefully round several elephants bulls, and gave a wide berth to a group of elephant cows, with tiny calves at foot; and to a couple of old *dagga* boys lying in the shade. There were the hoofprints of a rhinoceros, meandering out of the woodlands and into the scrub that surrounded them. I followed them for a while, but lost them in the scrub.

And, yes, there were carcases shrivelled by sun, spattered with vulture-droppings, and skeletons scattered by hyaenas: a zebra, beside a dry, hoof-pocked depression that once held water; an impala; an elephant calf, abandoned by its mother.

A few months later, though, I paid a fleeting visit to Mana in February, at the height of the rains. I huddled under the branch of an acacia and watched the storms swoop down from the Zambian hills. Rain-wraiths came writhing and dancing across the river, obliterating the islands and channels, bringing winds that shrieked through the trees and tore the leaves from the branches.

Brilliant emerald grass grew tall and dense where before there was nothing but dust; and there wasn't an animal to be seen: all gone into the hinterland, until they were driven back to the Zambezi as the pans and grass shrivelled and the long, dry months inched by once again.

My mind went back to the parks biologists, and the talk of 'managing' elephants and impala. Complicity in the death of one elephant had been enough for me, let alone several thousand.

It all sounded logical enough, in impersonal scientific terms, but I wasn't sure I wanted to be party to it, I thought, as I rediscovered the loveliness of Mana Pools. And – was it even necessary? We call them good years and bad years, our human perspectives distorted by preconceived ideas of the way nature ought to behave, but there's no such thing, really: just the eternal cycles of scorching drought and flooding rains, death and rebirth. That was all part of the beauty, too.

The business about the Mupata Gorge dam and the proposed destruction of Mana Pools came to a head. We at the parks department kicked up a fairly high-profile fuss about it all, and Mupata was eventually abandoned – or 'shelved', as its proponents preferred to call it – in favour of the Batoka Gorge, which lies just downstream of the Victoria Falls. I hadn't actually seen the Batoka Gorge – yet – but it was said to be long, narrow, formed almost entirely of bare basalt rock and populated mostly by crocodiles, so this seemed a reasonable trade-off.

But I was an odd species in the departmental ecosystem, neither fish nor fowl. I wasn't a steeped-in-the-bush field officer, but I wasn't a scientist either. I occupied a sort of hierarchical no-man's-land along with the bean-counters and storekeepers.

I began to think: maybe I am a mentally-challenged chimpanzee, sitting in my cage and grinning submissively at passing chief ecologists, scribbling pamphlets about the desirability of shooting 20,000 elephants, and being let out now and again to make films of people wobbling on top of dead elephants. It seemed an odd way to set about Saving Africa's Wildlife.

And khaki fever, I'd decided, was an overrated phenomenon. I resigned, even though it meant handing in the epaulettes and green beret, and went back to the wilderness – both in spirit and, more interestingly, in reality, as well.

Chapter Four

GOING DOWN THE DRAIN

The Batoka Gorge is several hundred feet deep, begins at the Victoria Falls, ends more than thirty miles downstream, and was carved out of solid black basalt rock by the floodwaters of the Zambezi River. It didn't sound particularly attractive, but I was still quite keen to see it as it had replaced the Mupata Gorge as candidate number one for damming and destruction. I therefore reacted with incautious enthusiasm to the telephone call I received not long after I'd left the parks department.

My caller had come straight to the point. 'I'm organising a rafting trip down the Batoka Gorge,' he said. 'Would you like to come with us and take some photographs?'

Another tourism outfit looking for cheap publicity, I thought. One of the less uplifting things I did to keep body and soul together after I'd left the parks department was to write articles about various tourist activities for a small magazine devoted to the oxymoronically-named 'hospitality industry.' The articles had to be wildly sycophantic, so that the magazine could touch the companies concerned for a page or two of advertising. Sometimes the companies would offer me free excursions in the hope of getting the sycophantic article without having to buy the advertising.

I knew that a couple of rafting companies were already operating in the Batoka Gorge. They did day trips from the luxury hotels at the Victoria Falls, and their brochures showed tanned, curvy blondes in tiny bikinis, waving happily as they swooped over innocuous little wavelets in brightly-coloured rubber dinghies.

I was as ill-trained for photographing blondes on rubber dinghies in the depths of a basalt gorge as I had been for filming people dancing on elephant carcases, but never mind, I could learn fast, I thought. And it would be a painless way of getting a look at the Batoka Gorge.

'Sounds great,' I said. 'Count me in. Which company are you with, by the way?'

Well, none, actually. My caller turned out to be Father James Channing Pearce, a Jesuit priest who taught at St George's College in Harare, an institution with a long history of wilderness exploration in its more eccentric guises. My initial burst of enthusiasm slowly turned to mounting horror as I listened to his proposal.

It involved over twenty teenage youths and three adults, with not a bikini-clad blonde in sight. It wasn't going to be a day trip, in between a couple of nights in a five-star hotel. James was planning to raft down the entire length of the gorge which, he said with apparent relish, included a large number of rapids of world-class size and malevolence. This would probably take the best part of two weeks. We'd be carrying all our provisions with us, and camping as and where we could.

Most ominously of all, the rafts would be built to James's own design, out of tractor-tyre inner tubes and long pieces of bamboo pole, all tied together with rope. So much for the flashy rubber dinghies as well as the blondes.

'We'll assemble them on the spot,' he went on. 'Each raft will have four sections, loosely tied together with rope, so it'll simply follow the shape of the waves instead of capsizing the way the inflatables do. We'll have two people on each section, eight people per raft, three rafts.'

'Nobody's done it this way before,' James concluded.

Nor since, I might add, and with good reason too. But it was too late to back down.

A few days later I found myself helping to carry several truckloads of innertubes, bamboo poles, ropes and food for two weeks down into the depths of the Batoka Gorge, just below the Victoria Falls, where the rafts were to be assembled on a tiny patch of sand deposited by a tributary stream. Dark basalt cliffs towered over us, devoid of vegetation except for a few fig trees clinging to precarious toeholds, blotting out all but a narrow slit of sky.

The thunderous roar of the Victoria Falls, half a mile upstream, echoed off the cliffs.

James exhorted us to tighten a lashing here, pump up a tube there, while he sucked a pipe clenched between his teeth. Finally the three rafts lay completed on the bank. James gave each of us a paddle, life jacket and – disturbingly – a plastic crash helmet, and held a briefing.

'We'll take the little ones on the fly. Bigger ones, we'll stop and recce first. Pick a route, steer the rafts through.' He strode about, puffing on his pipe, leaving a trail of smoke clouds behind him like a badly-tuned diesel engine. 'Right. Let's get at it.'

As photographer-in-chief, I occupied a privileged position on the starboard bow, or what passed for it on a craft that looked like the aftermath of a tornado in a bamboo plantation. Ian, one of the other adults James had press-ganged into acompanying the expedition, sat beside me and was responsible for actually skippering the thing. Behind us six teenage youths, all looking like triathlon champions or first fifteen rugger players, provided the motive power.

Things went quite nicely for a while. We bounced along over harmless little waves, all three rafts in single file and undulating gently as James had planned, and down playful little chutes of tumbling white foam. 'Left,' Ian called, as we entered the first of these. All the paddlers on the right stopped paddling, while those on the left dug in and gave it some wellie. The raft instantly slewed broadside-on.

'No!' Ian shouted. 'Turn left, I mean. Paddle on the right.'

'Sir. Mister Spong, sir,' said one young lad, 'wouldn't it make more sense to shout paddle right or turn left?' Everyone else stopped paddling to listen, while the raft slowly turned until we were going backwards.

'OK, OK!' Ian shouted. 'All paddle right! NO!' he yelled, as four left-hand paddlers tried to obey, and clouted their companions beside them around the head. 'I mean…'

'Paddle right means right-hand paddlers paddle. Right? Sir?' said the young lad. He looked vaguely familiar. A tiny, far-off, tinkling bell began to ring.

'Yes, Kloppers,' Ian said. Kloppers? The tinkling turned into an ominous, doom-laden tolling. The last Kloppers I'd met had a mountainous dad called Hansie, a pimply face, and an infuriatingly encyclopaedic knowledge of pipits. He'd filled out a bit, but you couldn't mistake that serenely confident air of someone who thinks he knows everything, and does.

'That's exactly what I mean.' Ian went on. 'Now bloody well do it!' There was an outbreak of random paddling, while the raft continued doggedly sliding backwards, undulated down the playful little chute and floated serenely downstream. Ian expanded on the definitions of left and right, assisted now and then by Kloppers, and I took the opportunity to study my surroundings.

Going Down the Drain

It was like going for a ride down a storm drain. Greenish-brown water, streaked with foam, ran between sheer black cliffs. The tiny dots of soaring birds – possibly the Taita falcons, which are one of the Batoka's claims to biological fame – were framed in the narrow slit of sunlit sky. There was, as far as I could see, nothing at all in the spectacular wildlife line. Except crocodiles, of which there were plenty.

They lay on flat basalt slabs and in tiny sandy indents at the feet of the cliffs. They didn't glide into the water as we passed, as crocodiles usually do, but seemed to be eyeing us in a sinisterly calculating manner. I glanced furtively at Kloppers. Just a little push…

The roar of the Victoria Falls, now some way behind us, had dwindled and died. Now, though, it was replaced by an ominous rumble that slowly crescendoed as we drifted steadily downstream. James pulled into the bank, and the rest of us brought up alongside.

'Real rapid coming up,' James said enthusiastically, 'Let's take a look.' We clambered off the rafts, onto the bank and down to the rapid.

It wasn't quite as easy as that. The basalt ledges that line the river in the bottom of the gorge are littered with boulders the size of small houses, and pocked with cavernous potholes. We struggled over, round and between these obstacles until we had a view of the upcoming rapid.

The river – this is the Zambezi, remember, the fourth largest river in Africa – narrowed until it was maybe thirty yards wide, became oily-smooth and sloped visibly downhill. It careered over a rocky lip and down a long, narrow chute, accelerating rapidly until it erupted with volcanic force into a mass of crashing white water. Some way further on it miraculously reformed itself into a series of immense standing waves. I stared at the sight in horror.

'Terrific!' James bellowed over the thundering of the rapid. 'If we KEEP LEFT we ought to miss that hole – not too far left, don't want to hit those rocks' – he pointed at what looked like a miniaturised version of Scylla and Charybdis – 'then OVER that wave and cross to the far side…' He went on in similar vein for a while, then turned to me.

'Sorry to say this,' he said, 'but I think you'll get better photos if you stay on the bank. Join us at the bottom of the rapid.' He indicated a patch of calmer water, just visible in the distance. I tried my best to look disappointed.

James and the others set off back to the rafts. I worked my way across the boulders and potholes – a couple of crocodiles did condescend to slip into the water as I did so – to a nice vantage point where I'd get a good view of what seemed likely to be mass suicide, and waited.

James and his band of paddlers hove in sight, sliding down the glassy-smooth stretch of water before it accelerated over the lip and into the chute. The raft hurtled down towards the looming maelstrom, hit the white water and disappeared. It reappeared a couple of seconds later, soaring vertically up the face of a huge standing wave, shedding paddles and crash helmets. It rose higher and higher until it hung poised in mid-air.

The fatal design flaw in James' undulating rafts suddenly became glaringly apparent. Instead of falling neatly forwards as the inflatables do in the glossy advertisements, the raft began to tip backwards and then folded itself in half, like an eight-man hamburger with arms, legs and a few remaining paddles sticking out of it. The hamburger roared over the rest of the standing waves, spinning like a top as it went, and disappeared from sight.

The second raft got stuck in a huge hole, where I could vaguely see it bobbing up and down, surrounded by walls of foaming water and deluged by sheets of spray. 'PADDLE!'

its skipper screamed, whenever he surfaced. It finally came hurtling out sideways, shedding half its occupants. They drifted off downstream, the bright dots of their crash-helmets vanishing as they were sucked down by whirlpools, then bobbing up and over the waves until they, too, disappeared from sight, followed by the raft.

The third raft appeared. Kloppers had appropriated my place on the front. Now you're going to get yours, I thought gleefully, and wound my camera on to capture the event. To my immense disappointment the raft curved gracefully round the watery wall-of-death on the outer fringes of the hole, soared up and over the volcano, and undulated over the ranks of standing waves, paddles dipping and flashing with the perfect timing of an Oxford eight when I've bet on Cambridge.

A broadly similar sequence of events took place at several more monster rapids. I'd click away on the bank, capturing an occasional sighting of glistening inner tubes and helmet-sprinkled water, then scramble over the rocks and potholes to what was left of the rafts. This was my job. I was happy in it. James, unfortunately, seemed to think I was being deprived of one of life's 'great experiences'.

'Poor Dick,' he observed. 'He hasn't been through any of the really good ones.'

There came a point when protestations about Duty and Getting the Job Done started to sound like abject cowardice, which it was. Off I went at the next chance of a great experience. Kloppers gave up his place – rather reluctantly, I thought – and sat behind me instead.

We entered the oily water-slide at the top of the rapid and began to gain speed. 'Paddle left!' Ian yelled. 'Paddle right,' Kloppers bellowed simultaneously. The raft careered straight on until we ran head-on into a huge wall of water that looked as high as a house. The impact knocked the breath out of my body. The raft flew up the face of the wave, while I clung desperately to a bamboo pole with one hand and paddled empty air with the other.

The raft hung suspended in mid-air for a second or two, then flipped over backwards. I lost my grip on the bamboo pole, fell several feet into the rapid, and plunged deep underwater. The current swirled me around like a sock in a launderette. I couldn't tell which way was up.

It wouldn't be the army after all, or man-eating lions, murderous trees, tropical hypothermia or hat-stomping elephants. It'd be death by washing-machine. I opened my eyes for one last desperate struggle for the surface and found I was already there, in a melee of floating paddles, helmets, upturned tractor-tyres, and teenagers whooping with joy.

Kloppers was bobbing along a few feet away, reclining idly in his life jacket and gazing up at the sides of the gorge. A couple of tiny dots were circling over the cliff-tops.

'Taita falcons,' I yelled at him. He stared at me.

'Why, hallo, sir. Thought I recognised you.' Kloppers turned back to the sky. 'Actually, they're black eagles. Far too fat for falcons. Much too big.'

'Oh,' I said lamely. 'So they are.'

Having had the great experience and survived, I would have been happy to call it quits and go home with the wet T-shirt to prove it. Why nobody got eaten by crocodiles, brained by falling rafts, drowned in a whirlpool or smashed to a pulp against the rocks, was – still is – a mystery to me. But a mountain goat couldn't have climbed out of that gorge. On we went.

Half the party went down with dysentery. They declined to the status of baggage, perching on their rafts in dumb misery, swimming for their lives when they had to, and disappearing regularly into such patches of straggly woodland as the gorge occasionally offered.

Going Down the Drain

As we progressed – sometimes by less than a mile a day – the gorge slowly became less forbiddingly steep, the rapids less intimidating, until they could barely be heard over the thundering of tortured intestines. We finally arrived at Deka Mouth, thirty miles downstream of our starting-point, got on a waiting bus and went home. As we reached Harare I, too, began to detect some untoward events within my own digestive system. I crawled into my flat, collapsed onto the loo and stayed there, on and off, for the best part of a month.

Dysentery provided ample time for reflection on the Batoka experience, between bouts of delirium.

'Stuff it,' I said to myself, at first. 'Dam it.' Ha, ha, very droll, I chuckled to myself, and was promptly punished with a spasm of abdominal agony. Later, though, I became capable of more rational thought.

The gorge had an immense if forbidding grandeur, and stretches of spectacular beauty. Sometimes, between the rapids, there had been long, limpid stretches of calm water, with little streams tumbling down from the black cliffs into gullies with aloes clinging to their sides and ferns growing in tiny crevices.

About halfway through the trip, where the gorge had briefly opened out into a wide bowl of rugged hills, we'd had to carry the rafts around the Moemba Falls. Once we'd recovered from this feat – which was comparable to transporting the sarsens of Stonehenge – we'd taken a little time to study the view from downstream.

The Moemba Falls are only a few feet high, but they are confined by a basalt cleft barely 15 yards wide. The Zambezi comes bursting through this cleft and over the lip of the waterfall with such force that the ground trembles underfoot. The air vibrates with a thunderous roar rivalling that of the Victoria Falls themselves. Rainbows hang in the spray, fading into an eggshell sky against a backdrop of sere brown hills, floating in the haze.

Most important of all, the Batoka Gorge was not only obviously and impressively wild: it was one of the few remaining parts of the Zambezi that hadn't been messed around in one way or another. Mana Pools shouldn't be destroyed by a dam, but neither should the Batoka Gorge and the Moemba Falls. There's too little wilderness left, and it should be cherished, wherever it is found, whatever its nature.

However, I still had the problem of writing truthfully about the trip itself without upsetting the embryonic white water rafting industry which, the publisher thought, might grow into one of his magazine's most lucrative sources of income.

'Experience of a lifetime,' I wrote, in a masterpiece of ambiguity.

Vicus had been right. However disgusting the Rhodesian war may have been, it did at least hold back a flood of overambitious developmental projects spawned by people who thought wilderness was wasted on elephants.

Proposals were put forward for four large hydroelectric dams on the Zambezi, including both the Mupata and Batoka Gorge schemes. Multinational companies wanted to mine uranium in the Matusadona, and drill for oil beneath the Mana Pools floodplains. The government department responsible for eradicating tsetse flies wanted to drench the Zambezi Valley with DDT – the chemical that had almost driven America's bald eagles to extinction.

Going Down the Drain

All these projects were abandoned in the end, but usually for reasons that had nothing to do with conservation: uranium prices were on the floor, there wasn't enough oil under Mana Pools, the donors wouldn't pay for the dams or the DDT. A small band of enthusiasts – myself among them – thought that the beauty of Africa's wildernesses was sufficient reason to leave them alone, but others didn't. Unless we could persuade them of this, the Zambezi and its wildlife would always be at risk.

I'd barely recovered from the Batoka Gorge rafting saga when I got another telephone call.

'I'm planning a canoe trip down the Zambezi and through the Mupata,' my caller said. 'Would you like to come?'

'These canoes,' I asked, cautiously. 'Have you built them yourself, out of bits of old motor car bodies held together with safety pins and supported by plastic bags full of empty beercans? Have you designed in your own anti-hippo-attack device, so that they fold up like clamshells, seal you inside and refuse to open again? Because if so, the answer's a big fat no.'

'What are you burbling on about?' my caller replied. 'What do you think I am, some sort of nutter?'

Thankfully, my caller was Mike Gardner, one-time director of tourism, gastronome and cheerful bon viveur; and the canoes, when we arrived at our launch point at Chirundu, thirty miles or so upstream of Mana Pools, were made out of good solid fibreglass, built in the Indian style, and well ballasted with South African wines.

The idea would catch on later, and by 1990 or so you could walk across the Zambezi on massed flotillas of canoes, if they hadn't been overturned by hippos fed up with being rammed in the backside and walloped on the head with paddles. Then, though, we launched on an empty river. The hippos were still amiable, and the crocodiles had the grace

111

to slide into the water where at least you couldn't see them wondering what you tasted like.

There was a familiar confusion over left and right paddles, and some of the canoes spent much of the first day rotating in small circles, but at least they weren't promptly engulfed by thundering white water. The more astute among us soon realised that you didn't actually need to paddle at all. It was far more pleasant just to drift along on the current, in what – in canoespeak – was called a 'leg-over'. This involves hooking your leg over the gunwale of another canoe, thus creating a catamaran, trimaran, quadrimaran and so on, until you run out of canoes and legs. It changes its meaning after sunset.

Thus, for several long, idyllic days: past Mana Pools, with its beautiful acacia woodlands; past the island where Dolf and I had been chased into the river, the carmine bee-eaters hovering in bright clouds over their nests; through mazes of tiny channels edged with purple water hyacinth; and through the Mupata Gorge itself, weathered granite instead of menacing black basalt; black eagles soaring over the cliffs and no Kloppers to correct me if they weren't; and the Zambezi running strong and deep, with occasional riffles that didn't even think of thundering.

And wildlife, of course: the impala and buffalo, the lions lying up under the Mana acacias and the elephants, swimming to the islands and playing in the pools; always elephants; all the things that make places like the Zambezi Valley what they are; that bring the backdrop of hazy mountain and sparkling river to vibrant life.

We camped al fresco, sometimes on an island, sometimes beneath a grove of mahoganies or acacias; and once, towards the end of the journey, beside a quiet pool a few yards from the Zambezi, overhung with majestic ebonies.

The trip was nearing its end but, Mike pointed out, he'd have to cart a lot of good South African wine back to Harare if we didn't do something about it fairly soon. We set about saving him the bother.

Towards the end of the evening Mike gestured expansively at the surrounding wilderness, chirruping with crickets and echoing with whooping hyaenas.

'What we need,' he said, rather slowly and carefully, 'ish a – a – Shamblezi Shoshiety to look after all thish.' Then he fell off his camp stool and went to sleep.

A Zambezi Society is what he meant to say, and we duly made one. I was elected founder-chairman, as I had more time on my hands than most. All we needed was a cause, since the Mupata dam idea had collapsed. It wasn't long in coming and when it did, it wasn't a place, or a vague idea. It was the rhinoceros – a strange, often grumpy, but oddly endearing animal for which I was already developing a lasting affection.

Rhinos are poached because their horns are highly valued by some cultures. Scarcely anyone, other than a handful of misinformed Western journalists, believes that rhino horn is an aphrodisiac. However, many Asian peoples think it has almost mystical medicinal properties, and use it to cure anything from piles by sitting on a stool with a hole in it, over a burning pile of ground-up rhino horn (safety warning – don't try this at home), to the common cold. And being stabbed with a dagger with a genuine rhino-horn handle is a high-status way to get killed in the Yemen.

By 1984 Zambia's rhinos had already been virtually annihilated. Now, it seemed, it was Zimbabwe's turn. A couple of parks department wardens told me that more than twenty rhinos had been shot and killed and their horns removed, not far from Mana Pools, and the figure was climbing by the week.

'We've been warning our bosses this might start happening,' one of the wardens said, 'but nobody listened. And nobody's doing anything. Can't you guys get something done?'

'After all,' the other one said, 'you do know the minister, don't you?'

While I was still in the parks department the Hon. Mrs Victoria Chitepo, heroine of the liberation struggle and Minister of Tourism and Environment, had been invited to open a new tourist camp on the fringes of Mana Pools. Protocol demanded that a parks officer should be present. Whereas there had been an unholy rush to go and watch Art and Martha solving Mana's elephant overpopulation problem, absolutely nobody wanted to go and watch a minister opening a safari camp.

Their loss, I thought, after the formalities had been concluded and I relaxed in a comfortable chair overlooking the Zambezi. Waiters rushed about, bearing trays loaded with gin and tonic. Mrs Chitepo sat a little way off, surrounded by assorted minions and tourism magazine hacks, chatting with the camp's manager. He detached himself from the group and came over to me.

'The minister,' he said, 'wants to go for a walk. She particularly wants to see elephants.'

'Fine by me,' I said cheerfully. 'Mind if I come along?'

'Ah, she wants you to take her,' he said. 'Alone.'

'What!?' I cried. Occasional meanderings around the Fothergill foreshore with a bunch of tourists were one thing. Deliberately leading a minister of state into face-to-face encounters with elephants was quite another, especially with two-and-a-half gin and tonics inside me. You needed a lot of experience to carry this sort of thing off, which I didn't have. I pointed this out.

'Shhhhh!' the manager hissed. 'I told her that.' Well, thanks, I thought, perversely. 'But she says she'd like to go with you.'

We were interrupted by the arrival of the minister herself. 'Ah, Mr Pitman,' she said happily. 'We shall go to see elephants. I know I'll be safe with one of my officers.'

The manager excused himself for a few seconds, then reappeared with an immense hunting rifle, larger and vastly more complicated than any I'd seen before. He thrust it into my hands.

'Better take this,' he said.

It looked as if it probably fired depleted-uranium shells. I thought about asking how it worked. That ought to change her mind, if anything would. On the other hand, I didn't want to be known evermore as the parks ranger who didn't know how a rifle worked. Maybe I'd find out as I went along, as I had with the camera, except I couldn't try it out on the minister, or even on a passing impala. Off we went, the minister and I, one of her bodyguards following a respectful few paces behind.

I decided to leave the rifle out of my calculations. Forget the hat-throwing business, as well. You don't want to get to that stage, not with a minister in tow. Besides which, the aerodynamic qualities of a parks beret left a lot to be desired. The badge threw them off-target.

Instead, I reviewed my own little arsenal of anti-elephant weaponry, which I'd secretly developed from my experiences on Fothergill Island, in direct contravention of the International Tour Guide's Treaty. For strategic defence, I decided to launch the long-range tigerfish multiple warhead. This involves crashing about through dead branches as noisily as possible, while talking loudly about cooking chicken in elephant dung before getting onto tigerfishing. Most elephants run for cover long before you get to them.

'Tigerfishing?' Mrs Chitepo said, looking at me as if I was barking mad, while we plunged through a thicket carpeted with dead twigs. She glanced around at the grey, dry soil. 'Here?'

'In the river, I mean' I burbled.

'Fish. I like fish,' Mrs Chitepo said. 'Much nicer than chicken cooked in elephant dung. Can you eat tigerfish?'

'Aaah, no,' her bodyguard put in, the first time he'd spoken. 'Too many bones. Too oily.'

Mrs Chitepo stumbled on a dry branch, which caught in her skirt and crackled nicely as it broke.

'Wouldn't it be easier,' she said, 'if we walked on that nice game path instead?' I was about to say we might bump into elephants if we did, then remembered this was what she wanted. We moved onto the game path. The bodyguard, whose natty dark suit was covered in dust and burrs, looked relieved.

At this point I saw the elephants – several of them, elephant cows and calves, dozing under a distant sausage-tree and largely obscured by shrubbery. I flipped the guard off the pipit ploy's firing button. This is a tactical weapon, which focuses a high-velocity stream of verbiage – and hopefully everyone's attention – on a small brown bird, giving the elephant time to wander off before anybody else notices it and starts banging on about getting closer. Its biggest drawback is that there isn't always a pipit handy. You have to be able to talk rivettingly about a lot of different little brown birds, sometimes for minutes on end. Also, you have to see the elephant before anyone else does. Unfortunately, I hadn't.

'There! Elephants!' Mrs Chitepo announced. 'Can we go closer?'

'NO!' I shouted, and added, hastily, 'Ma'am.' The pipit ploy having been neutralised by a conventional mark one eyeball, I went into a long and involved dissertation on elephant females, calves, fickle breezes, Art, dart guns, and dead elephants instead. I lent Mrs Chitepo my binoculars, and she studied the elephants thoughtfully.

'Lovely,' she said eventually. 'We can go now.'

And thank the good Lord for that, I thought, as we strolled back down the game path, the minister chatting as we went.

'Too many elephants' she said, happily. I had a sudden thought. Maybe it explained something. 'Too many', to Shona speakers, doesn't actually mean 'too many'. It means 'lots of'.

Maybe some minister had said 'too many elephants', and 500 parks rangers converged on the armoury…

The camp manager was waiting with an anxious look on his face. 'How'd it go? Find any?'

'Aah, plenty,' Mrs Chitepo said. 'But I felt so safe with Mr Pitman.' The manager subsided into stupendous relief. A waiter ran up with a tray full of drinks. I swapped the artillery piece for another gin and tonic. 'Cheers, minister,' I ventured. We clinked glasses. 'Cheers,' she said happily.

So, yes, I could claim to know her. Better by far than she knew me, in fact.

I hadn't managed to see any rhinos until I got into the Chizarira National Park thirty-odd miles south of Lake Kariba. Chizarira is one of Africa's finest but least-visited wildernesses. It's a glorious mix of wooded mountains, plateaux, gentle grassy valleys and deep river gorges. I'd gone there during my grand tour in between helping fix waterpumps in Hwange and spending five days driving to Kariba in the White Elephant. The park headquarters at Manzituba had been destroyed by guerillas and the staff were living in a hastily-built fort, like the one at Mana Pools. All they needed to make their lives complete was the arrival of a would-be wildlife writer. One young ranger summed it up.

'What? You haven't... brought any... chocolate cake?' he said incredulously as I disembarked from the armoured supply vehicle. He lost all interest in me.

'Probably just as well,' Nick Tredger said to me later. Nick had been deputised to look after me for the duration. Taking chocolate cake to Chizarira, it seemed, was like throwing a banana into a cage of starving monkeys.

Nick had organised a patrol into the remote western end of the park, largely for my benefit. This involved two armoured vehicles, one for parks and one for the army; assorted weaponry; and a small and unexplained dog. We set off along a rudimentary track, detouring round gullies and fallen trees.

It was mid-winter, and hadn't rained since April. Chizarira was wearing the subdued hues of the dry season, rustling beige grasses crackling underfoot, and the air filled with – to me – the most evocative of scents: buffalo dung mingled with drying leaves. The track ran through a shallow valley between red-brown hills topped with mountain acacias. Now and then it dived into shady tunnels through tall mopanes, and passed beside tiny springs, islands of green in an ocean of brown and grey.

The track finally petered out, and we set up our base camp in the shade of a large ebony growing out of an anthill. One of the scouts went off and shot an impala for dinner. The sun was warm, the breeze gentle, and the surrounding bush hummed and chirped with insects and birds. I dozed.

Going Down the Drain

So did the dog, its nose resting comfortably on a pile of impala entrails.

The sun set, and it grew dark and chilly. We went to bed early, lying in our sleeping bags under the stars. An hour or two passed before something woke me. A couple of scouts were sitting up in their sleeping bags and peering into the tall grass beyond the anthill, from whence came a soft rustling. Then several more scouts sat up and began to peel off their sleeping bags with enormous care.

'Aiee! *Chipembere*!' one of the scouts suddenly yelled. Simultaneously, a furious snort blasted the night to fragments. About fifteen game-scouts rocketed out of their sleeping bags, up the anthill and into the ebony tree.

I find it difficult to rocket out of a sleeping bag at the best of times. Mine was still tangled round my ankles when something very large came pounding and snorting out of the grass. It tore past the base of the anthill and vanished into the night.

It didn't count as actually seeing a rhino. It could have been a small tank, for all I knew. Nick materialised out of the darkness. 'Anyone get nailed?'

Hardly. They were all up the ebony, except me. One scout had climbed up so far that his branch had bent over until he was dangling upside down like a giant bat, three or four feet off the ground. Nick strolled up to him, and tapped him on the shoulder.

'OK, Farai,' he said, 'the *chipembere*'s gone. You can come down now.' The scout gave a squawk of surprise, lost his grip on the branch and fell heavily to the ground.

By dawn we were bitterly cold, our sleeping bags covered with dew. Nick and I set off on foot with half a dozen scouts and a couple of soldiers. We followed the last traces of the track for a mile or two, then veered northwards through luxuriant mopanes and onto a small plateau, where a trampling of elephant and rhino spoor surrounded a tiny spring. An hour or so later we found another spring, in gently rising woodland, and stopped there for the night.

Nick and I camped a little apart from the scouts and the army. Once again I woke up after an hour or so, this time to find Nick sitting up and staring hard into the tall grass beside the spring, which glistened in the starlight. There was a faint rustling in the grass.

Nick listened intently, then whispered: 'Not sure what it is. I think it might be…'

Whatever it was – whatever they were, as it turned out – made a sound like a *Star Wars* planet-blaster and came thundering out of the grass.

Nick turned to me, but I wasn't there. I was perched on a branch twenty feet up the nearest tree. Nick arrived beside me a microsecond later. 'Bloody rhinos,' he said. They knocked our camping stove over, showered our sleeping bags with dust and leaves, gave the scouts and the army a good fright, and went on their way. But I hadn't actually seen anything more than a couple of vague grey shapes in the darkness, so it still didn't count.

'Hell's teeth,' I said in the morning, studying the tree. 'How'd we get up there?' There wasn't a foothold more substantial than some knobbly bits of bark, from ground level up to the branch on which we'd taken refuge.

'Amazing what you can do, with a *chipembere* up your chuff,' Nick said.

Black rhino, he continued, often charge first and ask questions afterwards. As they're rather short-sighted, they may miss you altogether, and keep going into the far distance until they've forgotten what the question was.

Those with better memories may come back for another go. They can still be deceived if you pretend to be a small and unpalatable shrub, but this needs a lot of nerve. It's a chancy business, too, because a rhino that's missed you is quite likely to vent its frustration on what it believes to be a small and unpalatable shrub.

'A real tree,' Nick concluded, 'is a lot safer.'

In the morning we walked to a small stream, close to Chizarira's western boundary, and began to comb the game paths along its banks for snares. We had only gone a hundred yards or so when we found the first. Then another; and another. The scouts gradually became burdened with snares.

A few minutes later we came across the signs of a desperate struggle. The shrubs were broken, the earth trampled and scattered with dung, and the broken end of a barbed-wire snare had almost cut through the small tree to which it was attached. Nick examined the dung carefully.

'Rhino,' he said. 'Broken out of the snare.'

'Rhino? What are these guys after, the horns?'

'Not as such, I don't think. This is commercial meat-poaching. Completely indiscriminate, but they'll probably take the horns if they can. Bastards.' He paused. 'We need to find that animal. May still be alive, still got the snare round its leg.'

'And then?'

'Depends. Maybe get the capture guys in, take the snare off, keep an eye on it and see if it heals. Or, if it's beyond hope…' He shook his head slightly.

We located the remains of the rhino, ten miles away, lying beside a small pool. The poachers hadn't found him, and his horns were intact, but vultures had pecked out his eyes, and his hide was streaked with their droppings.

His hind legs were enmeshed in coils of barbed wire that had cut and gouged and torn at him as he ran, stripping the flesh from the bone until he lay down beside the waterhole and died. For a few sad and silent minutes I pondered the sight of the first wild black rhino I had ever seen.

There had also been a lot of rhinos in Mana Pools, before the killing began. I hadn't seen them there either, when Dolf and I had been confined to short walks on the floodplains, because they were mostly concentrated in the mopane woodlands and *jesse* bush further south. I had more luck later on, when I was wandering around the place on my own.

Several rhinos used to visit Chine Pool, which lies on the edge of the floodplain furthest from the Zambezi. The pool is only 20 or 30 yards across; its north bank gives onto open floodplain woodlands, but the south bank rises steeply into a patch of *jesse* bush.

There is a large and convenient anthill on the floodplain side, where I used to sit and wait for the rhinos to come down from the *jesse* and drink. This had the advantage of putting a narrow but comforting stretch of water between us. The only problem is that you can't see what's going on behind you, which is why I once found myself perched on its summit and surrounded by a herd of buffalo.

Chine is never boring. There's always something either drinking or meandering around nearby. Nyala – an uncommon, shy, smallish antelope, with glossy black-horned males and tawny, white-striped females – also like to occupy *jesse* thickets, and I've only ever seen them at Chine Pool. Sometimes, if I was lucky, a small group would emerge hesitantly from the bush and then come down to drink for a minute or two before trotting back up the bank and into the thickets.

Black rhinos came to Chine, usually singly, sometimes in pairs, drank their fill, and then fossicked around the pool for a while. Like most others watching rhinos for the first time, I thought: what strange creatures, as they bumbled and snorted around beside the pool, with little red-billed oxpeckers riding casually on their backs. How odd. How – prehistoric.

They must be uniquely well-adapted, if they haven't felt the need to change. But why have a horn on the end of your nose, for heaven's sakes, never mind two of them? Why be content with a little upper lip that looks like a failed trunk?

Well, why change something that's worked for millions of years? Rhinos and their ancestors have been an extraordinarily diverse and successful group. The earliest known forerunner of today's rhinos lived 50 million years ago. One ancient species, which lived in Asia, was the biggest land mammal ever known to have lived on earth, standing 20 feet high at the shoulder and possibly weighing 25 tons. Others lived in water and looked more like hippos. All in all, as many as 175 different species of rhino may have come and gone, of which five still survive today – three in Asia and two in Africa.

The black rhino – the species that was still so common in Chizarira, Mana Pools and the Matusadona when I first visited these parks – had already evolved into its present-day form when we humans were still wondering how to turn stones into something lethal, like axes and spears. If they'd had any intelligence, they'd have finished us off while they still could. Even the axes and spears were too much for species such as Europe's woolly rhinoceros, which survived into prehistoric times. Black rhinos fared rather better, but evolution failed to provide them with bullet-proof hides. And they aren't very bright, either, which doesn't help.

I got to know one rhino personally, near Mcheni camp and its magical mahogany forest. I made a point of looking for him, in the early mornings, and invariably found him browsing in the sunlit shrublands that flank the forest. I'd hide myself behind a fallen tree-trunk and watch him feeding. He'd reach for a succulent twig, delicately curl that odd little upper lip round it, bite it off and chew it with an air of total abstraction.

He gradually lost interest as the day grew warmer, standing almost motionless for minutes at a time while he pondered his next move. Then he would trudge doggedly out of the shrubs and through the mahogany woodlands to the Zambezi.

I would follow him at a respectful distance, sometimes detouring round occasional elephant bulls, always keeping his huge baggy-pants backside in sight as he ambled through the sunlit glades and onto the grassy floodplain beside the river. He'd find a hippo-trodden gully down to the water and drink for a few minutes; then, as the sun grew even hotter, begin to retrace his steps.

As he reached the enchanted forest his pace slowed even more until he came to a halt in the deep shade beneath some well-leafed mahogany. His eyes closed, and he swayed gently on his feet for a minute or two. Finally his legs gave way under him and he collapsed, fast asleep. I'd have taken him for dead if it weren't for his ears, swivelling like tiny radar scanners, and the tiny fountains of dust erupting beside his nostrils.

At first, I wedged myself into the fork of a nearby tree and tried to photograph him. My camera made the same sort of noise as Dolf's and the Fothergill tourists', and I winced every time I pressed the shutter release. But the rhino never even opened an eye. I got bolder, creeping across the crackling leaves and taking a few photos before walking away. Later – much later, in mid-afternoon – he'd finally wake up with such an air of apparent bewilderment that I came to think of him as a rhinocerine Rip Van Winkel. Then he'd struggle to his feet, spend a few minutes thinking things over, and amble back into the shrublands and start feeding again.

No: 'bright' isn't a word I'd use for an animal that sleeps like the dead while somebody who might have a rifle instead of a camera creeps up on them. Or for one that often charges on the slightest pretext when it is awake, but misses its target. I've sometimes wondered if George Bush studied rhinos, in his youth.

Gee Dubya may have a hide like a rhino, but rhinos don't. Even the adults have such delicate hides that you can accidentally poison them by putting them in a pen made of creosoted poles. And baby rhinos can die from diarrhoea with frightening speed, if you don't feed them the exact proportions of milk, glucose and vitamin supplements that they need.

You can have black rhinos eating from your hand a few hours after catching them. They mew like kittens begging for milk. They are, in short, a lot more sensitive and loveable than they look, which is largely why they've been such an important part of my life, on and off, for more than 20 years.

Actually saving them, though – or even getting anyone to admit they needed to, the minister included – was another matter altogether.

'Of course I remember,' Mrs Chitepo said, as I sat on her government-issue settee and drank her tea. 'Too many elephants. But I felt so safe!'

After a few more minutes of general chit-chat I got round to the matter in hand. The atmosphere, hitherto one of cosy reminiscence, grew cool.

'Rhinos? Killed? In Zimbabwe? Who told you that?'

I realised, with chilling suddenness, that I couldn't actually say that two of her own parks department officers had told me. They'd probably get into an awful lot of trouble. I skirted the issue and floundered on.

'We – that is, me, well, us, we'd like to help, do some fundraising, that sort of thing.'

The minister's air of faint irritation turned to a stony glare. I was, she told me, sorely misinformed. There never had been – never could be – any rhino poaching in Zimbabwe. And if – if – anyone even tried, her parks department could handle it. *Finish 'n' klar*, as local dog-English-Afrikaans puts it.

The conversation rallied a bit after that, but never recovered its early bonhomie. Mrs Chitepo continued to look as if she'd been bitten by her favourite chihuahua, and I slunk out of her office feeling as if I'd been given a good smack with a rolled-up newspaper.

This was, however, merely the first minor setback of many more to come during the black rhino story, especially when government officials were involved.

Chapter Five

THE PITFALLS OF MUZARABANI

People seemed to be making a habit of handing me pieces of complicated and sometimes lethal equipment I didn't know how to use, like film cameras and radar-controlled hunting rifles. It would make a nice change if someone handed me something I did know how to use.

It would be even nicer to use it on something constructive, like saving rhinos and elephants. Someone did, in the end – to wit: an aeroplane. But it was a long haul getting there.

If Mrs C had been chilly when I'd gone to see her about the rhino situation, my replacement at the parks department was downright arctic.

He'd been catapulted from game-scout to senior parks officer in a couple of years flat, occupied my old office, and enjoyed a rank so high he was almost in orbit along with the director. The carpet filled almost all the available floor space, and didn't have holes in it. A surviving pocket of baskets, wire, had apparently been located, and had undergone a 100 per cent population increase.

'I, ah, understand there's been some rhino poaching,' I said cautiously. 'Near Mana Pools. More than twenty animals.'

'A minor incident,' he said. 'All under control now. Don't worry about it. This is Zimbabwe, you know, not Zambia. Worry about real problems.'

'Such as?' I asked.

'Elephants,' he said. 'Too many elephants. Too, too many elephants.'

'Save wildlife, shoot an elephant'? It didn't have the makings of a classic wildlife fundraising campaign. He nodded at me dismissively as he took a file from one of the baskets, wire.

Another one-time colleague put things into perspective. 'We all know what's happening. We're just a bit sensitive about hearing it from you.'

'From me?'

'From people like you, I mean.' What, dedicated wildlife conservationists looking for something to be dedicated to?

'From…' – he hesitated, a pained look on his face, and possibly a blush, it was hard to tell – 'from white people,' he finally forced out, in a voice which sounded as if he was not only being strangled, but had a very large stone down his throat as well. There was a fair bit of racial stuff going on by then, but everyone was still being terribly polite about it.

The reconciliation bit was all very well, he went on, but when push came to shove people like me weren't exactly heroes of the liberation struggle. Me telling government ministers how to do their jobs was like the Taliban offering an advisory service to the US government.

'Just carry on and do it,' he went on. 'Raise some money, buy a load of boots and backpacks, organise a big handover with lots of reporters, pretend it was our idea all along and make her the star of the show. She'll love it.'

My Zambezi Society colleagues and I established a Rhino Survival Campaign, and leaked the news about the poached rhinos to the local press. Rhino fever swept like a bush fire across the country, or at least those bits of it still occupied by what was rapidly becoming a disempowered ethnic minority looking for a role. People wrote songs about rhinos. Other people manufactured rhino costumes and lurched around shopping centres rattling tins and scaring the daylights out of small children.

Since I was chairing the campaign's fundraising committee, I was deluged with invitations to address high-school assemblies and Rotary club lunches, daytime media briefings and select evening dinners at ambassadorial residences. Somewhere along the way, I agreed to the suggestion that we might invite international conservation celebs to visit Zimbabwe and publicise our efforts.

Some of them, I soon found, were not particularly pleasant people. They had talent by the truckload, but mostly for self-promotion. They all wanted to be filmed cuddling live baby rhinos or gazing sadly at dead ones, preferably by the BBC.

This wasn't always easy to organise, and I was still smarting from the remarks made by a celeb who'd only got five minutes of off-peak time on Zimbabwean television, when Gerald and Lee Durrell accepted an invitation to do a week-long fundraising tour of the country.

I didn't greet the prospect with much enthusiasm at first, I admit. But I warmed to them immediately. For one thing, they didn't start looking round for the cameras as soon as they stepped off the aircraft. They were conservationists first and celebs second, instead of having fashionably done things the other way round.

We wanted to show them something of the country's wildlife, but preferably not on foot as Gerald was already suffering problems with his hips. We organised a boat trip on the Zambezi with one of our more up-market tourist camps, not far from Mana Pools.

However, Zimbabwean tourism was still in the stick-and-string era then, and 'up-market' was relative. I was rather taken aback when I saw the home-made raft on which we were to commit two of the world's greatest conservationists to the perils of the Zambezi's hippos and crocodiles.

It consisted of two pontoons connected by a wide wooden platform, and looked like a floating bedstead. A couple of tatty canvas chairs were perched on the platform, and it had a small and suspiciously battered outboard engine on the back.

Mercifully, I didn't actually have to drive the thing. Jeff Stutchbury did. Jeff was a real Real Bushman, and something of a Zambezi Valley legend. He didn't have to tear the sleeves off his shirt to prove it.

'Welcome aboard,' Jeff boomed. Gerald settled gratefully into one of the chairs, his trademark white hair and beard ruffled by the morning breeze. Lee, slim and energetic, stood in the bows as we chugged slowly out into mid-Zambezi – which, at this particular spot, was a long way from the banks.

All went well enough for a while, as we meandered downstream. Elephants swam between islands on cue; hippos snoozed in the backwaters; fish eagles called from the acacias on the banks, and stooped after small tigerfish in the shallows.

'African skimmers,' Gerald said, indicating a flight of lovely birds scooping up water in flight with their beaks, like firefighting aircraft but vastly more graceful.

'Yes. Nest on the sandbanks,' Jeff replied.

'Lovely,' Lee murmured, taking in the scenery.

At this point the engine stopped, with a finality that suggested it might not be too keen to start again. 'No problem,' Jeff said cheerily. He fiddled with the fuel lines and pulled the string. The engine went *CHUFF chuff chuff* and sank back into silence.

'Almost got it,' Jeff said cheerily, and pulled the string again. This time the engine didn't bother to chuff. He took the cover off and began fiddling with the carburetter.

Meanwhile, the raft began rotating in the eddies, while purposefully drifting downstream at a steady four knots or so. Lee and Gerald got a slow, all-round panoramic view of mountains, islands, hippos, assorted storks and herons, a couple more elephants and a lot of crocodiles lying on sandbanks, but not of the camp whence we had set out. It had long since vanished upstream.

I leant over Jeff and said quietly, in his ear, 'Maybe we ought to radio the camp for help?'

'Radio?' Jeff said distastefully, as if I'd asked for lemonade in my Moet & Chandon. 'Haven't got a radio. Horrible things.' He turned back to the carburetter, now reduced to a small heap of its component parts.

I went into babble mode. '... and you see those buffaloes there, on that island, might see lions with them if we're lucky, lions do swim, you know, a lot of people don't think they can, but they do.' A variation on the pipit ploy, really, but more random, designed to divert attention from terrifying things that are actually happening, instead of merely imminent.

'Really? Can they?' Lee, a highly qualified biologist, said patiently. Jeff glanced up at me, a tad indignantly. He possibly thought babbling was his job on this trip if it was anyone's.

'And coming up here,' I went on, 'is a grey heron.' Gerald lifted his binoculars and studied it carefully as it flew past, with some difficulty since the raft was rotating away from the heron's flight-path and towards a herd of impala.

'Actually,' he said, 'I think it's a black-headed. It's got black under its wings.'

Bugger it, will I never learn? Gerald, however, said it almost apologetically, which makes a big difference.

I stopped babbling at that point, because Jeff had reassembled the carburetter and was pulling the starter cord. It broke.

'Damn,' he said, looking at the outboard as if he'd like to wrench it off the raft and hurl it into the river. 'Wonder if we've got another cord.' He dived into his toolbox. 'Nope. Have to try and tie it together.' He took the cover off the engine again.

'Hmmm,' Lee said thoughtfully – showing, I fancied, the first faint signs of apprehension.

At this point the raft broadsided into the branches of a submerged tree, deposited in mid-river by the rainy-season floods. We stopped abruptly, and the raft began to tip in the current. Chairs, coffee mugs and binoculars slid across the raft until they were brought up by the gunwale.

The raft tipped further as the current pushed against its underside, and seemed about to capsize and throw us into the river. Lee and Gerald grabbed the guardrails and hung on grimly.

Gerald seemed unfazed, as might be expected of one who'd once owned a boat called *Bootlebumtrinket* and had doubtless fantasised about sailing it up countless African rivers full of crocodiles. I, however, was undergoing agonies of the imagination. There had already been some nasty incidents involving upturned canoes on this stretch of the Zambezi. Getting Gerald and Lee Durrell drowned, chomped in half by hippos or eaten by crocodiles would make world headlines. 'DURRELLS DIE FOR ZIMBABWE'S RHINOS' was the sort of thing that came to mind. They wouldn't have to explain who the Durrells were. Nobody knew who I was, but they soon would.

But then the raft suddenly broke free of the obstruction

and crashed back down right-side-up. A makeshift starter cord survived a couple of pulls, the engine burst into life and it even kept going for two long hours as we plodded back upstream, painfully slowly, to Jeff's camp.

Most of the other conservation celebs would have packed their bags on the spot and gone home, grateful to be alive, but Lee and Gerald were cast in a different mould. We went on to Fothergill Island, and paddled around the Matusadona in canoes. After that we toured the country's urban centres, where Lee and Gerald played to packed houses and raised a lot of money for Zimbabwe's threatened rhinos.

After Lee and Gerald had departed, our fundraising committee bought a mountain of equipment, handed it all over to the parks department via Mrs Chitepo – who was as chuffed as had been predicted – and watched it all disappear into a big black hole.

To be fair, this wasn't Mrs C's fault. There were some powerful interests behind the poaching gangs, above the law and beyond the influence of a minister of environment. Increasingly, these interests played the 'race card'. Instead of getting medals for bravery when they caught rhino poachers, white rangers and wardens were thrown into jail. One ranger, who shot and killed a poacher during a fierce gun-battle, was charged with murder.

Some resigned. Others became reluctant to engage poaching gangs in the field, for fear of arrest and retribution. But many went on doing their jobs, because they were utterly dedicated to wildlife conservation and believed in what they were doing.

Conversations with those that remained followed a familiar path.

'Can't you get something done about it?' they'd say.

'Like what?'

'Well…' These discussions usually tapered off into a depressing silence. One of them didn't, though.

'Best thing we can do,' one of the wardens said, 'is to cut the horns off every rhino we can find. Then there'd be nothing to poach.'

It was a controversial idea. Dehorning a rhinoceros involves sedating it and cutting its horns off with a chainsaw. It's a crude, noisy undertaking, and stressful for the rhinos. It's also extraordinarily expensive, since it requires aeroplanes to look for them, helicopters to dart them from, and a week's supply of the necessary tranquillising drugs probably keeps Big Pharma in profit for a year.

But it's also vastly less terminal than a burst of bullets from an AK-47. 'You know the minister,' the warden said. 'Can't you…'

No, I couldn't. I was back in her good books after the equipment handover, and I wasn't keen to go through the whipped-chihuahua business again. I might have a go at her permanent secretary, though.

This worthy listened attentively enough, although he didn't offer me a cup of tea. The way things were going, I told him, there wouldn't be a rhino left in Zimbabwe in a couple of years or so. They were already nearing extinction in Mana Pools and fast going the same way in the Matusadona. These were two of the country's prime tourist areas, I pointed out. A rhino with its horns cut off might look odd in the publicity brochures, but it was better than no rhinos at all.

He thought for a few moments, frowning a little. Then: 'I really don't think you should worry about rhino poaching' he said. 'It's all coming under control now. Anyway, we've still got plenty of rhinos. Thousands of them. It'd take years to cut all their horns off.'

But the permanent secretary was saving the best until last.

'Also,' he said, 'you said something about using helicopters?'

'Well, yes. It's the easiest way to do it.'

'Helicopters are a problem. White men,' he said, with straight face and a voice that didn't sound even slightly strangled – the era of exaggerated inter-racial politeness had passed its peak – 'are going around in helicopters and stealing our rhinos.'

I mentally examined this statement, hoping to stumble across a hint of rationality, and found none. I could believe that some white men might be joining in the rush to steal rhino's horns, but not whole rhinos. Besides, the sort of helicopters used for wildlife work could barely lift two men and a lunch-box, let alone a couple of tons of rhinoceros.

Rational or not, the permanent secretary obviously wasn't going to be much help. Even worse, I'd probably cast myself in the role of prime suspect rhino-thief. As I shut his door behind me I wondered if he was picking up the telephone to find out if I owned a helicopter.

And there the matter rested, for a while. Other developments were taking place, which diverted my attention from the plight of the rhinos. The whole conservation scene was undergoing one of its periodic changes in direction, largely catalysed by the hordes of foreign-aid donors who had effectively recolonised the country since independence.

Few of these donors were interested in conservation – at least, not in its traditional form. They were interested in encouraging rural development. If wildlife could be rendered useful in the process, all well and good. But saving animals for their own sakes was rapidly becoming unfashionable, especially if – as in the rhino's case – they lived almost exclusively inside national parks.

However, there were still many animals outside the parks, co-existing uneasily with rural villagers who regarded them mostly as pests. Elephants were the main offenders, because they not only destroyed crops wholesale but sometimes killed anyone who tried to stop them. Until now, they had been regarded as 'problem animals', and usually got themselves 'controlled'.

These animals, it was thought, could be turned into productive members of rural society if the villagers were allowed to sell them to hunters and keep the money. This process had been christened 'sustainable utilisation'. As a result, the villagers would learn to love and cherish wild animals instead of killing them whenever they got the chance.

It came to the same thing in the end for the elephants – they merely got 'utilised' instead of 'controlled'. But it made a huge amount of difference to the donors. They poured millions of donor dollars into its achievement. Many conservation organisations were hurriedly turning themselves into rural development agencies. Meanwhile several organisations hitherto concerned with rural development suddenly developed a burning interest in conservation.

These developments had largely passed me by, as I'd been deeply preoccupied with rhinos. I was also hesitant about getting back into the elephant-shooting business, even for an apparently good cause. But circumstances dictated otherwise.

Muzarabani Rural District is a couple of hundred kilometres north of Harare, and lies mostly in the Zambezi Valley, where thatched huts and villages are dotted amid tiny fields of maize. Its southernmost portion consists of several hundred square kilometres of uninhabited river gorges and densely wooded valleys in the Mavuradonha mountains, on the summit of the Zambezi Escarpment.

Local peasants treated the mountains as a source of free cattle-grazing and firewood, while the commercial farmers who owned the land on its southern boundary used them as a conveniently-sited weekend picnic area. But the mountains also sheltered a fair-sized population of elephants, which periodically descended on the maize fields surrounding the villages below.

There were moves afoot to turn this island of wilderness – and its wildlife – to profitable account, for the benefit of Muzarabani's villagers. Probably means shooting elephants again, I thought, rather cynically. All the same, I accepted the invitation I received to attend the opening of what had suddenly become officially known as the Mavuradonha Wilderness Area. A few days later I found myself in a roadside lay-by, surrounded by forested mountains overlooking the Zambezi Valley, and face to face with the minister again.

There were, to be honest, a lot of other people around as well. There were tobacco-farmers in shorts and long socks, most of whom looked like Hansie Kloppers. There were a dozen or so representatives of the Muzarabani Rural District Council in dark business suits; and there was a large contingent of groupies in shapeless dresses and bolt-on dreadlocks who'd found their way into several brand-new conservation organisations that had sprung up like weeds when they found just how much money there was in turning elephants into useful members of village society.

There was also a small herd of cows, grazing peacefully on the grass that grew in the lay-by, and a bemused crowd of villagers who didn't look nearly as prosperous as the district council representatives and who clearly hadn't the faintest idea what was going on.

'Why, Mr Pitman,' the minister cried cheerfully, 'what a nice surprise to see you here. I thought you were down in Mana Pools, saving our rhinos.'

I thought of bringing up a few things about imprisoned wardens, paranoid permanent secretaries and helicopters, but was saved by a minion who intervened to say that the formalities were about to begin.

A local politician opened the batting. The Mavuradonha, he pointed out, was uninhabited for the very good reason that nothing other than elephants and some nimble-footed antelopes could live among its precipitous slopes and marshy valleys, let alone grow crops in it. Therefore, he said, the local villagers had decided to devote it to wildlife, and had asked the government to formally declare it a protected wilderness area.

The groupies were listening with rapt attention, interrupted by an occasional suspicious glance at the tobacco-farmers. The Hansies were listening with not-very-rapt attention, casting suspicious glances back at the groupies, and talking among themselves in between. The villagers, however, were listening in growing bewilderment and casting suspicious glances at the district councillors, farmers and groupies.

I started off by listening with rapt attention myself, but he went on for some time and soon shifted to the depressingly familiar theme of 'save villagers, shoot an elephant', so I began looking at my surroundings instead. They were very beautiful, if you like mountains, which I do if I don't have to climb them. That's just one of the nice things about Mana Pools and a lot of the Matusadona. You can wander around in them without having to climb anything except an occasional tree, and even that was becoming unnecessary now that all the rhinos were being killed.

The road and the lay-by were cut into one of the mountains. Its wooded slopes rose steeply on one side to bare granite cliffs, and plunged down to an attractive river-gorge on the other. Beyond the gorge, more mountains rose in forested ranks above more gorges, extending to a ragged horizon. If I craned my neck and peered down the gorge and round the edge of the mountain I could just see Lake Cabora Bassa in the far distance. Lake Cabora Bassa is Mozambique's answer to Kariba, and is another place that'll get a nasty shock if Kariba's dam ever falls down.

I suddenly realised that Mrs Chitepo was speaking, possibly had been for some time, and wasn't talking exclusively about shooting elephants. Instead, she was saying, the people of Muzarabani were at last going to participate in the great African tourism bonanza.

Tourism companies would fall over themselves to build luxurious lodges in the Mavuradonha Wilderness Area. High-rolling foreign tourists would arrive in droves and revel in its scenery and wildlife. Pounds and dollars would roll in and be converted into clinics, schools and libraries.

Elephants that persisted in stomping on people and eating their crops would still get themselves 'sustainably utilised' by hunters. However, those that behaved themselves and stayed within the Mavuradonha would be allowed to live long and peaceful lives. The net effect would be the same: more money for the villagers.

It would all be run by a management committee consisting of villagers, district councillors, commercial farmers, conservation agencies and anyone else who might conceivably have an interest in it. The committee would – in one of the politically correct phrases minted by the rural development business – be 'inclusive'. It would consult all stakeholders. Everybody would be happy.

And – the bunch of cherries on top of an elephant-sized cake – this was all being done, not by government diktat, but in accordance with the wishes of Muzarabani's people themselves. As their side of the bargain they had agreed to give up some bad habits of their own, notably those of roaming all over the Mavuradonha with their cattle, picking up firewood and poaching elephants.

Mrs Chitepo finally folded her notes and smiled at the assembled crowd. There was enthusiastic applause from the Hansies, a wild outburst of cheering and clapping from the groupies, and a stunning display of incomprehension from the villagers, mixed with a trace of alarm.

Afterwards I mingled with the farmers. One or two of them produced cooler-boxes from the back of their pickups.

'Well, that's that. At last,' said one, draining a bomber of lager in rather less than one go. His colleagues nodded in agreement. 'Been waiting for this for a long time.'

Odd, I thought, it's still only eleven o'clock. 'Getting this Mavuradonha thing sorted out,' he clarified, knocking the top off another bomber.

'All getting totally out of hand. We'd go up the hills and find a load of *mfazis* cutting firewood, couldn't have a skinny in the rivers without getting surrounded by cows and pop-eyed herdboys, you'd think they owned the place.'

Funny, I thought they did, according to all the speeches. I glanced round at the villagers, some of whom were looking less alarmed and more enthusiastic, since the ministerial party had brought out some cooler-boxes of their own.

'I wonder what they think of it all,' I said, carefully pronouncing 'they' in a manner appropriate to the company. I wouldn't want the Hansies to think I was going groupie.

'Who? Oh, them. God knows. Dunno if anyone's asked them.'

The Pitfalls of Muzarabani

The tourism idea had some appeal, even if a fair number of elephants were probably going to get shot as well. I decided to have a closer look at the Mavuradonha, especially if I could find a way of doing it without having to climb mountains under my own steam. Chris and Dawn Pohl, who owned one of the farms on the Mavuradonha's southern flank, lent me a horse, thus perpetuating my tradition of being offered things I didn't know how to use.

'Go through the gate at the top of the lands,' Chris said, 'you'll find a path that takes you up into the hills.'

The path rose gently at first, then more steeply, through a woodland of msasa, mfuti and beautiful wild jacarandas with delicate purple flowers growing from the rocky outcrops. The horse plodded upwards, while I relaxed and studied occasional glimpses of the adjacent stream valleys and wooded hills.

As the path grew steeper, it became confined to narrow ledges between slabs of weathered granite overlaid with mosaics of lichens and mosses. What Chris hadn't told me, possibly expecting me to work it out for myself, was that the path was made largely by elephants. I met one of them coming the other way, just as the path narrowed until it was less than two feet wide with loose screes above and a nasty drop below.

I drew back on the reins and said, 'whoa, there, Lightning', or something like that, a second or so after the horse had taken this decision for itself. Horse and elephant studied each other with mutual perplexity. Man studied both horse and elephant with apprehension and an absence of constructive ideas. Throwing myself off the horse and five hundred feet down a cliff into a dry streambed didn't count as constructive.

Then the elephant – goodness only knows how – rotated on the spot without any other visible motion, as if perched on a small turntable, and set off back whence it had come. I checked the horse's desire to try the same trick and carried on warily, until I saw the elephant's spoor going off down a branch line.

Rock-rabbits peered at me from the granite slabs as I passed; and I glimpsed a couple more elephants, browsing in the woodlands, before I rode between two soaring crags and emerged on the very edge of the hills, where they plunge three thousand feet to the Zambezi Valley below.

I dismounted, and let the horse graze on the sparse tufts of stringy grass that grew between the rocks. Stunted msasas, covered in lichens, clung to crevices in the grey granite, shrunken and bowed by the wind that moaned bleakly over the hilltops. It was eerily, desolately beautiful. But I gazed longingly towards Mana Pools, seventy miles away across the friendly, sunlit warmth of the Zambezi Valley, hidden behind a distant range of misty hills.

On the way down I emerged onto a grassy little plateau, surrounded by groves of wild muzhanjes, trees that grow delicious yellow plum-sized fruits. Several zebra and a couple of waterbuck were meandering around a tiny spring.

I dismounted and watched them for several minutes, while the horse grazed on the grass beside the stream that trickled from the spring. Then a line of women with bundles of firewood on their heads emerged from a thicket and began picking ripe muzhanjes. The zebra and waterbuck ran away.

I got back on the horse and walked him round the plateau and into one of the thickets, whereupon an innocuous-looking patch of grass, leaves and dead branches suddenly opened up beneath us like a trapdoor. Horse and rider found themselves standing stiffly erect with surprise, in a sheer-sided hole several feet deep.

Luckily, the horse didn't seem to have broken anything. In fact, it seemed remarkably blasé about it all. It began nibbling the grass around the edge of the hole, which was around nostril-level.

It was easy enough for me to get out of the hole. I rolled off the horse's back and onto the surrounding grass. Getting the horse out was a different matter. It looked slightly odd, I thought, as I surveyed part of its back and a busily-munching mouth protruding out of a hole in the ground.

Possibly feeling it was safer where it was, it refused to try and help itself in any way and carried on grazing instead. Not that it could help itself much, since – as I realised after some thought and a bit of fruitless giddy-upping – horses can't leap vertically upwards from a standing start. I'd have to excavate some steps.

This took a couple of hours or so of backbreaking work with a series of pointed branches that kept on breaking. The horse went on being happy where it was. I finally achieved a semblance of a staircase. It took a lot more giddy-upping and a fair bit of tugging on reins to get the horse to trust it, but it did in the end.

The horse studied the hole interestedly from above and then, while I was dusting myself down, decided enough was enough and set off for home alone at a leisurely canter. I walked back alone, treading on a thorn that penetrated my heel to the bone and later went septic. I would spend three weeks hobbling around, and added mountains and horses to the growing list of things I shouldn't mess around with.

The horse must have found a lot of interesting things to eat on its way down, since I'd almost reached the farm gate when I met Chris coming up to look for me. The horse's solo return had alerted him to the possibility that things might not be entirely rosy up on the mountain.

Chris and Dawn Pohl could blend in with the Hansies when they wanted to, but really they were a different breed. Chris was about the only tobacco-farmer at Mrs Chitepo's grand opening who wasn't built like a mobile mountain. He was built like a mobile telegraph-Pohl, as I almost said to him once but thought better of it. Dawn had the sort of figure that certainly didn't come from eating *koeksisters* and *boerewors* all day and keeping up with the boys in the bar all night.

And they weren't very wealthy. This was partly because their farm consisted almost exclusively of granite kopjes and lay in the Mavuradonha's rain-shadow. It was also partly because people like me scrounged deplorably on their extraordinary generosity and hospitality. They made bed, board and a fridge full of beer available without a moment's notice. Thanks, Chris; thanks, Dawn, wherever you are now. Better late than never.

And it was partly because they didn't adhere to the Zimbabwean commercial farmer's traditional mantra, which was: you can't farm in a zoo, let's go out and exterminate everything bigger than a shrew. Chris and Dawn liked having zebra, waterbuck, honey badgers, impala and even elephants wandering around on their farm. That they consumed the larger part of such crops as grew between the kopjes was something that came with the territory.

Their farmhouse was small, cosy and slightly ramshackle, and overlooked a small dam that Chris had stocked with bream and bass. We sat on the verandah. Thousands of fireflies danced over the dam, a blaze of twinkling meteors.

'Some nice sable herds in the Mavuradonha itself,' Chris said. 'Zebra. Waterbuck. Wonderful birdlife. Leopard. Lions, now and again, passing through, not resident, as far's we know. Maybe a hundred elephants or so, not many for its size.'

'But scenery,' Dawn said. 'Waterfalls. Lots of streams. That's what Mavuradonha means – the hills of water.'

That was a relief. I'd distrusted nice-sounding local names ever since I'd discovered that Matusadona meant – roughly – 'mountains of shit.'

'And it's wild,' Dawn went on. 'Get down into those valleys, the Tingwa, the Sohwe, the Msengezi, you could be a thousand miles from anywhere.'

'Except for the ladies picking up firewood,' I said. 'What was all that about an agreement? No firewood-gathering, no cattle-grazing and so on.'

Chris frowned. 'Dunno if we'll ever stop that. The management committee'll have to think of something.' He paused. 'They've elected me chairman, God knows why.'

So that they've got someone to blame, I thought to myself, if it all goes wrong? Sooner you than me.

'I'm co-opting you onto it,' he said. 'Have another *chiboulie*.'

My co-option wasn't entirely unwelcome, as I had already decided we ought to dip our toes into these rather strange waters by offering some sort of constructive assistance to the Mavuradonha. As the donor cash had already been sewn up by a lot of other organisations while I was fiddling about with rhinos, we had to find the money from the Zambezi Society's members.

'Forget it. I joined to help save rhinos, not to get eles shot by bloody hunters,' one of them said.

As I was in two minds over the whole business myself, he echoed my own secret thoughts with uncanny accuracy.

'We won't be,' I said, with slightly uneasy confidence. 'They want us to pay a manager to run the tourist camps in the Mavuradonha.'

Rob Clifford was an experienced parks warden who had decided to leave the department before he got himself imprisoned for arresting rhino poachers. I punted him heavily to the management committee as a suitable candidate. He got the job – something he only forgave me for much later.

We installed Rob and his wife, Shirley, in a decrepit caravan among the gravel piles of the abandoned Roads Department site, which – lying within the Mavuradonha itself, at an almost exact distance from both the commercial farms and the Zambezi Valley villages – was a sort of neutral no-man's-land between two worlds destined to come into disastrous collision in the not-so-distant future. Everyone thought it might make a nice campsite once the heaps of sand and gravel, a broken tractor and a lot of elephant dung had been tidied up. For now, it made a good base for committee meetings. I was duly summoned to one, soon after Rob had been appointed.

'I ought to get there early,' Chris Pohl had asked. 'Won't you pick up Mr Mhene on your way through?'

Mr Mhene was a district councillor who lived in a small and rather inexplicable pocket of peasant farmers next to Chris's farm, where he also tried to grow crops among a lot of granite kopjes, with much the same result.

I came across Mr Mhene already plodding slowly down the road, a couple of miles from the Roads Department site. He was a slight, bent figure with a trademark carved walking stick and a strong addiction to snuff. Being a traditional religious leader as well as a district councillor, he embodied two minor planets also destined for collision. Mr Mhene was successfully holding them apart, for the moment anyway.

'Thank you, Mr Dick,' he said as he painfully clambered up into the White Elephant. 'I am *madala*. An old man.' Mr Mhene never quite brought himself to use my first name unadorned. I never found what his was. He's always been Mr Mhene to me.

By way of small talk, I told him about the horse-in-the-hole episode, and the subsequent three weeks of limping around. He took a hefty pinch of snuff.

'It's the spirits,' he said, when I stopped sneezing.

'This wilderness area is all very well, but nobody's consulted the ancestors,' he went on. 'Everyone will have bad luck. We must consult the spirits.'

This, he said, would require a length of black cloth, some beer, and – the spirits having kept abreast of developments in modern society – quite a lot of money. I said my members would pay for it, furtively crossing my fingers. I'd pay for it from my own pocket if I had to. The next hole that opened up under me might be a lot deeper, and full of ancestors I'd no particular wish to meet.

The meetings were held in a hastily built structure of poles and thatch, surrounded by the piles of gravel and broken tractors. I was not very surprised to find that the committee consisted mostly of commercial tobacco-farmers.

They were slightly diluted by a trio of groupies, two enthusiastic conservationists including myself, and a representative of another odd breed: a well qualified biologist who'd morphed into a badly qualified sociologist to get his hands on some of the big donor money. This one had tried to grow his own dreadlocks. He looked like a Medusa who'd tangled with a combine harvester.

A small and beleaguered-looking contingent of local councillors sat on the periphery. There wasn't a villager to be seen.

'Mr Mhene,' Chris said, rather cautiously. 'On my way here I met a herd of cows wandering down the road. Tourists will come to the Mavuradonha to see elephants and sables, not *mombies*.'

A battery of eyeballs swivelled towards Mr Mhene. He took another huge pinch of snuff, and waited politely until the farmers sitting on either side of him had stopped sneezing. He smiled and nodded.

'Ah, yes,' he said. 'Cows are not allowed. The cows must go.'

This seemed unlikely, since everyone knew that most of the cows belonged to Mr Mhene himself. It led to a discussion on getting other people's cows out of the Mavuradonha, if not Mr Mhene's.

'I thought this point had been made to the local communities,' the combine-harvested biosociologist put in.

'It's one of the trade-offs for capacity-building and economic empowerment,' he went on, 'Wasn't it?'

Eyeballs darted around as if watching a ping-pong ball after a misjudged forehand smash. They came to rest on the councillors. There was a long silence. Few of them except Mr Mhene spoke much English.

'Wasn't what?' Mr Mhene said.

The biosociologist repeated himself, throwing in a bit more jargon about economic empowerment for good measure. Mr Mhene translated in a volley of Shona, a language that sounds like nuts and bolts being rattled around in an oilcan. His task was rendered difficult by the absence of Shona words for things like empowerment.

'Eeh, we didn't do that,' another councillor said at last. His own eyes swivelled towards the farmers. 'We thought you had.' There was an even longer silence. It was eventually broken by a small and bearded farmer, who looked a little like a ferocious garden gnome.

'Well,' he said, 'maybe we can still get the cows out of there. With the game-scouts. We've already discussed the need for anti-poaching patrols, because of the snares and pitfall traps. I still think it's a pity we can't give them guns, but I suppose a truncheon's better than nothing.' He paused, and glared at the councillors who'd objected to the guns.

'The game-scouts must promote the wilderness area,' he continued. 'They must go to the villages and tell the people about it. They must tell them not to graze cows in the Mavuradonha. We won't call them game-scouts after all. We'll call them' – he paused again, before producing his climax – 'ambassadors.' His own eyes came to rest on Rob Clifford. 'Neat, don't you think, Rob?'

'Weell,' Rob said, a bit dubiously. 'If you say so.'

'Good,' the garden gnome concluded. He glared at the councillors again. 'That's agreed then, wouldn't you say?' The councillors, who hadn't followed a word of it, nodded glumly. 'Yes,' they said, in chorus.

These meetings took place every month, but the ad hoc introduction of sensitive subjects such as Mr Mhene's cows soon led to misgivings on the part of the other councillors. Since the management committee fell under the district council, they said, its meetings should follow district council rules.

One of these rules said that 'new business' had to be submitted to the district council offices in advance of the meetings, and circulated to members in writing. This gave the councillors the chance to have a good long think about possibly threatening items – such as discussions on cows, firewood gathering, poaching, guns and truncheons – and suppress them.

Chris tried to circumvent this by various stratagems, including judicious visits to the council offices and the discovery that the chief executive officer, who seemed to wield more power than the councillors themselves, was happy to rubber-stamp most proposals. They then mysteriously appeared as previously-minuted items and could be dealt with under 'matters arising'.

But the councillors could still make life difficult, if they wanted to. WWF found some money to build a guest lodge, overlooking the Zambezi Valley where the Sohwe River tumbles over granite rocks and waterfalls into a limpid pool nestling between wooded hills. The villagers were supposed to make the bricks, cut the thatch and provide the labour, all free of charge.

This, it was thought, would give them a sense of pride in the whole thing. Of empowerment, even. Unfortunately, it failed to take into account the interests of several councillors who, foreseeing a need for tourist lodges and other developments, had already established brick-making and building companies.

Rob clattered all over the Zambezi Valley in his pride and joy – a little open Series I Diesel Land Rover, which was, I noted, in genuine showroom condition – looking for piles of brick and thatch and crowds of labourers eager to be empowered by building a lodge for free.

Instead, he found a lot of people fed up with ambassadors telling them to make bricks and cut thatching grass for nothing, and then getting bashed over the head by angry councillors when they did. The bricks didn't get made, the grass wasn't cut, and the lodge was never built.

Rob finally managed to build some small thatched shelters on the old Roads Department site, and to get the gravel piles cleared away. Dawn Pohl planted fig trees for shade, and grass lawns outside the shelters. But the income from the few backpackers who visited the Mavuradonha failed – spectacularly – to cover the costs of running the wilderness area, let alone save villagers from starvation.

The villagers were also getting fed up with ambassadors telling them about the benefits the Mavuradonha would bring them tomorrow, while bashing them over the head with truncheons for cutting firewood and digging pitfall traps today. To make matters worse, elephants persisted in wandering out of the Mavuradonha and into the surrounding fields.

The commercial farmers had a simple and direct answer when elephants got into their own fields: they shot them. This didn't go down too well with the groupies, who felt that shooting elephants was fine if it was done by villagers, but not by commercial farmers.

'In that case,' the farmers said, at one of the regular management meetings, 'we'll drive the elephants back into the Mavuradonha, and build an electric fence to keep them out of our fields. It'll cost us a bit, but we can't farm in a zoo, you know.'

One of the councillors spoke up.

'The elephants are eating all our crops, too. Can we have a fence on our side, as well?'

The answer to this seemingly logical question was far too uncomfortable to be made in plain English. All the eyeballs came to rest on the biosociologist, whose mastery of unfathomable jargon often proved useful in such circumstances.

'Of the many challenges involved in ameliorating issues of social equity in post-colonial rural Africa...' he began.

It was one of his finest efforts. It took him half an hour to say: 'Unlike the commercial farmers, you're so stone-poor that elephants in your fields are actually an asset. The Mavuradonha Wilderness Area isn't making any money, so better we get some hunters to shoot elephants in your maize fields, if you want to earn anything at all. That's what Sustainable Utilisation is all about. Oh, and by the way, I charge the donors four hundred US dollars a day to give you this advice, so there isn't any money to build you an electric fence anyway. So – no fence on your side.'

And he put it across so well that the councillor not only thanked him, but thanked the commercial farmers as well, for sending the elephants back into the Mavuradonha and thence into his own maize fields.

So the farmers built their fence and, always one to leap in feet-first where blithering lunatics fear to tread, I found myself sitting on a rock in the midst of a rather scrubby bit of bush with a couple of Mavuradonha ambassadors and several press-ganged villagers.

'What's happening,' I explained carefully, 'is that the elephant herds are being driven towards this fence.' I indicated a smart new electric fence, eight feet high, in the middle of a wide strip cleared of scrub that marched up the gentle hills on either side.

'The elephants,' I went on, 'will be driven through here' – I indicated a gap in the fence – 'and into the Mavuradonha. Once they have gone through, we will close the fence, and tomorrow, the electricity will be switched on.'

We settled down to wait beside the fence, a couple of hundred yards from the gap. As there were several other gaps up and down the length of the fence, all manned by similar little groups, the chance of any elephants coming through mine seemed fairly remote.

The ambassadors and villagers declared a temporary ceasefire, or cease-bash-over-the-head-with-truncheons anyway, and played *tsoro*, a complicated sort of draughts, perching the board on a rock and using bottle-tops as counters.

I brushed up on my small-brown-bird recognition skills for a while, then fell into a light doze. I was awakened by the sound of a small aeroplane, buzzing away nearby. It was, I saw, circling low over the bush, straightening up every now and then and flying in our direction before going back and circling again. Well, that looks like fun, I thought, what a nice way to see the Mavuradonha without falling into pits on horses.

My train of thought was interrupted by an ominous crackling in the scrub and an even more ominous chorus of trumpeting, as of a herd of very cross elephants on the move.

'OK, get ready, guys,' I said, 'looks as if they're coming through our gap after all.'

They didn't. The scrub shook and trembled as if hit by an earthquake. A huge dustcloud appeared, and about twenty elephants came thundering out of it at a smart gallop, hell-bent on coming through us instead. Actually, elephants can't gallop as such – their legs aren't made that way – but they certainly look as if they can when they're coming straight at you in a dense cloud of dust.

'Run!' I screamed, and found I was talking to myself, an abandoned *tsoro*-board and several bottle-tops still clattering down the rock. I joined the ambassadors and villagers behind a small outbreak of less scrubby bush, and peered round it.

The elephants screeched to a halt as they reached the fence. One of them sniffed curiously at the *tsoro*-board, then picked it up, threw it over his shoulder and trumpeted loudly. Then they all leant hard against the fence. Several hundred yards of it fell down with an earsplitting crash of breaking gum-poles and twanging of wire. There was some triumphant trumpeting. Then the elephants picked their way over the wreckage and disappeared into the Mavuradonha.

The little aeroplane circled overhead a couple of times. Someone waved happily out of the window. Then it flew off after the elephants. A long silence fell, broken only by a diminishing crackle of branches.

'Ah. *Endege*,' one of the ambassadors remarked, watching the aeroplane wistfully as it disappeared. 'I wish I could fly an *endege*.'

It was one piece of equipment I would know how to use, if someone handed me one.

The last straw for Rob and Shirley weighed several tons, and took the form of a very large tree that blew down during a midnight storm. It narrowly missed the caravan, but reduced Rob's Land Rover to a heap of scrap metal.

'When that happened,' he explained to me, 'I knew we weren't meant to be in the Mavuradonha.'

He'd been offered a job as manager of Fothergill Island. I tried to persuade him to stay in the Mavuradonha, but that Land Rover had been his pride and joy. Rob and Shirley left. 'Do come and see us,' they said, before they went.

After some disenchanting youthful experiences with motorbikes, I'd turned to aeroplanes instead. The aeroplane circling over the Mavuradonha elephants had been a Super Cub, an uncomplicated little device which I'd often flown in those long-gone days. I was swept by a wave of almost unbearable nostalgia and longing. It coincided, more or less, with my fiftieth birthday and a sense of now or never.

I took myself off to Charles Prince Airport, just outside Harare, and located a couple of young instructors who were willing to take on the job of retraining someone they probably thought should be learning to drive a wheelchair rather than an aeroplane. Thanks, Marks Hughan and Hess, wherever you are now.

One of the first things I did was to fly to Fothergill Island. The Matusadona had got a lot bigger since I'd last been there. After several years of drought, Lake Kariba had receded to reveal miles of gently-shelving shoreline on which succulent swards of torpedo-grass had grown. Fothergill was joined to the Matusadona by a broad causeway on which thousands of impala, several hundred buffalo, herds of zebra and waterbuck and elephant family groups were grazing.

Rob's house – a nicely-thatched, single-storey affair, surrounded with little mopanes instead of hulking great trees – was situated more or less where my old hut once stood.

Rob drove me to where the end of the island used to be. He had painstakingly rebuilt his Land Rover, and then spoilt the effect somewhat by painting it purple. 'Only colour I could find,' he explained, rather defensively.

'It's all the extra grazing,' he said as we parked on a gentle slope with a view of the extraordinary wildlife spectacle occupying several square miles of grassland where a lake used to be. 'Zebra and waterbuck all over the place. Buffalo and impala coming out of our ears. And lions.'

Lions had been something of a rarity when I'd been towing eager tourists around the place. Now, Rob said, prides of ten or more were commonplace. So were prides of Land Rovers full of tourists, I noticed. I could see several of them scattered among the buffalo herds.

I couldn't stay, because I had to get the hired Cessna back and I wanted plenty of daylight in hand in case I had to spend a lot of time looking for Charles Prince Airport.

Not long afterwards I got a telephone call from a parks officer who had so far managed to survive the earthquakes as racial tensions built inside the department.

'Why don't you become a volunteer pilot for us?' he said.

This seemed almost as improbable as becoming a tourist guide on Fothergill, but at least I could spell P-R-O-P-E-L-L-E-R (or is it -O-R?). I accepted, and went off to get checked out on Z-WMP, the department's Super Cub.

'Well,' my instructor said after we'd landed, 'there isn't much I can teach you about flying Super Cubs.'

I wasn't entirely sure whether he was referring to my superb piloting skills, or my supreme overconfidence.

Chapter Six

COMING THROUGH IN BUBBLES

It was a huge relief to get back into the good old world of macho Real Bushmen, after what an unreconstructed colleague called 'all that touchy-feely stuff' in the Mavuradonha.

During the early 1990s the British government provided the parks department with the funding to employ two wildlife vets: Mike Cock, who was English, and Mark Atkinson, a Zimbabwean. Both were highly experienced, extremely competent, and disinclined to mince their words when faced with paranoid permanent secretaries. They'd gone onto the offensive over the rhino dehorning business.

Moreover, they said, it was high time any such rhinos that remained in places like Mana Pools and Chizarira were moved into other places where they could be more easily protected, like the Matusadona. These places were given the snappy title of 'intensive protection zones', or IPZs.

There was a new permanent secretary, but he had been well trained by the old one. 'No,' he said. Asked to explain why not, he launched into the mantra about there being lots of rhinos left and capped it with the likelihood of theft by helicopter.

'Crap,' Mike and Mark said, in effect, and offered to prove it by trying to lift a fairly substantial permanent secretary with a small game-capture helicopter. He declined hastily, and agreed to their proposals instead.

Catching rhinos and carting them about the countryside is a complex and hugely expensive business. You need an aeroplane to find them with, the helicopter to dart them from and the drugs to tranquillise them with. You need several very large crates to put them in, and a socking great truck to cart them around once you've caught them. You also need enormous quantities of fuel, lots of smaller items like radios, and you need chainsaws. Since all this has to be transported to the scene of operations in the middle of the bush, it's like getting ready to invade Iraq. Unfortunately, Mike's British budget didn't run to this.

'No,' the American ambassador said when I tried to touch him for a few hundred thousand dollars. 'We haven't got a Rhino Act. We've got an Elephant Act, though. You can have the money to cart a couple of very small elephants around.' They were clearly saving up for Iraq.

'Yes,' the Norwegians and New Zealanders said. 'Well, a hundred thou or so anyway. Can't you use a smaller helicopter?'

I resigned myself to my usual role in rhino conservation, which was to scrape together the cash and then hang around on the sidelines while the experts did the work – or, even worse, film them doing it. I was therefore pleasantly surprised when I got a telephone call from the parks department, asking me if I would fly Z-WMP to the Chizarira National Park, to take part in a rhino capture and dehorning operation.

Was someone entrusting me with an item of equipment I actually knew how to use? I assembled a pile of tinned food, a stretcher-bed – won't need a tent, there's nice accommodation in Chizarira – threw some spare clothes in a bag and the whole lot into the back of Z-WMP and took off for Chizarira before anyone could change their mind. I landed at Manzituba, the parks station from which Nick Tredger and I had set out on patrol, many years before.

Mike and Mark were already there, along with an army of game-scouts, socking great trucks, and the foreign film crew that was filming events. Viv Bristow, a local capture expert, had also arrived with his very small helicopter.

This may be the point at which to admit that neither Viv nor I were Mike's first choice of pilots, which would have been along more macho lines. I'd never tried looking for rhinos from an aeroplane before. Viv had, but was middle-aged, slightly balding, and slightly overweight. Nor, to outward appearances, was he very macho or the sort of rakish bon viveur Mike often seemed to attract. However, appearances can be misleading.

Instead of taking me to the park headquarters, though, the scout who met me on the airstrip drove me several miles down a rutted little track to a small campsite with no buildings except a very smelly toilet block.

Mike greeted me. 'Ha,' he shouted, 'and about time too. What kept you? Put your tent up over there' – he indicated a small patch of unoccupied ground.

'No tent? No tent? What do you think this is, the Chizarira Hilton?' I might have found half the money for all this, but I was beginning to sense my new place in the scheme of things.

Viv Bristow appeared alongside. 'I didn't bring a tent either,' he sighed. He indicated the sloping thatched eaves of the toilet block, which extended down to a couple of feet above the ground and, I saw, already sheltered a neatly made-up stretcher-bed.

'You can cram in under there with me, if you like. It's on the upwind side. Some of the time, anyway.'

Mike glanced at his watch. 'OK,' he said, 'you ready to get airborne? Got some catching up to do.'

I stared at him in horror. The sun had already set behind the hills. 'Joke,' he said. 'Get going first thing in the morning.'

The film unit was composed of precisely the sort of bon viveurs that Mike often attracted. They had brought a cook with them, together with a lot of decorative female assistants whose functions were obscure. They'd also had the foresight to bring several large tents, one of which served as a dining room.

We sat down to a meal of fillet steak, washed down with French wine. 'Well,' their producer said, finishing off the last of his fillet, 'been a bit slow so far. I mean, we haven't actually seen a rhinoceros yet.'

'Oh, they're there alright,' Mike said airily. 'Just been a bit difficult finding them, without an aeroplane. Can't use the helicopter just to look for them, costs far too much. But we've got the Super Cub now. And Dick,' he added as an afterthought. 'He comes for nothing.' My perception of my place in the scheme of things changed even more. Get one free with every aeroplane.

Mike turned to me. 'Goin' to fly your friggin' arse off,' he said. 'Last stand-in we had just sat on the ground all day, too windy, too hot, too cold, altimeter's buggered, always some excuse.' I recognised the symptoms that resulted from frightening yourself so badly that you'll do anything to stay on the ground. Getting the twitch, older pilots called it.

The cook began to replace the entrée china with bowls of strawberries and ice-cream. 'We know there's rhinos in this part of Chizarira,' Mike continued, waving vaguely at the surrounding bush, 'even if we haven't actually seen any of the buggers yet. We'll get to them later, but we'll search the rest of the park first. Have a look at the Busi in the morning. We'll make an early start.'

By 'we' he meant me. After a night of fitful sleep, during which about a million game-scouts decided they needed to go to the loo, I staggered into the pre-dawn gloom while the rest of the camp slept. I found a functioning vehicle, drove myself to the airstrip, and fired up the Super Cub.

There were compensations. As I took off, the sun erupted over the eastern horizon in a blaze of light, on a clear, sparkly morning with the green buds just beginning to burst open in the mfuti woodlands. To the north, the ground rose, gently at first, then more steeply, towards the summit of the Zambezi Escarpment, glowing in the sun and cut with deep and craggy river-gorges. I swung the nose southwards towards the Busi River 20 miles away, and crept into the dawn sky.

Landmarks – ranges of hills, rivers, occasional park tracks – were easy to identify. I drank in the view, then took the Super Cub down to the treetops and swung around the hills and along little river valleys. It beat riding rafts through storm drains and falling into holes on horses, hands down. This was fun. I found the Busi, a fat sandy snake winding through floodplains dotted with billowing acacias, and waited for the first black rhino to pop out of the woodwork.

It didn't. A lot of large grey rocks did, half-hidden under the trees and pretending to be rhinos. Any fantasies of instant stardom – Mike, I've got six rhinos here, which one d'you want – began to fade as I zoomed over the umpteenth large grey rock to see if it had horns on its nose. There was precious little sign of anything else either, except an occasional elephant.

I tried radioing the camp where, by now, the vets and Viv were no doubt eating a leisurely breakfast, cooked by the film crew's factotum and brightened by the functionless film-persons. 'Aaaah, you are coming through in bubbles,' a voice observed in a Shona accent, then fell silent.

Coming Through in Bubbles

This is one of life's enduring technological mysteries. I can use a gadget the size of a small cigarette packet to have a conversation of crystal clarity with a colleague in Boonsville, Ohio. I can hear the things his wife is saying about me with even greater clarity, because it's two o'clock in the morning in Boonsville. In an aeroplane, equipped with a radio the size of an electricity substation, I come through in bubbles if I try to talk to someone 20 miles away.

I tried flying low enough to see under the canopies of the trees. This was fine, but I couldn't see under more than about two trees at a time. I climbed higher, but the sprouting canopies became opaque enough to hide whole herds of black rhinos. I flew on, up and down the riverlines, in and out of the valleys, that's the way the money goes, POP! goes the donor...

It all began to be slightly less fun. My eyes began to water, and my backside to ache. The radio crackled a little – the first sign of life it had shown for a couple of hours. Mike came through, apparently untroubled by bubbles.

'Nothing,' I told him.

'Keep going. Try harder,' he advised.

I did, until the bouncy little red balls in the sight glasses that constitute a Super Cub's hi-tech fuel gauges bounced themselves out of sight at the bottom of their tubes. The sun was hot by now, and the air turbulent.

It seemed a good time to land, refuel, and head back to camp for a cup of tea, or maybe even an early lunch and a siesta. As I flew over the camp Mike called me up again, startlingly loud and bubble-free. 'Let me know when you're airborne again,' he said, and switched off before I could reply.

Someone had taken the vehicle from the airstrip, so I couldn't drive back to camp anyway. I wrestled a barrel of Avgas into position and refuelled with a worn-out handpump that squirted some of the petrol into Z-WMP's tanks, and the rest of it all over me. This gave me an excuse to lie in the grass until the petrol evaporated and I could light a cigarette without turning myself into a Hindi funeral. Then I clambered back into the cockpit, flew back to the Busi, and began all over again.

I flew high, I flew low; I flew fast, and I flew slow. Sometimes I even flew sideways a bit and, if I could, I'd have flown upsidedown and turned over the large grey rocks to see if there were any rhinos hiding under them. I threw away any semblance of thoughtful planning and flew around with desperate abandon. There wasn't a sniff of a black rhinoceros. The turbulence was getting worse, and gusts of hot air blasted into the cockpit through the open windows.

After a couple of hours or so I climbed up to a thousand feet for a rest, whereupon the engine gave an apologetic cough, as if to remind me of something, then stopped altogether. Fuck! I thought constructively, then tore through the drills thoughtfully designed to take your mind off the upcoming crash. My eyes came to rest on the fuel tap. Super Cubs are so uncomplicated that you can't run them on both fuel tanks at once.

I turned the tap from the empty one to the full one and the engine started again, possibly even more relieved than I was. 'We got plenty of pilots,' Mike had said, in contradiction of my unlikely presence in Chizarira, 'but aeroplanes are expensive. Look after the bloody thing.'

By the time I'd almost emptied the second tank I was so stiff I doubted I'd ever walk again. My eyeballs felt gritty from peering down into the trees. The earpieces of my headset were meeting somewhere in the middle of my brain. My bladder was about the only bit of me that wasn't complaining, probably because I had thoughtfully stowed my water-bottle out of reach in the luggage compartment.

Three o'clock. I could fly to the strip, refuel, back here by four... just about the time when the odd rhino or two might be expected to stroll out from beneath the trees where they would have been dozing the day away.

Well, toughies. Finding a rhino this late in the day would have meant hanging around waiting for the helicopter, then spending another hour or more guiding the very large truck and its capture crate around the countryside, and probably scaring myself stupid by trying to land at Manzituba in the dark. I set off back towards the airstrip, radioed for a lift with all the authority I could muster, and landed. After a few minutes Mike arrived in his Land Rover, looking thunderous.

'I,' he said, 'am goin', personally, to paint a fuckin' rhinoceros on your fuckin' windshield. Then at least you'll recognise the sods when you see 'em. You're a complete waste of fuckin' oxygen. And fuel.' This annoyed me, since I'd got the money for the fuel.

'And you,' I replied, 'are a fucking stupid git. There aren't any fucking rhinos down there, and you fucking well know it.'

I had discovered a language an English vet could understand. His face dissolved into laughter, and he threw an arm round my shoulder. 'No, I don't suppose there are,' he said, 'but it was good practice for you.' He stopped laughing, and a shadow passed across his face. 'Trouble is,' he went on, 'the film crew's packed up and gone. Said there wasn't enough action.'

I murmured in sympathy but, privately, I didn't think this was much of a disaster – until we got back to camp and the implications became fully apparent. The film crew had taken all their imported wine, their fillet steaks, cutlery, linen tablecloths and napkins, refrigerator, womenfolk and – most appalling of all – their cook.

The true awfulness of our situation dawned on us when we realised we had ten tins of sweetcorn, another ten of baked beans, some palaeozoic bacon and a few warm beers between us.

'Bugger it,' Mike said, as a slow drizzle began to fall. 'They've taken the dining room as well.' Supper was a subdued affair, eaten in semi-darkness while we huddled under the eaves of the toilet block. Viv Bristow was particularly quiet. Helicopter pilots expect a certain standard to be maintained, and I wondered if he might not pack up and fly away in the morning.

Viv was indeed up at dawn, and announced his intention of buzzing down to a tourist safari camp in the Zambezi Valley.

'For breakfast, I suppose,' someone said snarkily. Viv smiled cryptically. 'To make a telephone call.' He thwacked off into the sky.

The day went on much like its predecessor. Mike asked – very nicely – if I wouldn't mind carrying on in the south of the park, just to check things out once and for all.

I was learning how to survive as a fully paid-up member of the testosterone club, instead of as a dabbling onlooker. I didn't tiptoe away into the dawn this time. I stuck the Super Cub's nose down, snuck up to the camp, opened the throttle wide and roared over the tents and trucks as low as I could get without hitting the radio aerials slung between the trees. That'll get the bastards to turn the bloody radio on, I thought.

Then I flew off to spend another eight hours or so in the air, burning up fuel and aircraft time at someone else's expense, which made up for a lot. There weren't any rhinos, just a lot more trees and grey rocks.

I landed just before sunset, and a waiting game-scout drove me back to our camp. As we arrived, a very large and dusty truck appeared behind us. It creaked wearily to a halt. Viv, who had returned sometime during the day, strolled up to the cab.

'At last,' he said to the driver. 'What kept you?'

The driver looked apologetic and began to unload the truck, together with a wizened little man who had been sitting silently in the passenger seat. Out came fridges, crates of beer and wine, boxes of meat and vegetables, awnings, tables, chairs, linen – an entire pre-packaged Hemingwegian safari camp.

Life took an immense turn for the better. The wizened little man turned out to be a cook of vast expertise and experience. During a gourmet meal of fresh meat, vegetables and dessert, Viv revealed that he'd telephoned his staff in Harare and told them to buy the food, load the truck and drive the two hundred miles to Chizarira by nightfall, or face certain death.

'Any bloody fool can be uncomfortable in the bush,' he remarked, glancing at the toilets, 'and I'm too old to be a bloody fool.' He glanced at me. 'Damn. Didn't think of asking for an extra tent for you.'

Not to worry. I know my place.

Mike and Mark still wanted to cover more of the Chizarira hinterland before focusing on the known rhinos in the north of the park, which were in a wooded bowl cut by several deep river-gorges. It made sense. It would be silly to miss an unknown pocket of rhinos while we had the invasion force in place. Funds wouldn't allow a second go, unless the Americans passed a Rhino Act and decided to give Iraq a miss as well.

Besides, it was certainly good practice for me. Apart from some forays into the Scottish mountains, most of my past flying had been of the suburban, 1,500-metre-long, tarred-runway variety. You didn't fly around southern England at

200 feet looking for rhinos, unless you wanted to get yourself certified insane.

I slowly began to develop 'bush eyes' – the ability to distinguish a glimpse of animal hide from a large grey rock, even if it did turn out to be an elephant instead of a rhino.

And I began to take in more of the magnificent Chizarira scenery. I took the little Super Cub into places it would have taken days to reach on foot. I flew down a particularly beautiful river valley, with my wingtips almost brushing the wooded slopes until they opened out into a lovely amphitheatre, almost like a miniature meteorite impact crater, with a tiny gorge at its far end.

Inside the amphitheatre the river had formed a sparkling pool, where a family of elephants was drinking and bathing. I throttled back and let the Cub purr round the walls of the amphitheatre a couple of times. The elephants looked up briefly, then went on drinking, splashing and rolling. I flew out through the little gorge and left them in peace.

It was late in the year, the trees slowly coming into leaf, hazy green against the brown grasses and grey granite rocks. I flew up to Tundazi, the great bald-headed mountain in the north-east of Chizarira. Tundazi is sacred to local people, forbidden territory. I flew round it at a respectful distance, looking for the huge serpent which, they say, lies coiled around its summit. I couldn't see it. Nor could I see any rhinos.

If you want to fly aeroplanes and live there are several things you don't do, besides forgetting to look at your fuel gauges. You don't fly on four hours' sleep. You don't fly around hills and mountains in bad weather. You certainly do not fly with the arch-prototype-granddaddy of all hangovers. Doing just one of these things is Russian roulette. Doing them all at once is about as insane as leaping off Nelson's Column in the belief that you're a pigeon. Luckily, there's a minor aviation god who is also concerned about the cost of aeroplanes.

There can be all kinds of pressures on operations like this one. Some stem from trying to save a sorely endangered species, with the weather gradually deteriorating and the leaf cover growing by the day, when there may not be another chance. Some arise from the frustrations of keeping less-than-new equipment in working order; some from watching time and money leaking away with absolutely nothing to show for it.

And some result from being isolated in the bush for weeks on end, like most of the rhino team. I'd only been in Chizarira a few days, but it was quite a long time to survive the smell of an overburdened parks department toilet. The idea of an evening at the safari lodge from which Viv had made his telephone call was attractive. I crammed myself into a Land Rover along with everyone else and we headed down into the Zambezi Valley. Viv declined to join us.

There are two subspecies of safari-camp host in countries like Zimbabwe. One is hotel-trained, knows little of the bush, and runs a tight ship geared exclusively to the needs of overseas clients. Unshaven wildlife capture teams in torn shorts and shirts with the sleeves ripped off have sometimes been told to go away from these places.

The other kind is a Real Bushman by inclination, often ex-parks, and returns to his roots whenever the chance arrives in the form of wildlife capture teams in torn shorts. He doesn't tell you to go away. If he did, it wouldn't be in those words. Instead, he welcomes you with open arms and the correct customary greeting, which is: 'Help yourself to the bar.' The correct response to this is to do so. Anything else is very rude.

Having made the customary greeting, Steve Alexander briefly pointed us out to his paying guests as part of the real Africa wildlife scene and then joined us in the bar. Things could only start to slide gently downhill.

It all began after dinner, with the mini-flares. These are little tubular gadgets that go off with a small 'pop!' and shoot a brightly coloured ball of fire into the air. Mike, Mark and Steve suddenly found caches of time-expired flares, which all went off nevertheless, creating a mini-firework display that went on for some time.

'Bugger it,' someone said. 'That's the last of them.' There was a longish silence while people tried to get their heads around this.

'I know. Tracer!' someone else said. 'Got lots of tracer bullets.'

Several magazines of tracer vanished down the barrels of parks-issue rifles, and reappeared as bright red streaks arcing high into the night sky. The crack of rifles echoed around the hills. The guests, who had rather enjoyed the mini-flares, crawled away beneath the cover of the table-tops and hid in their chalets.

'I bet,' Mike said to Steve, or it might have been the other way round, things were getting blurry round the edges, 'you can't let off both barrels of a double .500 at once and stay standing up.'

A double .500 is a very large rifle, more like a miniature artillery-piece, with a recoil to match. It's hard enough to fire one barrel without being blasted backwards into the next county, let alone both at once.

'Bet I bloody well can.'

'Bet you bloody well can't.'

This might have degenerated into a yah-boo-sucks

shouting match, except that somebody actually produced a double .500 elephant rifle.

'Ho, well, watch this, then.'

Whoever-it-was drew a careful bead on a portion of the night sky, and let fly. There was an enormous double explosion, and he ended up flat on his back on the verandah floor with a yelp of agony, clutching the .500 in one hand and a sore shoulder in the other. This was a difficult act to follow, so we quit before anyone could remember they'd got a few napalm bombs hidden away.

Some time in the small hours, we managed to drive back up the escarpment and arrived in our camp with a good deal of singing, shouting and roaring of engines.

'Right,' Mike shouted above the din. 'Be outta your shocking shart-fucks at farrow-spurt. I mean, be outta your spucking...'

'HE MEANS BE OUT OF YOUR FUCKING FART-SACKS AT SPARROW-FART,' Viv bellowed from his tent. 'NOW CAN WE ALL GET SOME BLOODY SLEEP?'

I awoke with sleep-deprivation and a king-size hangover, and squinted out from under the eaves of the toilet block. The dawn was grey and misty, and a howling wind bore flurries of drizzle. The hills were shrouded in low cloud. Impossible flying weather. I rolled over with a sense of relief, closed my eyes – even this quick glimpse made them hurt – and tried to go back to sleep. Five minutes later a jaunty and apparently hangover-free Mike appeared.

'Up!' he commanded. 'Up, up, up!'

'Forget it,' I muttered. 'Even your bloody sparrows are grounded.'

Mike glared at me stonily. 'They haven't got rhinos to catch,' he said.

I caught sight of Viv Bristow, still comfortably abed in his tent, one eye open. 'Try not to find one for an hour or two,' he said, smirking. 'Breakfast's not ready yet.' The eye closed.

I struggled wearily out of my sleeping bag. We would, Mike said, concentrate on the rhinos known to be lurking in the fearsomely rugged terrain below the all but invisible mountains. He also assigned a game-scout to the back seat of the Super Cub, on the assumption that he might know a rhino if he saw one, even if I didn't.

This poor trusting soul climbed into the aircraft without a murmur. The Cub lifted off the airstrip in about ten yards, assisted by the gale raging at us from the hills. My stomach stayed on the ground for a few seconds, then lurched skywards to join the rest of me and overshot. I pointed the nose more or less northwards, under a menacing roof of dark grey cloud trailing wisps that flashed past the wingtips. The bottom half of the escarpment was dimly visible as a near-black band ahead.

I edged towards the hills, over the granite outcrops and deep, sheer-sided gorges. As I did so, I realised that a tiny voice of past experience was trying to send me some sort of warning. 'You,' it was saying, 'are flying a small aeroplane, close to a large range of hills, in a very strong wind. Shouldn't you be worried about this?'

I should have been very worried indeed. The combination of mountains and strong winds can produce areas of extraordinary turbulence. Sometimes this turbulence is marked by ragged shreds of swirling cloud. Mostly, it's marked by ragged shreds of aeroplanes.

'Never mind all that,' I replied to the tiny voice. 'I'm much more worried about finding rhinos and keeping Mike Cock happy.'

Whereupon all hell broke loose. The Cub suddenly plummeted earthwards. The game-scout's clipboard came flying into my lap, after bouncing off the cockpit headlining.

I opened the throttle as far as it would go. Z-WMP pointed her nose valiantly upwards, but continued to hurtle downwards at a mile a minute. The granite crags, already uncomfortably close, ballooned beneath us.

Then the Cub halted its graveyard plunge with a wallop that felt as if we'd dived into a skip of wet concrete, crunching our spines into the seats, and rocketed skywards again.

The granite outcrops retreated at warp speed, and the low dome of grey cloud reached down to enfold us. It was slightly less unnerving to be in an aeroplane pointing steeply downhill while hurtling upwards like Burt Rutan going for the space-tourism prize, but not much.

I fought the aircraft round into a turn away from the mountain, and was about to cut and run for the relative safety of the airstrip and Mike's scorn when two things happened. The turbulence subsided to a level at which the Cub was more or less controllable. And the game-scout in the back seat, whom I had almost forgotten about, announced, clearly and calmly: 'Rhino.'

Bugger his bush eyes and the rest of him, I thought. Maybe he was mistaken. Maybe it was a large grey rock. Maybe I could bribe him to forget all about it. Instead, I asked, shakily: 'Where?'

'Down there,' he said helpfully.

It was, too – a rather dirty, mud-spattered rhino, pottering peacefully around a small clearing in the woodlands. But there's some good in everything, even if you have to look hard to find it. Viv and the others ought to be just starting on the eggs and bacon. I called for the helicopter with malicious delight. About ten minutes later the bright red Hughes 300 hove into sight, Viv and Mark on board, bouncing around just above the treetops.

'OK, visual,' Viv said over the radio. He flew low over the rhino and disappeared behind my wing. Mark called up a few seconds later. 'Dart's in,' he said. 'Keep an eye on it. We'll stand off until it goes down.'

'Roger that,' I said. I was picking up the terminology too, copying this and rogering that all over the sky.

Rhinos usually jump and run when the dart hits them. This one didn't even flinch. I circled overhead, watching it. The helicopter was out of sight. Minutes passed. 'Nothing's happened,' I volunteered.

'OK,' Mark said. 'We'll have a look. Give it another dart, maybe.'

He was back on the radio a few seconds later. 'She's gone down anyway. We're gonna land. Can you see the calf?'

Calf? A few unpleasant facts penetrated the mental fog, together with the creeping chill that accompanies the realisation that you may have screwed up, big-time. My rhino was very much up and walking. It didn't have a calf, either. I couldn't see the helicopter any more, let alone a bright red one landing in a clearing.

'Where are you, Viv?' I asked.

'Right below you, beside the rhino,' Viv said, with the undertone of stretched patience people use when answering silly questions while trying to land helicopters in a howling gale. I widened our circle a bit and there, clear as anything, was another clearing, another rhinoceros – this one flat out, dead to the world – and the helicopter settling daintily onto the ground.

As it turned out, there weren't just two rhinos in the same patch of woodland: there were five, all wandering about in useful little clearings. 'Clean 'em all up today,' Mike said, as he drove his Land Rover out to the scene of the action, 'why not?'

The wind continued to roar down from the hills, creating turbulence full of aerial devils and demons bent on giving a hungover, middle-aged novice bush-pilot the twitch. The game-scout in the back didn't know enough about flying to realise that he ought to be scared to death and unconscious from airsickness. We hurtled around the sky all day long, guiding helicopters to rhinos, the truck with its crates through the woodlands, and Mike and his Land Rover into a boulder-strewn gully.

'Copied that,' I said, when the hurricane of verbal abuse finally blew itself out.

'I'm landing to refuel and have a pee,' I told him, a little later.

The bubbles must have been back in action. 'Tea?' he shouted. 'Tea? What do you think this is, a bloody picnic?'

Shortly before sunset I landed for the last time. The game-scout had to help me out of the cockpit. I slowly straightened up, with a popping and crackling of joints and a kaleidoscopic swirl of rhino-shaped spots before the eyes.

'Eh, *madala*,' the game-scout said. Me? *Madala*? Shonas respect the elderly, but I still get unreasonably indignant at the suggestion.

'Thank you,' he went on. '*Ndatenda*. Nice ride. He glanced at the Super Cub, whose joints were also popping and crackling as the engine cooled. 'I wish I could fly an *endege*.'

Mike arrived in his Land Rover. The bumper, I noticed, was bent sharply upwards from his collision with a boulder. Here we go, I thought, and began framing a retort about drivers who were dim enough to depend on second-hand information from people trying to keep aeroplanes right-side-up, instead of using their eyes.

'Great day!' he said. 'Fuckin' fantastic.' He thumped me between the shoulder-blades, roughly where the Super Cub's rudimentary seat had already gone through the soft tissues and started on the bone. 'Well done, mate!'

It was like passing an initiation rite. I felt stupidly proud and unreasonably humble, all at the same time. Mike

Cock and Mark Atkinson were, after all, only the men who were ultimately responsible for saving every rhino left in Zimbabwe.

The Chizarira capture operation lasted almost four weeks, during which we plucked 14 black rhinos from the park and transported them to the Matusadona Black Rhinoceros Intensive Protection Zone. Nothing got killed. I'd possibly tried to kill a game-scout by flying him into a mountain, but he didn't seem to hold it against me.

Most of all, I loved being part of a team that was doing something useful, and I actually got quite good at finding rhinos, provided they were there in the first place. But it was tempered by a wider sense of overwhelming sadness. Once, there had been more than 500 rhinos in Chizarira alone. It was the same story in Mana Pools and the Chewore, the great Zambezi Valley wildlife areas. A pitiful handful of animals remained.

The final tally was something over 300 rhinos, and we would have lost even these, were it not for Mike and Mark's persistence in the face of almost overwhelming political opposition, physical hardship, and danger.

The other thing Mike and Mark did before letting the rhinos go in the Matusadona was to put radio-collars on them. These are placed round the rhino's neck, and contain a small radio transmitter, which emits a signal that can be picked up from a receiver in an aeroplane. It makes a barely-audible 'plink' when you first pick it up, rising to a frenzied 'PINGGG!' as you get closer. Putting them on rhinos was a bit experimental, since nobody had yet designed a radio-collar that a determined rhino couldn't rip off on a tree stump, but the actual tracking business was reasonably well tried.

I learnt how to do aerial tracking when the Matusadona's own aeroplane, its pilot and the park biologist were all simultaneously engaged on other business. Shirley Mason, who was Mark Atkinson's fiancée, helped me fit the tracking aerials onto the Super Cub on the Tashinga airstrip, one on each wing.

'They seem to plug into this little box,' I mused, 'in the back seat. Then you switch it all on and listen through the headset.'

'Sounds reasonable,' Shirley said. 'Then I tell you where to go, right?'

'Something like that.' I paused. 'Small problem. Z-WMP's intercom isn't working.' Shirley thought for a moment.

'OK,' she said. 'If I tap you softly on the left shoulder, it means "turn left gently". If I tap you harder, it means "turn quicker". If I tap you between the shoulder blades it means "go straight". Same on the right, as well.'

Yup, simple. We took off, climbed out over the lake-shore grasslands and then turned inland.

Shirley tapped me between the shoulder blades. After a few seconds, she tapped me gently on the left shoulder. I swung Z-WMP into a lazy turn. Then she hit me harder. I steepened the turn. I'd barely done so when she hit me very hard on the right shoulder. I'd barely got all the requisite controls up against their stops when she whacked me as hard as she could on the left shoulder again.

This was followed by a sensation akin to a regiment of Cossacks dancing all over my back in hobnailed boots. Make your mind up, Shirls. The Super Cub skidded and spun all over the sky, like a crazy-flying turn at an air show.

There was a wail from the back seat, audible over the engine noise. 'There are rhinos everywhere!' Shirley yelled despairingly. 'Things going plink and plock all over the place. I can't make head or tail of it all!'

Plock? Shouldn't go plock. OK, something's wrong somewhere. We landed, went to the park office and telephoned Richard Hoare, a radio-tracking expert.

I outlined the problem.

'Well,' Richard said. 'First of all, it shouldn't go "plock". Tune the receiver until it goes "plink". There's a little knob to tune it with. It's probably labelled "tuner".'

'As for the rest,' he continued, 'have you asked yourself why you have an aerial on each wing, instead of just one perched on the nose, other than avoiding having it chewed up by the propeller?'

No, not in great depth, I hadn't.

'And have you,' he went on, 'also considered why the little black box inside the aeroplane has a great big switch marked "left", "right", and "both"?'

'Um. Eeerrrr…' I said. There was a faint tinkle, as of pennies being lined up for a low-level cargo-drop.

'Exactly,' he said. 'You start by listening on both aerials. That way you find out if there's an animal around, somewhere. Maybe it'll go "plink" if it's a long way away, or "PINNG!" if it's quite close by. But that's all it tells you. So. Now you switch to 'left' and listen a bit.'

The pennies went into free fall. 'Ah-ha' I said. 'I think I…'

However, Richard was in full spate. 'Then,' he went on, as if explaining relativity to a nursery-school class, 'you switch to "right" and listen again. If it went "plink" on the left, but goes "PINNG!" on the right, you know the animal's to the right of you. So you turn towards it. And vice versa. But if it goes "plink" – or "PINNG!" – equally on both sides, then it's ahead of you. Or possibly below, or even behind you.'

'Got that?' Richard concluded. 'Shall I run through it again?'

No, I said hastily, amid the crash of pennies on a corrugated-iron roof. I get the picture. We'll go off and try it. When we did, we were rewarded almost instantly by the sight of a rhino – one of my rhinos, as I liked to think of them – pottering around in a riverbed and wondering how to get its collar off.

Chapter Seven

A TRUCKLOAD OF CHEETAHS

Things were looking up. I thoroughly enjoyed flying around the bush in small aeroplanes, helping to save rhinos at the British, Norwegian and New Zealand taxpayer's expense.

They were looking up on the financial front, too. I was still writing for the small tourism magazine, but it was doing quite well, thanks to Zimbabwe's boom in tourism and a lot of articles saying nice things about some fairly awful camps and lodges that had sprung up to cash in on the boom.

Thanks to this and the help of good friends, by 1992 I'd been able to finish the small thatched house I'd been building in Harare's northern suburbs, and even to buy myself another Land Rover which, having been made in 1969, was a lot younger than the White Elephant. Something had clearly gone awry in the design department, because it did nearly 50 mph on a good day. I drove it to Mana Pools, to see what fell off.

Most of the exhaust pipe did, for a start. The Mana Pools road had passed its apogee of over-improvement, and was well on the way back down. Immense corrugations traversed its surface, with an occasional huge pothole, as if a landmine had been missed by the post-war clearance teams.

The Land Rover – a sort of beigy-brown elephant with a black go-faster stripe this time – bucked, banged and reared like a small dinghy in a nasty chop. Odd, I thought, for Datsuns to damage the road this badly. I couldn't even get close to the speed limit; the Landy felt as if it would split apart at the seams.

I saw a tiny plume of dust far behind me, in my rear-view mirror. The plume grew to a tornado, spearheaded by another Land Rover. It hurtled past, apparently airborne, its wheels a vibrating blur on the corrugations. There was a thunderous clatter of overworked springs and shock-absorbers. It was towing a huge trailer, also apparently airborne, with six large canoes bounding around in their retaining straps.

As the dust-cloud thinned and I got back up to my safe operating speed of about fifteen miles an hour, a similar plume appeared, ahead of me and coming my way. A Toyota Land Cruiser this time, at the same awesome speed and with another trailer full of canoes.

Two realisations dawned, after I'd passed – and been passed by – half a dozen of these terrifying phenomena. One was that the Zambezi canoe safari business was doing rather well; the other, that it was probably responsible for the appalling state of the road.

Not just the canoeing business, either. Mana Pools was crawling with Land Rovers and Cruisers with tiered seats in the back shaded with frilly canopies. Beneath the canopies sat rows of tourists: ahead of them, unshaded, sat drivers in smart safari-company uniforms brandishing walkie-talkie radios.

I came across a pride of lion, lying up close to a buffalo carcase, beside the road where it descends from the mopane woodlands onto the Mana floodplains. Vultures perched in the trees, waiting for the lions to move off. The lions yawned, stretched, rolled on their backs, and the cubs leapt playfully on their mothers. I'd managed to enjoy this sight for less than five minutes when one of the frilly Land Rovers appeared.

Its driver shouted and pointed. There were squeals of delight from the tourists. The Land Rover drove off the road and parked itself several yards closer to the lions, neatly blocking my view. The driver gabbled into his walkie-talkie. Within seconds, it seemed, another four Land Rovers with the same logo appeared at high speed, drove off the road and formed an impenetrable semi-circular barricade round the lions, which got wearily to their feet and ambled off into the mopanes. The Land Rovers shot off in a collective dustcloud. The vultures grabbed their chance and fell on the carcase. I watched them for a few more minutes, then drove on.

Mcheni – which had expanded from one campsite to four – had been booked solid by tour operators, so I was stuck with Nyamepi, which was appalling. The barbecues, which had been barely visible amid the tangled undergrowth when I'd been at Mana Pools with Dolf, were barely visible amid the South African-registered bubblecruisers which were displacing the Datsuns.

Some of the South Africans had bypassed the bubblecruiser phase and bought large lorries instead. These disgorged small trail-bikes which were being ridden round the campsite by 12-year-olds, while their parents fired up portable TVs, found they couldn't actually receive any programmes in the Zambezi Valley, and watched kung fu videos instead.

I had to ask myself: was this what people like Dolf, Nick Tredger and all the wardens and rangers I'd met in 1978 had defended places like Mana Pools for? Fifteen years on, the parks had become tourist playgrounds, but all the money was being gobbled up by tour operators and high-level government officials who wanted bubblecruisers of their own. The Zambezi Society was still having to buy boots and backpacks for the game-scouts.

Mercifully, few of the tourists got out of the Land Rover and onto their own two unguided feet, even though – uniquely among Zimbabwean parks – this was still allowed. I packed a couple of sandwiches and a flask of tea, strolled across the floodplains to Chine Pool and spent a day beside my favourite anthill.

The years of drought had hit Mana Pools hard. Chine Pool had shrunk to a small expanse of muddy water surrounded by cracked dry mud deeply pocked with elephant footprints. Goliath herons stood on its margins, snatching up dying barbel. The *jesse* bush on the far bank had been reduced to a few frayed sticks, shredded by starving elephants, their hip bones protruding like hatstands. They stood listlessly in the shade of the acacias behind me, on the floodplains. No nyala came down. And no rhinos.

Next day, I walked through my enchanted woodlands, up near the Mcheni camps. They were as lovely as ever, with kudu browsing on the mahoganies and old *dagga*-boys lying up in the shade. But they were haunted by the ghost of the old rhino I'd followed around, back in the early 1980s, as he meandered down to the river and slept the day away beneath the beautiful trees. There were no rhinos left in Mana Pools at all. A handful of survivors had been moved into the intensive protection zones. All the rest had been killed by poachers.

Since things had improved on the personal front, someone was clearly due to come along and stuff it all up. I'd only had my 'new' Land Rover for a few months when a German aid agency offered the Zambezi Society the money for staff, an office, a computer and a brand-new Toyota Hilux.

This was all very well in its way – thank you, Deutsche Entwicklungsdienst, I don't mean to sound ungrateful – but it created some knotty issues. For one thing, it meant losing our amateur status. Amateurs are allowed – expected, even – to racket around the bush in aeroplanes and mess around with what some conservation sects rather disparagingly call 'single species' conservation.

Professionals are expected to sit in their offices and write opaque documents about 'stakeholder consultations', 'community capacity-building' and 'empowerment'. Sometimes, on a good day, they are allowed to talk about 'ecosystem integrity', and even about elephants, but only if they were being useful members of rural society, i.e. getting themselves shot by hunters, turned into ivory galleons and umbrella-stands and making a lot of money in the process.

On the other hand, I could give up writing nice things about nasty places without fretting about starvation in a country where the one queue you never see is a dole queue, because there isn't any dole.

The Hilux created a dilemma all of its own, since I'd often been very rude about donor-aid addicts tearing about in their luxury 4WDs. It stood glistening outside the wooden hut the Zambezi Society already shared part-time at the Mukuvisi Environment Centre, just outside Harare. It sang a siren song. I can do 80 miles an hour, it crooned, and that's uphill.

Look at my power steering and luxurious seats, it went on. Think how nice it would be to arrive at far-flung meetings nice and fresh instead of totally knackered from arm-wrestling that tatty old Land Rover for six hours while sitting on the carefully-designed instrument of torture that passes for its driving seat.

Ha. Got you there, I can fly to them now. The Hilux stopped singing for a few moments. Through thunderstorms? it said, incredulously. To stakeholder consultations in places where there isn't an airfield? Can't pick and choose, if you're going to be a professional conservationist. You've got to be there. Think of the image. Would Muzarabani people place their hopes and aspirations in the hands of someone who didn't aspire to anything more than a beat-up old Land Rover?

The whole song lasted slightly less than a minute, during which I managed to rationalise everything. You need to take it easy, I told the old Land Rover, you've earned it at your age. We'll trundle off to all the nice places like Mana Pools and let this young upstart do all the hard work.

The aid package, I suspected, would also turn me from happy-go-lucky amateur into anxiety-ridden donor-aid junkie, but *carpe diem*. I grabbed it with both hands.

Meanwhile, having done some community capacity-building and empowerment at Mavuradonha, I felt free to go out and look for another single species in need of saving. I didn't have to look very hard, because it was looking for us. A truckload of cheetahs arrived – almost literally – on the doorstep, looking for a home.

Cheetahs are among the loveliest of all African animals. They have become extinct over much of their former range; those that remain have lost a lot of their genetic diversity and thus become vulnerable to disease and reproductive problems.

Conservationists avoided this problem with species such as the white rhinoceros, which had declined to less than 50 individuals by the early twentieth century, by redeveloping its numbers as fast as possible over the following decades. Unfortunately, the cheetah's problem arose before conservationists had evolved.

The one place where cheetahs were thriving was on Zimbabwean cattle ranches. Here, lion and hyaena – which compete with cheetah for food and often eat their cubs as well – were exterminated long ago by the ranchers, in conformation with the philosophy that you can't farm in a zoo. Somehow, cheetahs either escaped this holocaust, or snuck back onto the ranches when nobody was looking.

Confronted with an endless supply of succulent and awesomely brainless prey, without any competition for it, cheetahs bred to the point of pestilence. As they were classified as a 'protected species', ranchers had no legal way of disposing them. Scores – maybe hundreds – of cheetahs were being secretly shot and their corpses stuffed down ant-bear holes.

Again, it was a telephone call that started it all. It didn't ring; bits of the twentieth century were penetrating even the Zimbabwean telephone system, which was more than could be said for a lot of overseas telephone calls. It chirruped, twanged, or burped, according to taste. Someone even came into our office, looked at the computer and the telephone and said something like, 'Why do you not connect the two together, so that you can send messages to people overseas at local call rates?' 'It's called u-mail, or something like that,' he went on.

I dismissed this as the ravings of a deranged mind, along with the other rumour I'd heard, of a little black box you could put in an aeroplane to replace the maps, pencils, protractors and rulers that kept falling off your knee and down through holes in the cockpit floor. The little black box, the rumour said, not only told you where you were; it told you where you'd been, where you were going, and how to get there as well. GPO, or something. Pull the other one.

Anyway, back to the twanging telephone. It was another senior white parks officer, still surviving, but on the brink of the abyss.

'We want,' he said, 'to catch some cheetahs before the ranchers stuff them all down ant-bear holes, and move them somewhere else. Matusadona, probably. See if they'll breed there.'

'Why Matusadona, particularly?' I asked.

'Well…' He gave it some thought. 'Why not? The whole place is one gigantic uncontrolled experiment because of Kariba.'

He went on, possibly realising this wasn't a very satisfactory answer. 'Got nice big open shorelines with a lot of impala on them, looks like good cheetah country. Why don't you go and find a nice place for a cheetah boma and build one for us?'

Bomas – holding facilities for captive wild animals – need some careful design, and can be expensive. What the department probably meant was 'you do the work and pay for it, and we'll take the credit if it's successful.' However, I put these unworthy thoughts out of my mind and zoomed off to Fothergill Island, where I met with Rob Clifford and a number of other tourist camp operators.

'Mmmm,' Rob said, 'dunno. Lot of lions around. Hyaenas, too. What if the lake comes up again and all the grasslands vanish? Anyway, who's going to pay for it all?' Eyeballs darted around, and came to rest on me.

'Mmmmmm,' another tour operator said. 'Be nice to give the tourists something else to look at, they're getting bored with all these lions and elephants. Wouldn't like to buy us some manatees, would you? Oh, well, cheetah it is, then. We'll chip in a bit.'

His own eyeballs turned to Rob. 'Build the boma on Fothergill, shall we? You've got a nice bit of foreshore.'

Really, we should have done a lot more by way of research and feasibility studies before embarking on a project like this. To salve my conscience, I mentioned the idea to a biologist friend. He wrinkled his nose, as if at a nasty smell. 'Predator relocations,' he pronounced *excathedra*, 'seldom work.' But we decided to do it anyway.

It was December 1992. Christmas was approaching, and Harare was slowly being submerged by a tidal wave of cheap Chinese crackers that didn't go bang, but showered you with incomprehensible Chinglish jokes instead.

'Spend Christmas and New Year with us on Fothergill,' Rob Clifford said, 'we need to start getting the boma built.'

I mumbled my heartfelt thanks and fled to Fothergill, only to find the cheap Chinese crackers had washed over into the Zambezi Valley. Rob, Shirley, a few of the Fothergill staff and I sat among the debris of Christmas dinner, wearing silly hats. Outside, thunder roared and rolled, and the rain bucketed down. Shirley fiddled with a cracker.

'Ah,' she said, 'what you have to do is pull the cracker doodab out first.' She applied her cigarette lighter to it. It went off nicely. 'Then just throw the rest of the bloody thing away.'

A rather similar 'Crack! Crack!' came from outside, during a lull in the thunder. 'Damn,' Rob said. 'Branch must have fallen on the electric fence again.' I'd noticed this fence when I arrived. It seemed to run round the camp's perimeter.

'Yanks,' Rob sighed. 'Sure, everyone loves elephants and lions wandering through the camp, but get someone eaten and then see what the lawyers do to you, the travel agents said.'

A Truckload of Cheetahs

Never again would Fothergill's clients know the thrill of falling over sleeping hippos in the middle of the night, or of being dragged out of their huts by lions, come to that. The new, vast and crystal-clear swimming pool had pumps and filters and you could see all the way to the bottom. The dead snakes were whisked out at dawn, long before most guests were out of bed.

In the morning Rob, Shirley, myself and another Rob – universally known as Baldric – jumped into the purple Land Rover and went off to invent a cheetah boma. We didn't think anyone had successfully caught wild cheetahs and put them in a boma before. Actually, they had, but with varying success, as we later found.

Lake Kariba had dropped even more. The lake was a distant blue line, far across the grasslands, littered with stumps and skeletal trees. Unlike Mana's gaunt and hunger-ridden animals, the Matusadona's wildlife populations were thriving. Zebra and elephant, fat as butter, paused to watch as we passed. One of the lion prides, Rob said, now had twenty members and was still growing.

'I thought we might put the boma here,' Rob said, stopping on the edge of the mopane scrub overlooking the grassy lake-shore. 'Include some mopane and that big anthill, and some of the grassland.'

'How big's this thing got to be?' Shirley asked. 'Cheetahs probably need exercise. How fast can they run?'

'Fifty miles an hour,' Baldric said. 'Best part of a mile a minute.' There was a short silence and some mental arithmetic.

'Half a mile long, then, for thirty second's exercise,' Shirley said. There was a longer silence while we pondered the implications.

'Make it round, then,' Rob said. 'Circular. A hundred yards across, say. Then they can tear around it as long as they like.'

'If we make it out of gum-poles with pig-mesh between them,' I said, 'the cheetahs can see out. That's probably important, they can see what they're in for.'

'And vice versa,' Shirley put in, looking at a herd of several hundred impala. 'Where can we get gum-poles and pig-mesh?'

'The veggie garden...' Rob began.

'Forget it,' Shirley said, defensively. OK, we'd buy the poles and pig-mesh.

'Thinking about it,' Baldric said, 'we'd better bury the poles and pig-mesh in a trench full of stones, stop anything trying to dig under it. But the lions might try to climb in. If we build it high, five metres or so, leave the pig-mesh a bit floppy at the top, they'll probably wobble about and fall off if they try.'

'And who's going to test that little idea?' Shirley said. All eyes rested on Baldric.

Digging a trench a yard deep and 300 round, filling it with rubble, erecting 50 enormous gum-poles, covering them with pig-mesh and getting just the right degree of floppiness at the top sounds like a lot of work but it isn't, not when you've got twenty-odd waiters and bedroom hands press-ganged into service. It took about ten days flat.

'Hell, Baldric, you OK?' Rob said as Baldric lay spreadeagled face-down in the mud. 'That was a helluva fall.'

'Well,' Baldric finally managed to gasp, 'I mean, if I can't, I don't think a lion could.'

Mark Atkinson stared at the truck parked at Viv Bristow's own wildlife holding facility just outside Harare.

A Truckload of Cheetahs

'When you said you could get a truck to move cheetahs with,' he said, 'I didn't think you meant a coal truck.'

'I didn't,' I said, 'but that's what turned up.' We studied it. Actually, it didn't look too bad, once the coal dust had been cleaned off, and you don't make lots of money out of coal – which our benefactor had – by carting it around in trucks that break down every day. Even so, it's over 200 miles to Kariba, and we'd said we'd be there by lunchtime. 'What,' I asked Mark, a bit hesitantly, 'if it does break down?'

'God knows,' Mark said. 'Hope we do it alongside a cattle ranch.' We turned our attention to the five cheetahs, which were lying quietly in their crates, watching the proceedings with calm detachment.

I'd never seen a cheetah before, wild or captive. Leopards – which most people find elusive – were my speciality. At Mana Pools they'd drop out of trees as I wandered through the magic woodlands, and run off. In Matusadona they'd gambol in the shoreline scrub, just for me; and I was once, rather unnervingly, stalked in tall grass by a leopard for some minutes. But cheetahs, never. I studied them in their crates, the beautifully-marked coats, finely-built legs and teardrop facial markings, and fell instantly in love.

'I've given them all a sedative,' Mark said. 'They're nice animals, in good condition. One of the females' – he indicated a small, slight animal – 'seems a bit thin. Maybe she's older than the others.'

We loaded the crates onto the coal truck, covered them with a tarpaulin and set off. I followed in the Hilux – the Land Rover, I reasoned, probably couldn't keep up with a coal truck. Helen Maxwell, a film-maker (I'd finally managed to get someone else to do it, thankfully) rode with me. Every now and then we overtook the coal truck, pushed on for a couple of miles, stopped to set up Helen's camera and hoped the coal truck would appear. It did. We got about eight sequences of a coal truck and a flapping tarpaulin roaring past at full throttle.

The prospect of being stranded at the roadside with a lorryload of cheetahs receded as the miles rolled by. Even more surprisingly, the ferry we had arranged for the journey across the lake was waiting at the right time and place. Kariba's notorious summer storms, which can whip up huge waves in gale-force winds, had receded for a few days and the ferry chugged across a calm blue lake towards the Matusadona hills. Rob, Shirley, Baldric and most of the Fothergill staff were waiting at a small bay near the boma, together with a largish crowd apparently consisting of every tour operator in Zimbabwe.

We drove the coal truck off the ferry and into the boma. You don't see many coal trucks on Fothergill, so that was a nice little film sequence all of its own. We unloaded the crates, and sent the coal truck back to Kariba.

Mark decided to put radio-collars on one of the males and the older female. He tranquillised them in their crates and fitted the collars, and we carried them into the shade beside the anthill to recover.

'OK,' Viv Bristow said, 'shall we release the rest? Boma gate's shut, is it?' He lifted the sliding gate on one of the crates, which held a big male cheetah. It stood up, looked out of the crate at its surroundings, and didn't like what it saw, which was a large circle of pig-mesh surrounded by a forest of camera lenses. It lay down and waited to be taken home again.

Viv rocked the crate gently. The cheetah shot out of the crate in a tawny blur and rocketed into the scrub behind the anthill, followed half a second later by a deafening hiss of automatic telephoto lenses. Cameras had got better over the years, but human reflexes hadn't. The remaining two cheetahs behaved in the same way, and a lot more photographs of half a cheetah-crate and some empty grassland got taken.

The two collared animals began to recover. The male got unsteadily to his feet, fell over, then struggled upright again and tottered weakly into the scrub. The female lifted her head a little, then flopped down again. We cleared the boma of crates and spectators – of whom there were far too many – and left the animals to settle down.

By early evening, four of the cheetahs had begun to explore the boma, pacing up to the wire mesh and gazing intently at the herds of impala on the grasslands. Lions can look majestic if they want to, which isn't often. Leopards exude power. Cheetahs are, above all, graceful. We studied them through the boma gate.

True professionals give their animals numbers, and say things like: we saw dear old Number Fifty-Three today. We'd even started doing this with our Matusadona rhinos. However, we gave our cheetahs names instead. More accurately, Shirley Clifford did.

'Blondie,' she said firmly, of the biggest male. 'And that little male with the big female – gotta be Clive and Louise' – a reference to friends with similar sexual dimorphism. She thought for a few moments. 'And Vitalstatistix,' – indicating the collared male.

'Hunh?' said Rob, Mark, Baldric and I, in chorus.

'Because we took his pulse and blood pressure and things while he was being collared.'

'Why the heck can't we just call him Joe?' Rob said.

'Because.' Shirley said, with the exasperated patience of an undervalued Asterix addict. 'You can call him VS for short, if you like.'

'Let's go inside,' Rob said. 'We can always come out if it worries them.' We slipped quietly into the boma and sat down on a log. VS drank from the small concrete pan we had built, then lay down beside the anthill. Blondie, Clive and Louise ranged across the boma, giving us an occasional wary glance. Blondie suddenly walked up to a dead tree-trunk, raised his tail and scent-marked the tree with urine. Clive did the same thing a minute or two later.

The small, slight-collared female, who hadn't been named, still hadn't got to her feet.

We watched her through the following day. The other four cheetahs were bursting with health, roaming the boma and staring longingly at the impala. The small, sick female staggered to the pan, drank for a couple of minutes, then lay down again. By sunset she was so weak she could barely lift her head. We decided to put a drip into her. We went back into the boma and found her by torchlight.

'Careful,' Rob said. 'She might try to bite.' He put a blanket over her head. Shirley and I held her legs and tail. Russell Gammon, a Fothergill guide, slipped the needle into a vein in her foreleg. Shirley stroked the cheetah's head while we gave her two full drips.

We decided to watch her throughout the night. I drew the first shift, and the third; and after Rob, Shirley and Russell had gone I settled down in the boma close to our poor, sick cheetah, with a flask of tea and some sandwiches, and waited out the hours.

All the other cheetahs were fast asleep. They lay companionably close to each other round the foot of the anthill, stretched out like domestic cats on a fireside rug. The lull in the storms continued. From the boma 20 miles of shoreline stretched away to the west, without an artificial light to be seen.

Kariba's vast canopy of stars curved overhead and sparkled like diamonds down to a crystal-clear horizon. The balmy air was filled with the night-sounds of the Matusadona: crickets chirring, jackals calling, now and then the trumpeting of an irritated elephant and the distant grunt of hippo down by the water, far across the drought-bared shore. It grew cold after midnight; the sounds faded and the bush fell silent except for the rhythmic snore of an elephant – a long, echoing rumble – lying down somewhere close by.

The sick cheetah was breathing slowly and regularly. I felt her pulse, in the deep recess of her thigh, and it seemed a little stronger. Then the loom of headlights stained the sky over the rim of the lake-shore bush. Rob took over from me, and I went back to the camp.

I was back at the boma at sunrise, with the cool morning light spreading over the blue lake and the Matusadona hills rain-washed and green in the background. The cheetah's respiration and pulse seemed stable, Rob said. He left, and I sat beside her on the bright red sand, now pockmarked by the spoor of the other four cheetahs, which had woken up and were pacing around me.

Half an hour later her breathing suddenly faltered. I felt for her pulse: it was weak and fluttery. She convulsed, and voided her bowels on the sand in a thin, watery stream that soiled her beautiful coat. I drove to the camp to get a new drip and some help. Rob came back with me. We tried desperately to get the drip going, but her veins had collapsed and her pulse was almost gone.

With one final convulsion, at three minutes to seven, she died.

Later that day I drove back to Harare, her corpse in the back of my truck, covered with my bush jacket. I delivered her to the vets for post-mortem, and in a few minutes she was an unrecognisable wreck of meat, hide, body parts and globs of congealed blood. This didn't tell us anything.

I wished we had simply buried her in the quiet of the Matusadona, in the red sand beneath the bright emerald mopanes.

The Zambezi Society had moved out of the shared wooden hut and into a nice new brick and tile office that we'd built a few yards away, on the other side of the Mukuvisi's car park. I had bought a bigger desk, to try and accommodate a torrent of invitations to workshops to discuss subjects like gender issues and rural community empowerment.

Most of them eddied round the desk for a few days, then overflowed into my wastepaper basket. The 'workshop' – which had become a defining characteristic of donor-driven conservation – was, I soon found, one of the most time-consuming substitutes for intelligent thought ever devised.

If you do have an intelligent thought, you are expected to express it in five words or less on a piece of gaily-coloured cardboard and stick it on the wall – or, better, on one of the pinboards produced by some on-the-ball entrepreneur specially for the workshop industry.

This doesn't really matter, because most people likely to produce intelligent thoughts avoid workshops like the plague. It's like having the operating theatre cleaners turn up for a meeting on open-heart surgery while all the surgeons are on the beach in the Bahamas. They're a substitute for actually doing anything constructive, which is why they're called workshops. There's a hint of hammer on steel, the clatter of machinery, the ambience of rolled-up sleeves and the running of sweat, which stops everyone feeling guilty about not getting anything done.

A Truckload of Cheetahs

One afternoon, while I was drafting a polite refusal to yet another workshop invitation, an attractive lady with a notebook and ballpoint pitched up to interview me about rhinos. She handed me her card. Sally something-or-other, it said.

'It'll make a change from having to be nice about ghastly tourist camps,' she said. Oh? It turned out she'd taken up more or less where I'd left off. A thought struck me.

'Why not write nice things about us instead?' I asked. 'You know, get us in the newspapers without having to pay for it, that sort of thing.'

Unfortunately, I was dealing with somebody with some sense as well as good looks – a combination that I hadn't often come into contact with. She smiled. 'Just contact me when you've got something to say.' She did her interview and left. I spent a little time wondering how to entice her into the vortex of workshop invites and gave up, since no easy answers came to mind.

I turned my attention to scheming how I could get back to Fothergill and play with the cheetahs instead. Fate played into my hands. There was a break in the weather, Tashinga's aeroplane was broken, Fothergill was close to Tashinga, and the rhinos needed tracking. I threw the rest of the workshop invites into the wastepaper basket, jumped into the parks department Super Cub and headed for Tashinga. Gary Douglas, the Matusadona's second in command and regular pilot, met me on the airstrip.

'The Maule Rocket's playing up again,' he said, referring to the park's own aeroplane, a French job that seemed to have been made on a Monday morning after a long weekend on the absinthe. It had already dropped one pilot in a brickfield and another in a small pan in the Zambezi Valley. It had been rebuilt each time, but the gremlin that lived in the engine had merely gone into hiding, to re-emerge later when the banging of panel-beating hammers had ended.

'It takes off and climbs nicely,' Gary said. 'Then the motor stops. Then it starts again after a few seconds. Then it stops again in a minute or two. Seems to need a little rest now and then. Had a hell of a flight, getting it down to Harare.' I'll bet.

He was carrying a little black box, with a small viewing-screen on it. 'Tells you where you've been, where you are and where you're going. I just press this little button when we find a rhino, and it stores its exact position, give or take a yard or two. It's called a GPS. Neat, eh?'

We took off in Z-WMP and got down to the tracking. Everyone was getting quite good at this, since we'd sorted out the left/right, plock/plink confusion. The intercom had been fixed as well, which helped.

'Look,' I said at one point, after we'd found Number Sixty-Eight. We didn't actually have 68 rhinos, we had about twenty with radio-collars on, but they get named after their radio frequencies. 'Down there. An osprey. Don't see many of them.'

Gary peered out of the window. 'No ways,' he said. 'Ordinary fish eagle, not quite mature.' He held forth on the differences between fish eagles, ospreys and palm-nut vultures for a minute or two, interspersed with an occasional 'left a bit' while Number Sixty-Six plinked away in his headset. A thought struck me.

'Don't know anyone called Kloppers, by any chance?'

'What, young Joubie? Sure, great ornithologist. Doing his doctorate on the *Phalacrocoracidae*. Comes to see us sometimes.' Oh, does he now.

We scooted round the rhinos in about two hours flat. I dropped Gary off at Tashinga, and flew to Fothergill. Mark Atkinson was there, checking up on the cheetahs; and Rob and Shirley drove us to the boma. 'Pouf,' I said as we approached. 'What the hell's that?' It smelt like a roomful of tomcats and dead rats.

'Can't get rid of it,' Rob said. 'We feed 'em with an impala every other day or so, take the carcase out by midday, but the smell just hangs around. Plus, the males have been scent-marking everything in sight. Hyaenas have been showing a lot of interest.'

'Lions? Any problems?'

'Not yet.'

'And that?' I indicated a small thatched shelter, on top of four gum-poles about twenty feet high, just outside the boma.

'We're manning the boma every night,' Rob said. 'Just in case.'

We went into the boma. Blondie paced around us, a few yards away, sometimes veering in for another look. VS retreated into the scrub, then re-emerged, circled us a couple of times, then lost interest and lay down close to Clive and Louise, who were dozing together beside the anthill. I lay down beside a fallen log to photograph them.

'The books say cheetahs don't go for people,' I heard Rob say, from somewhere behind me. 'Let's hope Blondie's read the books.'

I glanced over my shoulder, to see Blondie sniffing intently at the soles of my shoes. I was reminded of the elephant at Mana Pools. There's no such thing as a small cheetah, either, when it's standing over you with a hungry look on its face. After a few seconds he moved off. I got my photos, and rejoined Mark, Rob and Shirley. Mark had got his photo too: I've still got a faded print of it. It reminds me never to wear white tennis socks with my trainers, if I want to look like a Real Bushman instead of a stupid Pom who's tripped over a log with a cheetah in pursuit.

'Staying over?' Rob asked. He indicated a small thunderhead, showing above the summits of the

Matusadona hills. 'Time's getting on, you don't want to be dodging storms.' I battled briefly with my conscience – there was a workshop to go to in the morning – and lost, as usual. I volunteered to man the boma for the night. After supper I drove myself back there with a sleeping bag and a flask of tea, and settled down on top of the platform.

The cheetahs all went to sleep. I lay awake for some time, enjoying the night sounds and the starlit view across the grasslands. Now and then the ghostly shape of an elephant ambled up from the distant lake-shore and disappeared into the bush. A pair of eagle owls duetted somewhere in the bush, *huuu-hu*, *huuu-hu hu*. I was instantly transported back to my little hut and Zizi, sitting on her perch; so much change since then – the lake would have been flooding the boma – yet so much the same. I drifted into a light, peaceful sleep.

I was woken by a not-too-distant clap of thunder, and peered out at the sky. The moon and stars had vanished, and lightning was flickering across the massing clouds.

I heard the sound of an express train, roaring towards me across the bush. Wind: it went from flat calm to storm force in an instant, and rain with it, solid sheets that came in through one side of the platform and out the other, except where it was intercepted by obstructions, such as me. Searing blue lightning-bolts struck the trees and lake-shore around me, with an explosive 'Crack!' followed by a moment's eerie silence. The bush was flattened by the gale. Thunder roared and rolled continuously.

If you hear it you aren't dead, I told myself. Yet. I was perched on the highest point for some distance, and linked to several hundred square yards of well-grounded pig-mesh. I couldn't remember enough physics to decide whether I was uniquely well-shielded from lightning, or a prime candidate for instant vapourisation, and I wasn't inclined to find out empirically. I threw myself down the steps, ran into the bush, lay down in the sheets of floodwater flowing across the sand and buried my head in my arms while the storm raged around me.

The rain eased after 20 minutes or so, and the thunder began to fade away. I crept back up the stairs to the shelter. The usual night sounds were silent, but the frogs had erupted into a deafening chorus, shouting with joy from every tiny rain-filled puddle. The cheetahs were sleeping round the anthill. I spent the rest of the night shivering in my sodden sleeping bag and hoping I'd tied the Super Cub down properly.

I had, although the rain had got in and soaked the seats. No matter: I wasn't about to take off anyway. The Matusadona hills were shrouded in low cloud, left over from the storms.

Gary Douglas telephoned from Tashinga: could I give him a ride back to Harare? His aeroplane had been fixed, the mechanics said. He'd get his game-scout to drive him to Fothergill. Fine, provided the weather clears, I said. Rob and Mark went out and shot an impala while the rest of us had breakfast, and we went down to feed the cheetahs.

As the boma was high enough to stop lions jumping in, it was also high enough to prevent us simply throwing a dead impala over its fence.

'This,' Rob said as we dragged it through the gate, on foot, 'is where we hope they've all read the books.'

All four cheetahs came at us, pacing slowly and steadily forward with their heads low and hackles bristling, then standing their ground and snarling. We dropped the impala and backed off slowly, and the cheetahs instantly lost interest in us.

Blondie fell on the carcase first, while the others hung back. Surprisingly soon, he stood up, his muzzle red with blood, and retreated to lie down and wash himself.

'VS next,' Shirley said. VS, too, ate alone, then retreated; and finally Clive and Louise together. They seemed to eat sparingly, even daintily; but their usually elegant bodies became fat and rounded, their bellies like over-inflated footballs. They all relapsed into somnolent inactivity. By midday the impala was already too old for their taste: lions and hyaenas may like their meat well-hung, not to say revoltingly decomposed, but cheetahs like it fresh. None of them objected when we removed the impala's remains.

'Jeez,' Shirley said, wrinkling her nose. 'Need to scrub this place with Dettol. A couple of thousand litres ought to do it.'

Gary Douglas arrived. The weather, which had been drizzling on and off throughout the morning, cleared slightly. We had a light lunch – you didn't need anything much on top of a Fothergill fillet-steak dinner and sausage-and-bacon breakfast, unless you wanted a belly like an overfed cheetah – and took off through the puddles, covering Z-WMP in gobbets of red mud. Curtains of drizzle still shrouded some of the Matusadona, but the cloud had lifted off the hills to reveal patches of sunlight. I called Kariba, and went through the routine – Z-WMP, two on board, Fothergill to Charles Prince, all that sort of stuff.

The rain seemed to have got into the radio. Kariba came through in bubbles. 'Urgle burble blup blup plock,' they replied. I pressed on across the Matusadona flatlands, up over the mountains and into the sun-dappled uplands. After half an hour or so the bush slowly turned to farmland.

'Nice airstrip down there,' Gary mused over the intercom. 'I think it's…'

He was interrupted because Z-WMP's engine chose that moment to explode. The whole aeroplane shook like a St Bernard after a bath, and a strong smell of hot oil and shredded metal flooded into the cabin. The normally invisible propeller clunked to a highly visible stop.

' …Solera Farm,' he concluded.

'Well,' I said lightly, doing my best to compete in the sangfroid stakes. Gary was used to engines that stopped, but this one wasn't about to start again after a little rest. 'We're about to find out.'

We glided down, round and in. Solera Farm it was, with a functional telephone to boot, and a genial farmer and his wife who gave us tea and cakes while we waited for someone to come and pick us up. He offered us his own aeroplane to go home with, but I declined. It was covered in about an inch of dust, had a flat tyre, and bees were flying in and out of the cabin. Once in a day was enough.

'D'you know,' Gary said, over the tea table, 'I saw at least three kinds of plover on your strip, as we came into land.'

Well, hell, Gary, I didn't notice that, maybe I should have done but I was preoccupied with landing an aeroplane with an exploded engine – something you don't get to try again if you get it wrong first time. I've never been that good at multi-tasking.

The Super Cub's engine hadn't actually exploded, as it turned out, not in the strict sense of the word anyway. It merely sounded as if it had. An exhaust valve had broken and gone on a tour of the engine, doing a lot of damage as it went and ending up by jamming a piston.

'Oh, they do this sometimes,' one of the maintenance engineers said. Well, that's all right then, isn't it? I thought it might have been something I'd done, although I couldn't for the life of me think what.

While this was being tended to, I went to a couple of workshops, even though I count myself as reasonably intelligent. A lot of workshops are held in up-market hotels and there is such a thing as a free lunch, believe me, when donor money's involved. Workshops gobble up huge amounts of cash that could be better spent on doing something useful like moving cheetahs around, I reflected as I stuck up another profound thought on a pretty coloured card and watched it getting binned by the facilitator. I didn't know how we were going to pay the capture bills we'd got already, let alone raise funds for further translocations. We hoped to release at least 15 animals into the Matusadona to create a 'founder population' with a reasonable chance of survival. Possible donors frequently reminded me of the dismal failure rate of predator relocations.

The component parts of Z-WMP's engine being dispersed around several workshops – real ones, that is – I drove to Kariba and thence by boat to Fothergill. The weather was clear, calm and hot, and my spirits rose as Fothergill's long, low profile rose above the horizon. We piled into the purple Land Rover and drove to the boma.

'Pace, pace, pace,' Rob said. 'That's all they were doing, round and round. Bored stiff. Never ran, just paced.'

'Need exercising,' Shirley said. The cheetahs watched expectantly as we arrived at the boma. Shirley picked up the volleyball whose presence in the Land Rover, I thought, had been incidental.

'Blondie!' she called as we went into the boma. 'Catch!' She hurled the volleyball.

Blondie tore after it at full cheetah throttle as it bounced across the boma and off the fence. He caught up with it and gave it a mighty swipe with a paw. Clive rocketed out from the scrub, but VS hit him with a shoulder-tackle and gained possession. He dribbled the volleyball round the wire until Blondie arrived in a snarling blur and kicked it into touch at Shirley's feet. She picked it up and threw it again.

It hit the anthill with all four cheetahs in pursuit. They fell on it as it bounced to the ground, and it disappeared beneath a whirl of spotted fur and whiplashing tails. There was a bang and a loud sigh of escaping air. The scrum dispersed, revealing Blondie with a deflated volleyball between his forepaws. He prodded it. Then he nibbled at it, before getting up and ambling off in disappointment.

'Bugger,' Shirley said, 'that's the third. Only got two left.'

'No problem,' Rob said, 'I've ordered another six, ought to get here tomorrow.'

'Shit,' I said, 'what do those things cost?'

'No idea. You'll find out when you get the bill.'

I volunteered to man the boma for the night, the weather seeming to be set fair for a day or two. I was woken from a light sleep by the sound of cheetahs spitting and snarling, followed by a loud twanging of pig-mesh. I groped for a torch, and turned it on in time to catch a glimpse of a tawny shape disappearing into the bush. I got into the Land Rover parked at the foot of the platform and drove round the boma. There was nothing to be seen, and the cheetahs soon settled down again.

'Big male lion,' Rob said, when I showed him the large dent in the pig-mesh in the morning. 'Took a good run-up to it, too,' he said, indicating the huge pug-marks in the sand.

'Can't have thought about it very hard beforehand,' he went on. The lion had obviously failed to appreciate the implications of the pig-mesh between himself and the cheetahs. 'Bet he's got a nasty headache.'

The cheetahs were due for release in a couple of weeks. We discussed how to do it over breakfast.

'Suppose we just open the gate and let them get on with it?' I suggested, helping myself to another two fried eggs and bacon at Fothergill's expense.

'I'm not sure they'd actually go,' Shirley said. The cheetahs were getting too used to the easy life in the boma, being served impala without the bother of having to go out and hunt them, and idling their lives away playing volleyball.

'I know,' Baldric said. 'We'll keep them hungry for a day or three. Then we'll shoot an impala, and drag it round the boma and out of the gate. That ought to do it.'

'And who's going to try that little…' Shirley said.

'Rob can,' Baldric said hastily.

'Maybe I'll drag it with the Landy,' Rob said.

The weather closed in again, and the morning planned for the release was cold and damp. Andy Searle, the Matusadona warden, arrived from Tashinga with his wife, Lol. It drizzled until nine o'clock, then cleared up a little. The tracks were lined with puddles, the usually brilliant green grass dulled under a grey and featureless sky. The weather matched the mood: we would be sad to see them go. If they went, that is.

'OK, ready,' Rob said, as he finished tying a dead impala to the back of a Land Rover on a long rope. 'Open the gate, Baldric.' He drove in.

Blondie and VS fell on the impala before he'd gone more than a few yards, with Clive and Louise trotting along behind. Rob began to drive back towards the gate.

'So far, so good,' Baldric murmured. As Rob got to the gate, though, Blondie and VS latched grimly onto the impala and dropped to a low crouch. We were treated to the spectacle of two large and hungry cheetahs being dragged bodily along on their bellies and out of the gate, with Clive and Louise still in pursuit.

Clive and Louise suddenly realised, with horror, that they were actually outside the boma. My God, they thought, lions, tigers and manatees. They ran back inside and hid in the scrub. Rob stopped the Land Rover. Blondie and VS chewed away happily.

'And now?' Shirley said.

'Umm.' Baldric said. 'Tow it round the boma again?'

'Better we just back off and wait a while,' Rob said. We did. Clive plucked up the courage to go out through the gate before breakfast disappeared forever, whereupon VS stood up, licking his lips. He ambled back through the gate and lay down contentedly beside the anthill. Louise sat inside the boma and stared dumbly through the fence at Blondie, Clive and the swiftly disappearing impala.

Word had got around and the boma was coming under siege by frilly Land Rovers from all the tourist camps that had sprouted in the Matusadona. The tourists' average age was going up in line with prices, as copywriters searched for synonyms for 'Untamed Eden', 'Wildlife paradise' and 'Zillion-star luxury', without much obvious success. Cameras were getting noisy again as bifocals clashed against viewfinders: the spectacled in search of the spectacular.

'I'll get rid of them,' Andy Searle said, setting his parks beret at a determined angle. He did. We left a Fothergill guide to watch over the scene and left the cheetahs to sort their own lives out. By three o'clock all four animals were outside the boma, lying in the grass a few yards from the impala's remains.

Blondie stood up as the sun kissed the distant hills across a shining lake. He stared across the bay, and started walking. The other three followed him. They walked steadily and purposefully, across the wide grasslands, and were lost to sight in the gathering twilight as they neared the mopanes lining the far Matusadona shore.

The boma stood sad and empty, the pan dry, the cheetahs' pug-marks fading in the windblown sand. But on the second morning after the release we found the remains of an impala on the grasslands, a few yards from the mopane scrub. Early morning rain had washed the spoor away, but the impala's head, neck and legs were untouched – the signature we had learnt to expect. Someone was learning, out there.

Chapter Eight

BUNG-HO, BIGGLES

'Nice story, that,' said Sally whatever-her-name-was. 'Ought to get some coverage.'

'Excellent,' I said. 'Maybe someone'll give us some money to carry on. You sure you don't want to work with us? Get to do some proper work, instead of the ghastly tourism thing?'

I thought I detected a flicker of indecision. 'Can you pay me?' she asked. I told her what the budget would stand. She frowned.

'I do actually need to eat,' she said. 'Not much, granted, but at least I can afford butter on my crust on two Sundays a month, as things are. When I'm not being force-fed fillet steak by tour operators, anyway.'

OK, so we're into sardonic repartee as well as common sense and good looks, are we? I turned back to the computer, which was connected to the telephone and displaying a message from someone I'd never heard of before.

'Look at that. Electronic mail, it's called,' I said proudly. 'E-mail, for short. Send stuff all over the world for the price of a local...'

'Oh, that,' Sally whatever said. 'Everybody's got it.' She peered at the screen. 'Mm. Spam.'

Spam? Luncheon meat? What's that got to do with anything, I thought. But she left before I could display any more Stone Age ignorance.

The Mavuradonha Wilderness Area went on not building lodges and not making any money either, without much help from me. Such tourists as did visit the place promptly fell down the waterfalls and got themselves killed, which led to mutterings about railings and warning signs on one hand, and black cloth and beer on the other.

The colliding worlds got closer. Chris Pohl decided to build a lodge on his farm, since the Mavuradonha wasn't building its own. He was instantly fired from his chairmanship, on the grounds that he was trying to sabotage the wilderness area by nicking all the high-rolling tourists that weren't pitching up and Mr Mhene took over. Z-WMP was reassembled, and seemed to work nicely. Gary Douglas's aeroplane didn't. 'Damn thing still stops,' he said. 'Joubie Kloppers thinks it's something to do with the fuel lines.'

'Kloppers?' I said, incredulously. 'What does he know about aeroplanes?'

'Doctor Kloppers now, if you please. He's doing stuff on *Accipitridae* in South Africa. Eagles, vultures, that sort of thing,' he added unnecessarily. 'Follows them around in thermals in a nice little Husky.'

'Husky? What's that?'

'Sort of Super Cub on steroids. Anyway, he knows someone who really knows something about engines. I'm going to take it down there, get it fixed once and for all.'

'What, by road?'

'Nah. Fly it down.'

Well, sooner you than me. I went off in Z-WMP and tottered nervously around the Matusadona, tracking rhinos and hoping the engine wouldn't explode again. I landed at Fothergill for lunch, as had become my habit.

'Louise had a couple of cubs,' Shirley said. Fantastic. This was what it was all about.

'But they got eaten by something,' Rob continued. 'Lions, probably. Or hyaenas.' Elation turned to gloom. However, it reverted to elation again when I got back to Harare and found a letter on my desk. It stuck out a mile, because it wasn't a workshop invitation, or another donor rejection. It was on Fauna & Flora International's distinctive yellow stationery, and it offered us money not only to pay off all the existing cheetah capture bills, but to incur a lot of new ones as well. At last. I sighed with relief, and set wheels in motion. Two weeks later we had five more cheetahs – a big male, a female and three already-weaned cubs, old enough to look after themselves – in the boma.

They were, we soon found, of a very different disposition to Blondie and the others. They purred and chirruped at each other in the scrub – a fascinating sound, the chirruping, an extraordinarily bird-like call – but went in for a lot of spitting and snarling whenever we entered the boma. They were also a lot less inclined to play volleyball – and a good thing too, said some of our parks department colleagues, who had watched some of the previous goings-on with silent disapproval.

For some reason, the Matusadona lions suddenly launched a series of mass attacks on the boma. It became ringed with their spoor, and pocked with huge dents where they charged at the pig-mesh. Why apparently intelligent animals never learnt the futility of trying to barge through pig-mesh with their foreheads is one of the project's great mysteries. Maybe one of them had tried climbing in over the wire, and had fallen off as per plan.

Rob had stationed one of his apprentice guides at the boma and equipped him with a hunting rifle, to fire over the lions' heads, and possibly at them if they tried to climb the stairs up to the platform. One evening – I was spending more time on Fothergill than I was in the office – we were just getting onto the dessert when a fusillade of shots echoed faintly from the direction of the boma.

'Uh-oh,' Rob said. 'Here we go again.' We set off hurriedly, with Rob's own hunting rifle and a bundle of mini-flares of the kind with which we'd entertained Steve Alexander's guests. As we approached, our headlights picked out a large lioness lying on the edge of the mopane scrub and peering intently into the boma. Inside, the cheetahs were sitting alertly by the anthill, staring back and snarling deep in their throats.

'Try a flare over her,' Rob said.

'Won't it set fire to the bush?'

'No ways. We've had a fair bit of rain already.'

The flare arched high over the bush, and lit the scene with an eerie red glow. The lioness watched it with mild interest, and turned her attention back to the cheetahs.

'Give her another. Lower. Just over her head.' This time she got to her feet and stared malevolently at the Land Rover which – since Baldric was in the midst of rebuilding it – consisted of little more than a chassis with some seats and an engine. Rob's hand hovered between the gear-shift and the stock of his rifle. Then the lioness turned and retreated into the bush.

The apprentice guide on the platform was trying to attract our attention. He looked harried, and the top step was barricaded with a sleeping bag draped over a pile of broken branches.

'Down here, by the steps,' he shouted. 'Three more.'

We inched the Land Rover as close as we could. 'OK, keep your head down,' Rob shouted. 'Flares coming.' The guide hurriedly ducked out of sight.

Three flares merely produced the leonine equivalent of a slow handclap and a sarcastic request for an encore.

'Try and bounce one off the gum-poles while I put a round over their heads,' Rob said. I took careful aim and let fly. Rob's rifle went off with a deafening crash. The flare missed the pole and bounced off one of the steps. It flew up into the shelter and fell down again beside the lions.

'Fuck!' came a terrified squawk from the shelter. The lionesses got up reluctantly, stared at the fizzling flare for a couple of seconds, and vanished.

A couple of days later, Rob was taking the remains of an impala out of the boma when a young lion appeared, clamped its jaws round the impala's forequarters and set about dragging both impala and Rob into the bush.

'It seemed wisest to let go of my end and let him have it,' Rob said, when he described the incident to me afterwards.

The lions returned with reinforcements. So did we, with an arsenal of flares and rifles and a fleet of Land Rovers. One vehicle snuck up through the bush behind the boma and attacked from the rear with a broadside of flares and a barrage of shots fired into the air. This looked and sounded sufficiently like serious warfare to send the lions out onto the grasslands, where another two Land Rovers were waiting. They chased the lions for half a mile, firing more flares and heavy artillery over their heads.

An occasional lion continued to hang around the boma, but the rest went off to breed another generation of warriors. The cheetahs didn't seem particularly worried when lions did come, and it was probably useful training for the big, bad world outside.

These cheetahs finally got named a day or two before we released them. Mark Atkinson decided to put a radio-collar on the adult female. He darted her, fitted the collar and we waited for her to recover.

As she tottered to her feet the male, seething with frustration after sharing accommodation for several weeks with an unappreciative mother-of-three, took advantage of the situation. He leapt on the staggering female in a paroxysm of unbridled lust. It didn't get him anywhere, because she instantly collapsed under him and refused to budge. We chased him off.

'Bonk,' Shirley said. 'That's what we'll call her.'

'Her? Don't you mean him?'

'Nope. He's Fred,' Shirley said. We gave up. The youngsters merely became 'Bonk's Cubs'.

Fred, Bonk and Bonk's Cubs stayed close to Fothergill after we released them, and we often saw them. Bonk's Cubs seemed to be getting thin. We watched them carefully, and soon found why. Whenever Bonk tried to stalk an impala, the cubs launched a wildly premature attack across several hundred yards of open grassland. The impala would make a leisurely assessment of the situation, then bound away with a contemptuous lack of urgency. After a while, however, the cubs learnt to leave the heavy stuff up to Bonk while they practised on birds and hares, and their condition slowly improved.

By now we had released nine cheetahs into the Matusadona. They hadn't yet bred successfully, but at least they were surviving. But we still needed more, to establish a useful founder population.

And then the wheels fell off. Catastrophe piled on disaster. It began with the arrival, in Kariba, of six cheetahs – two adults and four juveniles – jammed into two crates. They were thin and listless, their coats dull, wet with urine and matted with faeces.

They were unaccompanied by anyone other than a driver. It had taken him two days, he said, to make the journey from a ranch in southern Zimbabwe.

'But I had to stop and sleep on the way,' he continued, and cast a despairing glance at the crates. 'What could I do? Nothing to do. Just drive, boss said.' Most capture teams were sensitive in their animal handling. Some were appalling. The mood of the times had sparked a lively trade in animals-as-commodities, and some dubious people had leapt on the bandwagon.

'We ought to send this lot straight back,' I said.

Rob studied them thoughtfully. 'And then? Another two days on the road, then what?'

Down the ant-bear holes, probably. I saw Rob's point. He and Shirley knew how to look after cheetahs by now, if anyone did. We took them to Fothergill and put them in the boma. They lay hidden in the scrub, listless and silent, for the rest of the day, and emerged hesitantly the following morning.

'That one's limping,' Rob said, pointing at one of the juveniles. By evening he was lying down, and only moving with difficulty. Rob telephoned Mike Cock. He promised to get to Fothergill in the morning.

Some of the lions came to the boma that night, but the guard soon dispersed them. By morning, however, all four cubs were lame, and one couldn't walk at all. Mike arrived, and tranquillised it.

'Broken leg,' he said, after a careful examination. He didn't need to say more. There's no future for a crippled cheetah. He put her down while the rest of us stood sadly in the background.

Mike tranquillised another cub. 'Same thing,' he said. 'Look at this.' This time the break was open and contaminated. He put this cub down as well.

He darted a third, a female. 'Swollen hock,' Mike said, 'but it doesn't seem to be broken. She's got a chance.' We moved her into a hastily-built pen near Rob's house, for intensive care and left the fourth cub – with less severe symptoms – in the boma.

'My fault,' Rob said bitterly, as we carried the pathetic little corpses out of the boma. 'Shouldn't have let lions get anywhere near the boma last night. Probably panicked the cubs.'

'That's got fuck-all to do with it,' Mike said, speaking with the ominous calm I'd learnt to expect from him, before the explosion. 'Healthy young cheetahs can cope with that. I made a couple of phone calls last night.' The explosion came. 'Fuckin' bastard fast-buck merchants. Been keeping those animals like that for bloody weeks. Saw you coming. Pricks. You paid 'em anything yet?'

I nodded dumbly.

'We should go down there, blow those turds away and get the money back.'

We laid the dead cubs gently down in the back of Rob's Land Rover. Shirley stroked them sadly. Around us, the impala and zebra grazed quietly on the grasslands. A fish eagle called, a tiny dot high in a deep blue sky: I'm-over-here, where-are-you?, and his mate answered from a nest in a dead tree.

'OK. Here's what we do,' Mike said, more calmly. 'First off, no more juveniles and cubs. Secondly, Mark or I go down and look at any cheetahs that are caught. We supervise management and transport. That's fine, my budget'll run to the mileage and so forth. Then we travel up with them, all the bloody way.'

'What about bringing them up by air? I put in. Mike looked at me.

'Even better. Can you afford an aeroplane big enough to do it?'

'No. But I'll find one.'

The little cheetah with a swollen hock that we moved into the pen beside Rob's house captivated everyone she met.

Nobody was more captivated than Baldric. He named her Pebbles and moved in with her.

Baldric's real job was to be a mechanic-cum-guide, but he was a sensitive dreamer by nature. Rumour had it that he agonised over the post-traumatic sufferings of abused gearboxes to the occasional girlfriend who passed briefly through his orbit.

Sometimes, his contemplative tendencies led to lapses of logical thought. After weeks of painstakingly overhauling a Land Rover he'd take it into the Matusadona for a test drive and arrive back in camp hours later, tired and footsore.

'What broke?' Rob asked.

'Nothing,' Baldric replied. 'Goes like a bomb. I forgot to put fuel in it.'

Which, of course, was why he was called Baldric. Now and again he had to go off and fix a vehicle, since Fothergill's ageing clients weren't inclined to go searching for the spectacular on their Zimmer frames. Otherwise, he sat in the pen and talked to Pebbles. In a couple of days she was feeding from his hand. During the night she would wake him up with a swat of her paw, then leap over him and race after her volleyball.

The cub we'd left in the boma also went lame, and had to be put down. Mark Atkinson's post-mortem revealed several broken bones. The two adults – Barney and Wilma, Shirley had graduated from Asterix to the Flintstones – recovered fully. But Pebbles' future occupied us endlessly. Could she ever make it in the wild? Or should she be kept captive for life? If so, where?

In the end we decided to put her back in the boma for a while. If she continued to thrive – as she was, under Baldric's care – we would put a radio-collar on her and let her go. Then we could recapture her if she didn't cope.

We released all three animals on a warm June morning. Barney and Wilma attacked the impala carcase furiously as Rob towed it round the boma and dropped it outside the gate. Pebbles followed hesitantly a minute or two later. She ate for a while, then lay down beside one of the wind-burnished lake-shore tree-stumps. Baldric, who'd been watching with stoic resignation, squatted close by and talked to her, but some wild instinct had been reawoken and she moved away from him.

Barney and Wilma moved off across the grasslands just before sunset, but Pebbles stayed close to the boma. We tracked her through the night. I returned to Harare in the morning, while Rob, Shirley and Baldric continued to track her. Sometimes they saw her. She seemed to be coping.

Then, without any warning, she vanished. All efforts at tracking her failed. A week later she reappeared on Fothergill as suddenly as she'd gone, but she was desperately thin and limping badly. Mark Atkinson tranquillised her, and found the small bones of her feet ruined beyond repair.

Maybe we'd released her too soon; maybe she'd been through so much stress, before she arrived at Fothergill, that she'd never have recovered enough to cope with life in the wild. Pebbles was put down.

VS disappeared. After burning up a lot of fuel we tracked his radio-collar to a hut in the settled lands west of the Matusadona. A parks department raid found he'd been snared and killed.

'Two,' Mark said over the telephone. 'Male and a female. Any luck with the aeroplane?'

Yes, as a matter of fact – a twin-engined Cessna 401. The crate, I'd calculated, would just go through the cargo doors with an inch or two to spare.

'Same people who lent us the coal truck,' I said. I sensed a slight hesitation on Mark's part. 'Well, it went fine, didn't it?' I said defensively.

'OK. Euan Anderson,' – another British vet – 'can go down with it. Send your film-maker too, if there's room.'

There was. The Cessna flew to a ranch in southern Zimbabwe to collect the cheetahs, with Euan and Helen Maxwell on board, while I flew straight up to Fothergill in Z-WMP. Rob, Shirley and Baldric were there, of course, and most of Fothergill's other guides. So were Amy Merz and Bob Coen, then working together as general journalists for CNN, plus a holidaying local hack who was taking a keen interest in the proceedings.

The twin-engined Cessna arrived overhead early in the afternoon. I radioed the pilot from Z-WMP, parked beside the airstrip.

'Helen's just going to film the boma and the lake-shore,' I told the gathering crowd, 'then they'll come in and land.'

Amy set up her camera a couple of hundred yards down the strip, just outside the runway markers. The rest of us clustered beside Fothergill's makeshift pole-and-shadecloth hangar, and waited. After a few minutes the Cessna reappeared, pulling round in a steep turn for a pass along the strip. It arrowed in low and fast from the lake, roared past and swept up into a climbing turn. The undercarriage came down, and the pilot lined up for a landing. I glanced at the windsock, out of habit.

'Christ,' I muttered to Rob, beside me. 'Coming in downwind. Going to do another pass, maybe.'

The Cessna came in high over the threshhold, and I expected to hear the roar of full power as its pilot either started his pass or looked at the windsock. But it descended steadily.

It flared, and the wheels touched, almost halfway into the strip and going horribly fast. Plumes of dust flew up from its wheels.

'Open up, go round again!' my instincts screamed at the Cessna, 'there's still time!'

Instead, the nose dipped and the aircraft swerved violently as its pilot stood on the brakes. It flashed past Amy Merz, still filming, the wingtip a yard or so from her head.

There comes a point when you know, with a detached calmness and clarity, that the situation is irretrievable and there's going to be an accident. I've watched several people crash during my sporadic flying career. I ran to Z-WMP, to make a Mayday call.

'Fuckin' Ker-ristmas! Watch out!' someone yelled as the Cessna hurtled towards the stunned crowd of onlookers. The pilot swerved the aircraft away from them, and crashed through the fence at the end of the strip. The nose wheel tore off, and it skidded to a stop a few yards from Fothergill's staff houses. Flames instantly flickered under the fuselage, and a wisp of smoke rose into the air.

Helen's head and shoulders appeared in the emergency exit near the Cessna's tail, which was cocked high above the ground. She leapt out with her camera. Euan followed, falling heavily and gashing his head open; then the pilot. I ran to the wreck. The others were already there. Flames were licking up the sides of the fuselage, and the cabin was filling with dense smoke.

Half the cargo door was already open – it doubles as the emergency exit – but the other half wasn't. It needed a special key, which was kept in a small retaining strap inside the aircraft near the door. We leapt on the wing and groped inside, retching and choking in the poisonous smoke. The key had leapt out of the strap and vanished.

We scratched and tore at the cargo-door until our fingernails and hands bled. 'An axe!' someone shouted. 'Get an axe!'

The flames suddenly flared up. 'Get off!' someone else screamed. 'She's going to blow!'

We tumbled off the wing and ran. A platoon of Fothergill waiters arrived at the double, carrying axes and fire extinguishers. We advanced again, with the fire extinguishers. We might as well have used toy water pistols.

The dry grass caught fire and some of the mopane-shrubs began to flare up. 'Oh God, the houses!' Rob shouted. 'Get a tractor, someone. And rope!'

Someone ran and fetched a tractor. Rob rushed through the smoke and burning grass, leapt up through the flames and onto the aeroplane, looped a rope round the tailplane and jumped off. The tractor growled; metal crumpled and tore as the wreckage slid backwards through the remains of the fence and onto the airstrip, leaving a trail of blazing fuel.

A rescue helicopter arrived. Helen and Euan, his head wrapped in a bloody bandage, declined a transfer to hospital. The helicopter clattered off back to Kariba, shrouding the scene in dust through which the flames leapt and flickered like a scene from the *Inferno*.

Miraculously, the tanks never blew. The wreckage burnt fiercely until the fuel was exhausted and the flames died down, leaving a tangle of blackened, twisted aluminium.

Two charred bodies were revealed, curled up together in the remains of the crate. Someone – possibly the local hack – raised a camera.

'For fuck's sake,' someone else said – possibly Rob – and dashed it angrily out of their hands.

Rob, Shirley, Helen, all the others and myself slumped in Fothergill's lounge, sore, bleeding, smoke-blackened and tear-streaked: never again, we said, when we finally said anything at all. That's enough. Finish.

'And for Christ's sake,' Shirley said, eyeing a hovering guest in spotless Vogue safari gear. 'Don't ask me for decaf coffee now. We haven't got any.'

This disaster drove two things home to me. The distraught pilot went through the awful process of bureaucratic enquiry that eventually reveals the obvious: he got it wrong. All pilots do, from time to time. Outsiders like to allocate blame, but don't understand how one tiny error of judgment can suddenly turn into a full-scale crisis. Often, I realised, we get away with it through sheer luck. Sometimes, we don't.

The other was that playing God with helpless animals isn't something to be taken lightly. Sport hunting, 'sustainable utilization', cheetah relocations all sound just fine on paper, or on the workshop pinboards. But the reality of these things can be appalling. We balance it against our ideas of some greater good. But, I was beginning to think, we sometimes get that wrong, too.

We consoled ourselves with the knowledge that these cheetahs would almost certainly have been shot if they'd remained on the cattle ranches, but it was a long time before the shock wore off and we could take a more balanced view of events.

We had a half-completed project, and the money to go on. We really had no choice other than to try again. But, to cap it all, this was when we discovered that someone had caught and translocated cattle-eating cheetahs off ranches before. It was in South Africa. They'd put them into a national park, and the cheetahs had eaten everything there, as well.

One good thing came out of it. Sally whatever-her-name appeared in my office, carrying a newspaper.

'Well,' she said, 'I can see you're perfectly capable of getting yourselves in the papers without my help.' She unfolded the newspaper. 'It says…'

'I know what it says. It says 'ZIMBABWE'S LAST CHEETAHS DIE IN AIRCRAFT HORROR BLAZE'. Bloody lie, hundreds of them still getting stuffed down ant-bear holes.'

She folded the newspaper again. 'I've been thinking,' she said. 'Looks as if you need help, with that sort of thing going on. What if I worked for you two days a week – strictly two days only, mind, Thursdays and Fridays preferably – that'll put butter on the crust for one Sunday a month. I'll make up the rest with the ghastly camps and the fillet steaks.'

A-ha! Gotcha hooked. Once you're in this business, you're in. Sucked into the vortex.

'Fantastic,' I said. 'Wouldn't like to go to this, would you?' I passed her an invitation to a workshop that proposed to undertake a stakeholder evaluation of the impact of capacity-building funding on the empowerment of rural women.

She glanced at it and tossed it back. 'No ways. See you next Thursday, then.'

The next aircraft – an Islander, this time – landed without incident, and disgorged two more cheetahs. The sight of these healthy animals, roaming the boma and playing with their volleyball, began to exorcise the ghosts that had been haunting us. Then Jill, Jane, Rambo and several unnamed cheetahs – even Shirley Clifford's imagination finally ran dry – were also caught, moved and released.

We saw cheetahs more frequently, hunting on the Matusadona foreshore or loping through the bush, as we released more animals. Several litters of cubs were seen by the tourist guides who regularly walked and drove through the park. We began to feel that the project was worthwhile, after all. In the end we reached – and even slightly exceeded – our target founder-population. We called it a day, and waited to see what happened next.

What happened next was a power struggle at the parks department between its existing senior staff and a small but powerful mafia of political stooges. Exactly why this happened, at this particular time – in the mid-1990s – isn't easy to determine. There had already been some heavy-handed harassment of white parks officers, but things had generally been ambling along fairly amiably within Zimbabwe as a whole.

Whatever the root cause, the political stooges won and swiftly set about making life difficult for any officer who failed to match their standards of political conformity or spectacular incompetence. Unlike previous events, though, it was all very even-handed from a racial perspective. Almost all the department's experienced officers – white and black – either bowed to circumstances and left, or found themselves reassigned as ranger-in-charge (Aquatic), head office plumbing.

Andy Searle, who had been the Matusadona warden during the cheetah relocations, was one of the few who braved things out. He was posted to the Hwange National Park, where he was accused of stealing 2,000 Zimbabwean elephants and flogging them to Botswana. It was not clear how he was supposed to have accomplished this.

'I think I'm supposed to have driven them across the border with an aeroplane,' he said with his usual shy chuckle. This made a sort of warped sense, in a country where rhinos were being stolen by helicopter. Meanwhile, Mike Cock and Mark Atkinson got accused of stealing the rhino-horn sawdust from their dehorning activities and flogging it to North Korean diplomats.

These trumped-up charges faded away when it became clear that the alleged perpetrators were determined to stand their ground, instead of meekly allowing themselves to be forced out of the parks department. But life for these officers had become, as Andy put it, a little tedious.

Together with several other volunteer pilots, I got a duplicated letter banning me from setting foot – or bum, I suppose – in Z-WMP, on pain of arrest and disembowelment. Animal capture was stopped. Radio-collaring was stopped. Just about everything else was stopped.

While the axe was still falling, we managed to slip an MSc student into the Matusadona to do some of the research we ought to have done in the first place. Reduced to its essentials, her report said: you're either going to have to keep on putting more cheetahs in, or take some lions out. This was depressing.

Also in the shadow of the axe, Mark Atkinson had brought a tiny abandoned rhino calf to Tashinga and installed it in a boma for hand-rearing and, it was hoped, eventual release into the park. He flew it in by helicopter, which was possibly a mistake, in view of the suspicions of successive permanent secretaries. He and Mike Cock headed for more appreciative countries.

They couldn't stop us in the Mavuradonha, though, because it wasn't a national park.

'Stakeholder evaluation this, stakeholder fucking consultation that,' Richard Hoare – the wildlife vet who'd taught me radiotracking by telephone – said contemptuously as we sat round a damply spluttering fire in the Mavuradonha campsite.

'What about actually getting something done, for a change?' Richard went on. He picked up a wire-mesh gadget lying beside the fire and addressed it. 'Steakholder,' he said, 'what do you think?'

'It probably thinks it's time you guys got this bloody fire going properly,' Sal said.

Sal – or Sally Wynn, as her new Zambezi Society business card put it – had rapidly become one of our mainstays. The part-time, two-days-a-week business had soon gone out of the window, and I'd even persuaded her to go to a couple of workshops, although she'd insisted I went along as well, which hadn't been the idea.

I'd taken her with me on a couple of bush-trips, but conventional Sophie-trapping tactics hadn't worked. She'd looked at me very oddly when I materialised from my strictly separate tent, wearing a shirt with sleeves ripped off to reveal tanned biceps and a hunting-knife dangling casually from my belt.

She wasn't a Sophie at all, in fact. She put up stoically – if not totally enthusiastically – with day-long trips in the old Land Rover; and there wasn't, she said, anything wrong with ancient long-drop toilets, or even buckets in the bush, that couldn't be taken care of with a bit of down-to-earth determination.

As a result, our own worlds had inexorably moved closer, culminating in dramatic collision when Sal finally moved into my cottage and rummaged around in the clothes cupboard as she tried to make room for her own – not inconsiderable – wardrobe.

'Ah-ha!' she'd cried. 'These can go.'

'NO! Not those! They're my, um, best bush shirts.'

'How on earth did all the sleeves get torn off?'

'I – er – I…' Dangerous to try and explain. It didn't look as if I was going to be doing much of the tanned-bicep number in future, anyway. The shirts joined a growing pile of broken sandals, trousers with flared bottoms, torn jeans and divorced socks. Similar scenes were played out in the kitchen, bathroom and garden shed.

Other established orders were getting overturned, too. 'Who's cooking, anyway?' Sal addressed the circle round the fast-expiring Mavuradonha campfire. The Zimbabwean faces, black and white, registered unanimous shock and horror. Cooking was one of the rare issues on which both local cultures were united. Women always did the cooking. Their eyeballs darted around wildly.

'I will.' Loki Osborne, a vast and bear-like American, got to his feet. 'Chapatties with the curry?'

'What the stakeholders think,' Loki said, answering Richard's question as he rolled the chapatties out with an empty wine-bottle, 'is that it'd be nice to grow something without having it eaten by elephants. Right, Ignatious?'

Ignatious nodded. He and Loki were busily persuading the local peasantry to grow chilli peppers instead of maize. Elephants aren't keen on eating chillis. Then, the thinking ran, the peasants could sell the chillis and buy maize with the proceeds.

For some inexplicable reason – not entirely trusting either the World Trade Association's assurances or the infinite growth potential of the chilli pepper market, maybe – the peasants still wanted to grow some maize as well.

Ignatious and Kinos, Loki's other assistant, came up with a novel idea. They got the peasants to make briquettes out of elephant dung laced with chilli, place them round the maize fields and set fire to them. The elephants' eyes watered so much they couldn't find their way to the maize fields, and the villagers downwind got a good clearout of the sinuses.

The chillis might deal with elephants where they shouldn't be, but didn't answer another important question: where could they be, other than getting themselves managed wholesale or fenced off inside the Mavuradonha? These were options that fell outside the preconditions of the stakeholder consultation workshops.

This was where we came in. Our job was to find out where and how elephants moved around the place, when they weren't nailing maize fields and villagers, and create some elephant movement corridors. We were 'saving Muzarabani's elephants' – a possibly quixotic exercise in a country that still wanted to blast half its elephant population into oblivion, but never mind.

Sal and I took off into an achingly lovely sunrise to look for elephants in the Mavuradonha hills – an act that wasn't quite as simple as it sounds.

The Muzarabani airstrip lay in the Zambezi Valley, half a mile or so from the feet of the Mavuradonha mountains. It looked like a rutted cart track and was lined with unpruned trees, scattered with small but vicious thorn bushes, and dotted with potholes, squashed beer cans and empty fertiliser bags. Halfway along it was a rusty iron pole from which, possibly, a windsock once flew.

Another cart track crossed the airstrip near the rusty pole, its approaches hidden by dense scrub. It enabled tractors, cows, motorcycles and pedestrians to access the adjacent banana plantation. As hardly anyone else was insane enough to try and take off from the strip, other than an occasional crop sprayer – a branch of aviation with an impressive fatality rate – local people had mostly forgotten what it was for, and didn't look before they crossed.

Z-WMP had become a wistful memory, since the parks department had banned volunteer pilots. We'd hired a small and ageing Cessna instead.

'Why are you doing that?' Sal had asked, as I clambered onto the wing-strut and lowered a wooden dipstick into the petrol tanks. 'Isn't that what fuel gauges are for?'

'They don't work,' I said briefly, hoping she wouldn't get onto the flaking paintwork, dented fuselage and torn seat covers.

Now, engine running and checks completed, we sat at the end of the airstrip, ready to take off.

'What if a tractor comes across?' Sal asked.

'Well, you said a bit of risk was part of the fun of being in Africa,' I replied. 'Anyway, what you can't see can't hurt you. I've got the sun in my eyes.'

'Alright, go on then. *Hals und Bein bruch*, Baron von Whatsisname.' My library contained a lot of books about real and fictional wartime flying aces, but I'd drawn the line at having them thrown out along with the shirts, so Sal contented herself with some gentle derision instead.

'*Richthofen*,' I said defiantly, and opened the throttle. The Cessna trundled along in a leisurely fashion, weaving gently as we followed the ruts. By the time we reached the rusty pole we'd only gained enough speed to create a very small fireball if a tractor materialised. The Cessna finally heaved itself into the air and inched its way up the three-thousand-odd feet of the Mavuradonha mountains with a good deal of grumbling and whining.

Beneath us, slowly receding, lay a mosaic of tiny fields interspersed with patches of forest and thatched villages with chickens pecking around them. The just-risen sun highlighted the mountaintops and cast the valleys into deep shade. Halfway up, the Sohwe River plunged over a waterfall in a silver shower and into a limpid pool.

As we breasted the mountains, the Mavuradonha itself opened up before us. Ridge after ridge, clad with mnondo and mfuti woodlands and cut by deep river-gorges, stretched to the horizon, unbroken by game-viewing tracks and frilly Land Rovers. Through the intercom I heard Sal gasp with wonder.

'Wilderness. Real wilderness,' she said.

Flying aeroplanes is better than falling into holes on horseback in one way, I thought to myself, but you can't smell the wilderness and the elephant dung. You can't let the sand trickle through your toes. You're detached. You're not part of the action. Some people are never happy. I put these thoughts aside as we buzzed the campsite to wake everybody else up and set off to look for elephants to collar.

'What you have to do,' I explained carefully to Sal as we went, 'is to learn to look through the trees, pick up a bit of movement, texture…'

'Yeah, sure,' Sal said. 'Got at least two in sight right now, just deciding which one's easiest.'

OK, clever clogs, bet they're large grey rocks. They weren't. We selected one of them, half a mile from our campsite, looking forward to another day's peaceful browsing and blissfully unaware of the bizarre events about to befall him, if all went as per plan.

Usually, the actual darting would be done from a helicopter, but our budgets didn't run to that. Richard and his team were going to do it on foot. I radioed him. He set off into the woodlands with Andy Wilkinson, a hunter whose job was to shoot the elephant if everything didn't go as planned. This would, of course, be the elephant's fault.

We guided Richard and Andy by radio until they could see the elephant for themselves. They were close enough for the elephant to hear their radio, and possibly set about ruining our day along with his own. 'I'm switching off,' Richard whispered. We circled aimlessly overhead.

The elephant suddenly appeared to leap a couple of feet in the air, as if stung by a hornet. It spun round, ears wide, and set off at a shambling trot. The radio came to life again.

'Dart's in,' Richard said. 'Do you have us visual?'

'Affirmative. Visual with you and the elephant.'

'Wilco, old bean,' Sal murmured. 'Bung-ho, Biggles.'

The elephant trotted down a gentle slope, stopped and swayed gently for a second or two, then collapsed. Loki and his assistants appeared, burdened with radio-collar, hammers and spanners. They fitted the collar, Richard injected an antidote and the elephant got up and wandered slowly away, tentatively exploring its new collar with the tip of its trunk and possibly thinking: what the fuck sort of a hornet was that?

'Shall we do the other one while we're at it?' Sal asked. 'I've still got it vis... buggerit, it's catching – I mean I can see it. You guys and your bloody jargon, what's wrong with plain English?'

Bang goes another bit of Real Bushman macho, along with the bush shirts. We did the other elephant. Went like clockwork, nothing to it. Piece of old tacky, as we say in these parts. We gave ourselves a few hours off and went for a swim in the lovely little pool below the Sohwe waterfall. Kinos greeted us when we got back into camp.

'There's a *nzhou* that's been in the campsite all afternoon,' he said. There was, too. It was busily uprooting all the shrubs and lawns Dawn Pohl had carefully planted.

'Well,' said Richard, who'd just sat down in his camp chair, 'I could pot that from here. Shall we do it?'

Of course. He duly potted it. It set off down the campsite's access track at the precise moment the only tourists we'd yet to see came trundling along it in a campervan. The campervan skidded to a halt. There were a few moments of eye-to-eye confrontation between woozy elephant and astonished tourists. Then the elephant collapsed squarely in front of them and rolled on its side.

We arrived a few seconds later, brandishing rifles, dart guns and the axe we use to clear away obstructive branches and brushwood. The axe must have looked particularly sinister.

The tourists got out. 'Hey,' one of them shouted, 'what the hell d'you think you're doing? Supposed to be a non-hunting area, the leaflet says.'

They calmed down as Ignatious showed them the radio-collar, the hammers and spanners and the dart sticking out of the elephant's bum and – the way to the campsite being comprehensively blocked – they took a lively interest in the proceedings thereafter.

'Need to knock up a portable road sign if this sort of thing's going to happen often,' Richard mused as he draped a damp cloth over the elephant's eyes and Loki and his crew set to work. '"Beware of Falling Elephants", something like that.'

The last elephant I'd been this close to in similar circumstances had a bullet through the brain and Art and Martha dancing on its corpse, and I'd been in no mood to look at it closely. This one was healthily and refreshingly alive. One of its ears still flapped idly, and it snored regularly and loudly, with the sound of a deep bass drum roll.

I ran my hand down the massive tusks, streaked with brown and chipped by long-ago battles, and hoped they wouldn't end up as ivory table-lamps. I felt the soft pads of its feet, crazed and cracked like dry mud; stroked the wiry tail-hairs and left them firmly in place; studied the delicate little trunk-tip, just like a black rhino's, but perched on the end of several feet of massive musculature. The elephant-scent was sour-sweet, a compound of dung, chewed shrubs and the oozing trickle from its temporal glands.

Meanwhile, the elephant was undergoing a number of indignities, besides being walloped flat and having a radio-collar made out of several feet of heavy canvas conveyor-belting fastened round its neck with spanners and hammers.

'OK, nearly finished,' Loki said. 'Kinos, your turn at the lucky dip, I think.'

Kinos took his shirt off with a resigned expression. He knelt down behind the elephant, took a deep breath, and plunged his arm up to the shoulder into its waste disposal outfall. The tourists' Canon EOS's whirred and whined. Kinos pulled his arm out again, clutching a handful of wetly steaming dung.

'Great,' Loki said. 'Stick it in a bag. Doesn't smell of chillis, I hope,' he added. Finding out what elephants ate was all part of the project.

'OK, transmitter check,' Loki went on. Someone produced a receiver. It plocked a bit, then PINNGed satisfactorily.

'Antidote's going in,' Richard said. 'Move away, everyone.' The tourists backed their campervan away, while the rest of us took to the bush. He eased a hypodermic into one of the great veins in the elephant's ear, and walked away.

The elephant stirred, struggled to its feet and shambled off. Flying aeroplanes is fun, but you need to come down to earth now and then. It felt good to be trying to save elephants, for no other reason than that they are huge, gentle, intelligent beasts, with a damn sight more right to be there than we had. By morning he was back in the campsite, exercising this right over Dawn's shrubs and grass again.

Sal and I, however, were back in the aeroplane. Once again an elephant presented itself within a few minutes, its rear end sticking out of a thicket. Once again all went like clockwork. Up to a point. This elephant neither leapt, nor did it run away when Richard fired the dart. Nor did it fall down. It leaned against a tree and swayed as if mildly drunk.

Sal and I watched with some alarm as Richard and Andy walked right up to the elephant. There appeared to be a short discussion. Then the radio came back to life.

'You're not going to believe this' Richard said sheepishly. 'The bugger's already got a collar on. It's one of the ones we did yesterday.'

The tranquilliser hadn't worked, of course, because the poor animal was still full of yesterday's antidote. Richard gave it another dose and off it went. God knows what it thought this time, unless it was about moving to a neighbourhood with smaller hornets. We monitored him carefully for the next few days, in case he suffered any ill effects from his tranquilliser overdose, but he went about his business as if nothing had happened.

'Yeah, OK,' Loki said beside the campfire, agreeing to make the chili con carne that night after another outbreak of darting eyeballs. 'Anyway, who was responsible for that little snafu?'

The eyeballs swung back into action, bouncing down the wildlife conservation hierarchy from two PhD's (Richard) to one (Loki), to pilot (five 'O' levels) and finally to Sal (BA but novice elephant-spotter).

'Well,' she said, a little defiantly, 'it had its head stuck in that bloody thicket.'

All the elephant's fault, then.

We didn't do any more double-dartings, but elephants became steadily harder to find as we penetrated less easily accessible parts of the Mavuradonha. On one infamous occasion, Sal and I spent eight hours circling inside a granite-walled gorge while Richard pursued an elephant on the ground.

Every now and then Sal lifted her eyes from Richard and the elephant, only to see a granite crag apparently about to come in through the windshield. 'Eek,' she said, which made a change from 'tally-ho Ginger', and hastily went back to elephant-watching. We gave up in the end. Richard was exhausted, and Sal and I had run out of concentration. We were lurching round the sky like a drunken vulture. We called it off before Richard got killed by the elephant, or I flew us into a cliff-face.

'Done fifteen now. You know, I think that's enough,' Richard finally said. This was our fifth excursion, and we weren't in the Mavuradonha campsite any more. We were in one of several little patches of forest in the Zambezi Valley, which had – rather oddly – survived among the cattle and cultivation. A surprising number of elephants were holed up in these patches, stockpiling gas masks and planning mass attacks on the maize fields through the burning briquettes of chilli and elephant dung.

The Mavuradonha's night sounds of frogs, crickets and hooting owls were replaced by a distant chorus of sneezing elephants and villagers. We weren't sitting round a spluttering campfire any more either. We were sitting round a flying-saucer affair perched on top of a gas bottle and known, obscurely, as a 'scottle'.

'I'll cook, if you light it,' Sal said to me. I turned on the gas and stuck a match through one of several holes in the bottom of the flying saucer. There was a small explosion, and flames shot out of all the holes, as if it were about to lift off and head for Tatooine. It changed its mind and sat there rumbling gently.

'Chicken stir-fry do alright?' Sal said.

'Great,' Loki said. 'Want some chilli?'

'Put it in yourself, later,' Sal said hastily. 'So what now?' she went on.

'Start tracking 'em,' Richard said. 'Us from the air, Loki and his merry men on the ground.'

Through one of those wonderful comeuppances that make life worthwhile, Z-WMP had turned out not to actually belong to the parks department. It was loaned to them by a benefactor who had strong opinions on what constituted reasonable and well-focused use. This didn't include carting illicit fish, poached game meat and hash cookies all over the country. They took Z-WMP away from the department, and sold her to us instead.

We said goodbye to the ageing Cessna with some relief. Z-WMP had fuel gauges of a kind, even if you had to look at them now and then if they were to be useful. We spruced her up, fitted her out with tracking aerials and receivers, and put her to work.

Tracking the Mavuradonha elephants proved exceptionally easy at first, because none of them went anywhere. Richard and I flew up from Harare every ten days or so, and took turns at the flying and tracking. He'd fly up and down from Harare, since he's got a pilot's licence as well as the two PhDs. Then we'd change places, and I'd fly while he did the tracking, since he was a lot better at it than I was.

'Umm,' he'd muse, somewhere over the mountains, 'left a bit, OK, straight, OK, circle... there he is, gone about half a mile since last week.' Loki caught some of the bulls red-handed in the local maize fields at night, but they were all safely tucked up in the Mavuradonha valleys and the Zambezi Valley forest patches by morning.

And then they vanished. Evaporated, seemingly, overnight – all the bulls, and some of the cows. Richard and I widened our search until we were sitting directly overhead the Mozambique border, 40 miles from the Mavuradonha.

'A-ha!' Richard said from the back seat. I'd heard the faint 'plink' too, since Z-WMP now not only had an intercom, but the radiotracking receiver was also wired in to the pilot's headset via yet another little black box. I hoped the plink came from the aerial pointing into Zimbabwe. It didn't. It came from a vast and featureless expanse of Mozambiquan bush extending all the way to Lake Cabora Bassa, which we could see quite well from our current position.

If Z-WMP's engine chose to explode in Mozambique, it'd be a long enough walk home without having to explain what we'd been doing there in an aeroplane festooned with radio aerials and black boxes that look as if they'd been designed to call in a nuclear strike. I don't know the Portuguese for 'looking for elephants'. Even if I did, the Mozambiquan army probably knew the Portuguese for 'pull the other one, mate.'

We flew across the border, hoping we weren't in range of a Mozambiquan radar scanner. After a nerve-wracking hour or so we'd found most of the truant elephants, and we scuttled back into Zimbabwe. So did the elephants, a week or so later. They all turned up in their old haunts as suddenly as they'd gone, munching away as if nothing had happened.

But how on earth had they got to Mozambique? And back, for that matter, since we didn't catch them in the act. Quantum entanglement? Elephant-holes in space-time? If so, it would save us the bother of all the elephant movement corridor business, but I had to admit it seemed unlikely.

Luckily, our Dutch donors were happy to pay for more aerial radio-tracking – and several other things as well – to help us find out.

Chapter Nine

NOBODY MUST TALK
TO MR MHENE

By 1998 it had started raining properly again, after nearly two decades of drought, which was one of the reasons why it was difficult to pinpoint exactly how our elephants got to Mozambique and back. Loki couldn't get around on the ground, since much of the Zambezi Valley was flooded. Every time Richard and I took off, we'd run into a wall of thundercloud over the Mavuradonha, and have to turn back.

Lake Kariba stopped going down and came all the way up again. 'Bloody hell, look at that,' I said to Sal as we flew over Fothergill Island, which had changed hands. Rob Clifford had moved on. Fothergill would still admit wildlife conservationists in torn shorts, but only if they could produce several hundred American dollars in used notes.

'The boma,' I went on, half-turning to Sal in the back seat and getting poked in the eye by a fishing rod in the process. You can get two fully-assembled, non-collapsible rods into a Super Cub, but you have to work at it. Sal appeared to be wearing fishing-reels for earrings.

The old cheetah boma – still standing, I noticed, we must have done a good job when we built that thing – was half under water. The lake-shore looked much as it had done in 1979, when I first washed up on Fothergill and explored the Matusadona's creeks and bays. We flew on, and landed at Tashinga. The parks department could stop me flying over the Matusadona looking for rhinos and cheetahs, but it couldn't stop me flying to it. Especially since we were still giving them money.

Mark Atkinson had started something when he took that little abandoned rhino calf to Tashinga. Imire Ranch, in the Zimbabwean Midlands, had its own small population of black rhinos, which was breeding as fast as it could go. Imire had a surplus of rhino calves.

'We'll have 'em,' the parks department had said enthusiastically. 'They're ours anyway. All rhinos are ours. We'll take them to Tashinga, rear them by hand and let them go in the Matusadona. Now, who can we find to pay for it all?'

Several thoughts occurred to me when faced with this proposition, the first being: what's the point of moving rhinos into the Matusadona, if they're all going to be killed by poachers?

Another was: who, precisely, are the poachers? There was a strong suspicion that some members of the mafia that had hijacked the parks department were getting stuck into the rhino-horn trade. This had been reinforced by a curious conversation I'd had with one of them, just before the department's palace revolution.

'Oh, you don't have to worry about rhino poaching,' one of them had said, in an uncanny echo from years before. 'It's all stopping now.'

Well, I'm glad to hear it, I'd thought, but how can you know this with quite such certainty unless you've been involved? Even more curiously, the rhino poaching did stop – for a while, at least – when the mafia took over. Had they been masterminding it to make the previous management look even less competent than themselves?

I dismissed this idea. It seemed to need a talent for planning and foresight that was all too painfully absent from the department's operations under its new management. They'd possibly done it for the money, if at all. But why the rhino poaching ended when it did is still one of the great unanswered questions.

My final thought was: hand-rearing baby rhinos is a perilous business. They get diarrhoea – and several other things as well – at the drop of a hat, and die overnight. We might get the blame if it goes wrong, but at least we'll be able to retain an involvement in rhino conservation and keep some sort of handle on events. We agreed to pay part of the costs. The Matusadona tour operators were still doing well, even though all their game-viewing tracks were under water. They were carting the spectacled around in boats with frilly canopies instead. They could afford to stump up too.

We decided not to actually give the department the money itself – something that the mafia would have much preferred. By now its top guns were wearing three Rolexes on each wrist and driving two bubblecruisers at once. No, we'd buy the vitamin supplements and glucose and milk powder, nuts ands bolts for the warden's Land Rover and overalls for the rhino handlers, and we'd get it all to Tashinga. The mafia retaliated by making us request permission to buy every single thing. In triplicate. In advance.

Two could play at that game. We designed our own request forms, since the department had imposed a regulation but failed to create the necessary infrastructure. We made them extraordinarily complicated. We forgot to number them, or staple the sets together. Nut, bolt, washer and split pin consumed four sets of forms. We fired off an average of six sets a day.

I'd wait a few days, then go to the parks head office and drum my fingers on some clerk's desktop while he searched desperately through the muddle of unanswered letters and overflowing buff folders spilling out of baskets, wire, six.

'Eeeehh, can't find it,' he'd say, and go off to see if Mr Muparanga had it. He'd come back fifteen minutes later, looking harassed. Sometimes he'd find one copy in Mr Muparanga's office, but not the other two. Mostly, he wouldn't find any at all.

'Maybe Mr Sithole's got them.' I'd put on an encouragingly expectant face. 'But he's on leave,' the clerk went on. 'His office is locked.'

I'd change the expectant look to one of exasperated disappointment. 'This,' I'd say with heavy emphasis, 'is really urgent,' and I'd deliver a short lecture on the fragility of baby rhinos and the international implications for the parks department if they started dying all over the place.

It didn't matter too much because we'd already shipped the stuff to Tashinga anyway. Zeph Mukatiwa, who'd somehow escaped the general purge of the competent and become the Matusadona's warden, was a great collaborator.

'Eh! Thank you!' Zeph said as I exhumed Sal from beneath a pile of vitamin supplements, glucose, baby-bottles and teats. The luggage compartment behind her seat was fully occupied by tackle-boxes, bags of clothes, bird-books and a large cardboard box full of worms. One has to get one's priorities right.

'Stocks were getting low,' Zeph continued. 'Any problems with head office?'

'Usual story. You bought this lot yourself, if anyone asks.'

Zeph spat expressively. 'They are baboons.' He said that, I didn't. Whites would get disembowelled for even thinking it. 'Come see the totos.'

It was still early, and cool under the mopanes and terminalias as we strolled from the airstrip to the rhino bomas, set in a small patch of cleared *jesse*. A huge cattle-weighing machine stood in front of the bomas.

'All well?' I said to Edwards, the parks technician overseeing the rhino calves.

'Very well,' he said. 'You're just in time.' He called to his assistants. 'OK, open up.'

The assistants swung back the heavy boma doors. Four baby rhinos with nubby little horns peered out of the doorways. Then they trotted out and formed a line in front of the weighing machine.

'Wait, Chewore,' Edwards said to the biggest. 'Shungu first.' Shungu trotted into the weighing-machine. An assistant took notes. 'Out, Shungu. In, Chewore.' Chewore trotted in as Shungu came out: and so on, all four of them. Sal and I watched, transfixed.

'Time for exercise now,' Zeph said. 'And learning how to browse, too.' A handler called them, and set off into the *jesse*, the little rhinos meandering along behind him and taking experimental mouthfuls of leaves from the low-hanging branches.

I took the opportunity to pump Zeph for information. How many men did he have on the ground? Fifteen, he said, half of them on leave at any one time, and half of them too sick to patrol. HIV/AIDS was picking them off one by one. No replacements; all recruitment frozen by the mafia.

And were rhinos still being killed by poachers? Unfortunately, rhinos don't stay dehorned. They grow them back again.

'We haven't had a poaching incident for some time now,' Zeph said. 'Seems to have stopped.'

We left Z-WMP tied down on the airstrip, and Steve Edwards took us across to his tourist camp by boat. Msango Lodge lies on an island in the Ume River, which forms the Matusadona's western boundary. Msango is one of the nicest lodges in the whole of Zimbabwe, partly – from my perspective, anyway – because Steve Edwards is another ex-parks bushman who welcomes impoverished conservationists.

Not that I was actually wearing torn shorts any more. Sal had seen to that. They'd gone the way of the sleeveless shirts. Besides, she'd said, they're obscene. They're so short you might as well walk around naked. Now I had to wear shorts that came down to my knees and flapped wetly round my legs when it rained.

Steve – the only person I knew who'd been more or less chomped in half by a hippo and survived – uttered the traditional greeting. It still being lunchtime, we restricted ourselves to a couple of Cokes. I remarked on the paucity of buffalo and zebra Sal and I had noted as we flew over the lake-shore grasslands, now reduced to a thin strip between bush and water.

'Almost all gone,' Steve said. 'Half of them starved to death as the lake came up, the rest nailed by lions. Lions almost all gone now, too. Ought to give the cheetahs a chance, at least. Still see one or two, now and then.'

The decline of the lions was not entirely a tragedy. They'd become altogether too much of a good thing. They'd killed and eaten a trainee British guide, which made international headlines, and a Tashinga game-scout as well, which didn't. The Matusadona was back to where it was when I first saw it, almost twenty years before, but with the added complication of a lot more tourists in search of the spectacular.

Steve lent us a canoe. 'I'd give you the game-viewing boat' he said, 'but I've got to take some clients out.' We packed the fishing rods, worms and a cooler-box into the canoe. 'Go to the park if you like,' Steve said, 'but there's a beautiful little bay on the other side of the river. Settled lands, but you wouldn't know it.'

Sal and I set off across the Ume – a wide, gentle river-valley flooded by the lake, dotted with tiny islands and set against a distant backdrop of soaring mountains. I trailed a spinner over the stern, a task that involved abandoning my paddle.

'Bit faster,' I said to Sal. 'Take us past that weedbed.' She cast a glance at me over her shoulder, of the kind I'd got used to in aeroplanes, a sort of raised-eyebrow frown.

'Yes, sir,' she said. A small tigerfish hit the spinner as we canoed past the weedbed. Not a fizzing-reel number. I brought it alongside, unhooked it and let it go. I swapped the rod for my paddle, since the crew was idly reclining in the bow, scanning the approaching shore with her binoculars.

'Hmmm. Hippo. Just off the point. Go right.'

Yes, ma'am. Kariba hippos hadn't taken to overturning canoes yet. Biting chunks out of powerboats was their thing; but better to be safe than sorry. We passed the hippos, rounded a promontory and found ourselves in a beautiful secluded bay. Its banks were lined with steep red cliffs, shelving to gentle grassy shores. Figs grew on the cliffs, their exposed roots crawling over the sandstone like tentacles, searching for a hold in tiny crevices. Impala grazed on the grass, mirrored in the glassy-calm water. They glanced up curiously as we passed, then grazed again.

'Up there,' Sal commanded. 'Quietly.' We paddled over a submerged sandbar and into a tiny, shallow lagoon. Its muddy shores were trampled by elephants and hippos, and scattered with dung.

'Ought to be some bream in here,' Sal said. She didn't share my passion for tigerfishing. Bream, she said, were much nicer to eat than tigerfish. 'Never mind all that catch-

and-release sport-fishing crap,' she'd continued. 'Hook and cook, that's the way.'

She picked up her own rod and opened the worm box. There was a squawk of dismay from the bow. 'Where've all the worms gone?'

I instantly guessed where the worms had gone. Out through the holes in the box and into the bottom of Z-WMP's fuselage during the flight from Harare, that's where they'd gone.

Sal scrabbled around in the box and found a worm stupid enough not to have cleared out while the going was good. She cast it into the lagoon. Her float bobbled around a bit, then vanished. She struck. A tiny bream rocketed out of the water and landed in the canoe with uncanny precision. Mr Crabtree would have been proud of her. She unhooked it, let it go and raked around in the worm box again. That's another thing in favour of tigerfish. You don't have to mess around with worms to catch them. Metal spinners don't cover you in muddy earth and green worm-crap.

Just then the bush beyond the grassy fringe shook, and a questing trunk appeared, turning like a periscope.

'Shhh,' Sal said. Shhh yourself, it's not me who's banging on about absconding worms. The periscope disappeared and the bushes parted to reveal a majestic bull elephant. He stood a while, trunk and one forefoot swinging idly, then plodded down to the water and drank. The tip of his trunk wriggled around with a life of its own as he sucked up gallons of water; then he threw his head back and put his trunk in his mouth. Some of the water dribbled down the hairs under his chin and splashed back into the lake. The rest vanished down his throat with the gurgle of an emptying bathtub.

'Lovely,' Sal whispered. 'Shhh,' I said. We'd only got fifteen yards of foot-deep water between us and the elephant. It's amazing how fast a canoe can move with an elephant up its stern, but you can't get it up a tree.

The elephant looked around warily, as if about to do something very undignified, which he was. He was mentally taking all his clothes off. Then he knelt down on his forelegs, paused a moment, and let the rest of himself collapse sideways into the muddy water. He wriggled and squirmed with delight. He rolled right on his back and waved his legs in the air. Then he rolled onto his other side and thwacked his trunk around, sending sheets of water high into the air. Muddy spray splattered onto the canoe. Then he rolled back onto his belly for a rest and prodded the mud absent-mindedly with his tusks.

A slight movement in the canoe caught his attention. My fault, I'd got a tigerfish spinner hooked in my ear. The elephant stared at us guiltily, like a High Court judge caught playing with his teddy bear. He stood up and mentally put his clothes on again. He sucked up a trunkful of mud and squirted it over his back, which is what dignified old elephant bulls are supposed to do. Then he gave us a last reproachful look and plodded back into the bush.

Don't worry, old chap, I won't tell anyone.

And not for the first time I thought: how the hell can anyone pay ten thousand quid to march up to something like that, blast its brains out and bolt its head to the wall of their trophy room. For fun.

Then a little voice in my head reminded me about the tigerfish and bream. At least we eat what we kill, I told it firmly. Yes, the voice went on, but the villagers eat the elephants killed by the hunters. They're hungrier than you are.

We paddled back out of our tiny lagoon, into the bay and down a wide creek dotted with drowned trees. The sun was getting low, and shone from a cloudless, brilliantly blue sky. The drowned trees turned to flashing fire. We shipped our paddles and drifted on the shot-silk water. The first of the dikkops called, *TIEEU-tieeeu*, *teu*, *teu*, *teu*.

'Ought to be getting back,' Sal said reluctantly.

'Wouldn't it be lovely to stay out here,' I said, 'in our own boat.'

'Mmmm,' Sal said. 'Depends. Biggles in an aeroplane's bad enough, without Captain Bligh in a boat. Anyway, we can't afford a boat.'

The tranquillity was abruptly shattered as Steve appeared round a bend in the creek, at the helm of a raft of the kind on which I'd almost got Gerald and Lee Durrell killed. He hove alongside.

'Let's get the canoe on board,' he said. 'We'll take you back.' Raft technology had improved over the years. It had an electric starter, there was a small spare engine hanging on the transom, Steve had a radio hanging on his belt, and his clients reclined in non-tatty chairs and sipped gin and tonics from what looked like real glasses. We accepted lift and drink gratefully, watched the sun go down and chugged back to Msango.

Steve dropped us back at Tashinga, early on the following afternoon. It was scorchingly hot and windless. The little rhinos were trotting across the airstrip behind one of the handlers.

'Bath time,' the handler said. We dropped our kit in a pile beside Z-WMP, and followed them through the narrow strip of bush and onto the lake-shore.

The baby rhinos broke into a gallop when they saw the water. They plunged in with mews of ecstasy, and rolled and snorted and wallowed in the cool water. No abandoned dignity here: they were like kids in a paddling pool. Then they got out and ran around and tumbled in the mud and poked each other with their nubby little horns.

The handler called them. 'Home now.' They formed up in line again and he led them away. We strolled back to the airstrip. Sal opened Z-WMP's door and was instantly enveloped in a greenish gas cloud created by the putrefaction of two hundred dead worms. It was a low-tech biological weapon, just what Africa needs, maybe we can patent it.

'Pfwaaargh,' she said, staggering backwards holding her nose. 'I'm not going anywhere in this thing until you've cleaned it out.'

'Can't,' I said, peering inside the luggage compartment with my cap held over my nose. 'All gone down under the floorboards, can't get at them without taking half the aeroplane to bits.' And thus back to Harare. We tried opening all the windows, but the airflow simply sucked up the smell from beneath the floorboards and made matters worse.

'Pfwaaargh,' Richard Hoare, our wildlife vet and elephant-tracking expert said as we opened Z-WMP's cockpit doors at Charles Prince Airport, prior to flying off to Muzarabani.

We'd finally caught our elephants in the act of moving between the Mavuradonha and Mozambique. The little forest patches in the Zambezi Valley were the key to it all. They were hurtling between them at night, through areas of surviving mopane woodland, and snacking off the maize fields en route. Then they'd catch their breath in Mozambique for a while before coming back the same way. Exactly why they went on these sudden walkabouts was a mystery. Since it was mostly the bulls that did so, we surmised it had something to do with lust.

'What the hell's that smell?' Richard went on. I told him.

'What do you think this is, a bloody fishing smack?' he said. 'Can't you get them out?' Not without taking half the aeroplane to bits, I told him.

'So we smack into the hills with the controls jammed by several hundred dead worms,' he said. 'Look great in the accident report. What a way to go.'

Well, we weren't going to mess around in the hills this time. We were going to mess about over the forest patches instead. Our project was undergoing its own uncontrolled transformation, from a rinky-dink little elephant-collaring jaunt in the Mavuradonha to a transboundary natural resource management project, encompassing elephants, forests, villagers, a big chunk of Zimbabwe and Mozambique, and a certain amount of gender equality and empowerment as well.

It was very sexy, in spite of being universally called TBNRM for short, and the Dutch Embassy thought so too. They'd given us money to do some research on the forests as well as elephants, since their respective futures seemed to be inextricably linked together, but not to do the empowerment bit. Someone else would have to pay for that.

Once Richard and I had done the reconnaisance and returned with Z-WMP intact, the next step was to take a look at the forest patches on foot, to assess their overall composition, condition and role in the lives of Muzarabani's elephants and villagers.

The patches were called 'dry tropical forests' – oddly, since they are wet forests really, which is why they've got huge buttressed trees and curtains of lianes instead of straggly little mopane-bushes. They also have some rare trees and plants, which makes them the Zambezi Valley's answer to the tropical rainforests.

As aeroplanes were no longer involved, Sal and I were demoted again to hanger-on status. We blundered over the buttressed tree-roots and through curtains of lianes while from the thickets ahead of us arose a muffled chant that sounded like the prelude to pagan forest sacrifice.

'Pterodactyls, diarrhoea, clogs, dong, DEAD!' it seemed to say. Sometimes there'd be a lengthy silence followed by the boom of a heavy rifle.

The liturgical chant emanated from an invisible but multi-talented bunch of biological PhDs ahead of us including Fay and Kevin Dunham, botanist and zoologist respectively; an ornithologist; and Richard Hoare. They were shepherded along by Jane Hunt, a wildlife guide with immense knowledge of botany, zoology and ornithology, and one of the most accurate guns in southern Africa. Each member of this group was charged with calling out a certain feature of the forest when they saw it, which Richard then noted in his clipboard.

'*Pterocarpus*,' the chant actually went, prior to distortion by a hundred yards of flesh-tearing thornbushes. '*Xylia*.' 'Log.' 'Dung.' Then – rather sinisterly – 'Standin' DEAD!' from Kevin, in a funereal bass and the remnants of a British accent that had survived the journey from somewhere north of the Thames and through many years in African forests. Sometimes, even more sinisterly, he intoned: 'Stag-headed emergent!' These are trees in which dead branches stick up through a still-living canopy. The standin' dead are, well, standin' but dead.

The crocodile of chanting biologists suddenly stopped, and Sal and I almost tripped over the ornithologist. Ahead of us, glimpsed through the lianes, an elephant was busily uprooting a small shrub.

'No idea what it is,' Fay said, peering at the shrub. Botanists are as fond of elephants as anyone else, but don't take much notice of them unless they're uprooting rare shrubs.

Shrub and elephant lay in our direct path. These transects have to be done in a straight line, otherwise – the scientists tell me – the statistics go to pot. Besides which, Fay wanted to have a good look at the shrub.

'Jane,' she said, 'please get rid of it.'

'*VOETSAK*!' Jane shouted. The elephant paused, glanced up, and went back to the shrub. You don't hurl hats in that sort of forest, they don't go more than a couple of yards before hanging up on a branch. She raised her rifle and fired over its head. The elephant fled, taking the shrub with it. It went off amid a crash and crackle of standin' deads being downgraded to logs.

Fay shook her head over the small hole where the shrub had been. 'Last of its kind, no doubt,' she said. 'We'll never know.'

We finally emerged from the dry forest into a maize field. Fay, who dresses like an Edwardian butterfly-collector and skips nimbly over tree-roots and through thornbushes, looked as if she'd been for a stroll in St James's Park. The rest of us looked as if we'd spent three hours falling over tree-roots into thornbushes.

Jane propped her rifle against a small tree and sat down, mopping her brow. 'Six rounds of four-five-eight ammo,' she said. 'D'you think the donors'll pay for it?'

'That's the end of it, anyway,' Richard said. 'Five forest patches, we've got some idea of what's going on.'

'Lot of rare plants being exterminated by elephants, that's what's going on,' Fay said. 'Can't we get the wretched things out of there?'

Many villagers whose crops were being uprooted by marauding elephants would have agreed with her heartily, but that wasn't the point. We were trying to save forests and elephants. Also, 'reconciling human–elephant conflict' was a major conservation growth industry, and would go down the tubes if the conflict was reconciled by getting rid of the elephants.

A spirited debate ensued between plant and elephant specialists. It was inconclusive, other than that both plants and elephants would have a hard time if the forest patches got chopped down by the villagers.

Which, curiously, they hadn't been. Barring the occasional hut and maize field, the forests seemed to be looking after themselves quite nicely, in spite of being surrounded by villagers who'd chopped everything else down.

'So. What now?' Richard said. 'We've done the science, or will have once we've sorted this lot out' – he held up the clipboard – 'now what about actually conserving some elephants? Or forests, come to that.'

I sensed a minefield in the offing, and tried to choose my words carefully. 'I'm not entirely sure how we're going to do that,' I said.

'Up to the villagers, really,' someone said. 'Need to talk to them a bit more.'

'Stakeholder consultation, then?' Richard said. I nodded, and a collective sigh rose over the maize field and wafted away on the breeze.

One reason why a lot of these forests had survived was because they were sacred. Mr Mhene, it turned out, was their spiritual guardian. He'd taken me into one of them already.

'Mr Dick,' he'd said to me, at the forest edge. 'Please take off your socks and shoes and kneel down.' He moved aside a little, took off his own shoes and socks, and began to clap his hands and chant the ritual that would persuade the ancestral spirits to let us enter the forest. Finally he said, 'We can go in.'

Once inside, I was tempted to liken the forest to a cathedral. Vaulted arches of huge trees rose above aisles of waterworn gullies lined with dense shrubs; and banners of lianes hung from the branches like ancient battle-flags. Maybe the cathedral is inspired by the forests: nature formalised and turned to cold northern stone.

Mr Mhene elaborated on his traditional religion as we went. Its god – *Mwari* – made the world, he said, but your ancestors can screw it up for you good and proper. They can be nice to you if you behave, but I got the impression that they'd far rather give you a hard time. Be stingy with the beer at their funerals, and you're in for a lifetime of creatively malicious misery.

What he didn't say, but I'd already gleaned from others, was that you can also get them to stuff someone else's life up if, for instance, they accidentally grow nicer maize than you. You have to ask the ancestors nicely, using the right words. The downside is that other people can do the same to you. This creates a meek, well-behaved society paralysed with fear and devoted to growing inferior maize.

We eventually emerged on the far side of the forest, where a lot of people were busily hoeing their fields. Actually, they weren't real people at all. The rapidly-growing donor aid industry had rebranded them as a rural community – a pre-packaged bundle of stakeholders who supposedly think alike, act alike, love each other to pieces, and produce unanimously constructive answers when consulted. That's the mythology, anyway.

Traditional religion could have been a splendid way to save the forests, if everyone had been happy to spend their lives being screwed around by vengeful ghosts. Unfortunately, they weren't, as Mr Mhene lamented. Many of his constituents were turning to Christianity, which promised them immunity from malevolent ancestors in this life, and maybe in the next one as well.

'They have no respect,' Mr Mhene said sadly. 'They are making their fields in some of the forests.'

Some of them, he went on, weren't above filling an old blunderbuss with gunpowder and rusty nails and blasting elephants into bite-sized snacks. Exactly why Mr Mhene hadn't got his great-great-great-aunts to bring them out in boils before pushing them into pools full of crocodiles was a question I felt I shouldn't ask.

Since the villagers only had droughts, floods, vindictive ancestors, groupies, elephants and Mr Mhene to cope with, we brought the heavy artillery of the Global Environment Fund (GEF) to bear on them as well.

God knows why we got involved with the GEF in the first place, except that the German donor agency was tapering off its support and I was duly turning into a hopeless donor-aid addict.

The GEF didn't like buying vehicles or paying salaries. It didn't like mileage, and it didn't like expenses. It didn't even like forests and elephants very much, unless they provided 'sustainable livelihoods'. A lot of elephants were already doing this, but the forests weren't, as evidenced by their largely pristine condition. This presented us with the rather awful notion of having to suggest that local people should get in there with an axe and start making a living out of the forests – something, we felt, Mr Mhene might not like very much.

Since I was temperamentally unsuited to doing stakeholder consultations, we employed someone who was. I sent Tendai Warambwa off to Muzarabani to ask its villagers how their livelihoods might be rendered sustainable, preferably without chopping down the forests. As the GEF didn't like vehicles, he had to do this in an old Land Rover that had come to us via the British Army and Iraq, Act One, and looked like it.

He disappeared for several days, then reappeared with a clatter of worn big-end bearings. The Land Rover was covered in dust, and the green paint – which the army had hastily slapped on over its military camouflage before handing it to us – was flaking off. This gave it a sinisterly green-and-brown mottled appearance. It looked even more military than before. Tendai looked harassed. I wondered if he'd been arrested for being a mercenary. This wasn't so.

'They won't even talk to us,' Tendai said, 'until we give them tea and ess.'

'What's that?' Sal asked, glancing up from an Outlook Express in-box clogged with spam, virus warnings and gigabyte photographs of dogs and babies belonging to total strangers.

'Transport and subsistence,' I explained. 'T & S. Used to get it in parks. Make sure you get invited to a few out-of-town meetings every month, go on a moped and claim mileage for a Land Rover, camp in a tent and fudge up a bill from the local Sheraton, if there's one handy. It was the only way we underpaid parks officers could survive.'

By now a plethora of instant experts had been attracted by the opportunities the stakeholder consultation industry presented for the alleviation of their own poverty and the acquisition of a PhD at someone else's expense. The peasants, however, were getting poorer by the minute as they were spending most of their lives going to meetings and being consulted instead of growing crops. They wanted to be paid for it. The groupies had probably put them up to it. However, the GEF didn't see it that way.

'Pay them to come to meetings?' they said. 'Good heavens, no. Whatever next?'

Circumventing counter-productive stipulations by donors is all part of the game. We withdrew a sackful of the GEF's cash to pay T & S to the peasants, debited it against an innocent little project budget line called 'contingencies', and Tendai clattered off again. He was gone rather longer this time. I wondered whether the Land Rover had found the Valley and its monstrously corrugated dirt roads altogether too much, after the forgiving sands of Iraq.

Tendai finally reappeared. He poured himself a cup of tea, handed me an expenses sheet and sat down with the air of someone settling in for a long haul.

'Do we have to pay the district councillors T & S as well?' he asked.

'I dunno. Why not?'

'Because they already get paid T & S by the council. But Councillor Mudariki said he wouldn't come unless he got T & S.'

I shrugged. 'Fine. We can do without him.'

Tendai frowned. 'He told his people they mustn't come either, so they didn't.'

'Oh.'

'Well, I went to see Mr Malika – he hates Councillor Mudariki – and he told his people they must come. I gave them some T & S.'

'OK, so what then?'

'They're the traditional ones. They wanted Mr Mhene to be there. They said they couldn't do anything about the forests without Mr Mhene.' He paused.

'It took me all day just to find Mr Mhene, and then everyone else had gone home. Mr Mhene says he wants to kick all the new settlers out and put fences round the forests.'

'But that's colonial. The GEF'd go ballistic.'

'Don't worry, it can't happen. The people who are living in the forests are Councillor Mudariki's lot. He told Mr

Mhene there'll be war if anyone tries to throw his people out of the forests. He wants to build lodges in them, serve local meals, make a lot of money out of tourists.'

'Mr Mhene'd go ballistic if we did that.'

'Actually, he thought it was quite a good idea. He could be the head guide.'

'So what do you think?'

Tendai mentally drew himself up to his full height. 'I'm a Christian,' he said. 'I can't encourage this sacred forest stuff. I think we should build the lodges and get Councillor Mudariki involved and let him kick all the people out.'

'But you just said he wouldn't.'

'He'll have them out in a flash, if he gets to own the lodges.'

I felt myself going down for the third time in a sea of incomprehension, and struck out desperately towards more familiar shores.

'Did they say anything about elephants?

'Oh, yes, quite a lot, but only when I talked to them privately, outside the meetings. They'd like them all to be shot. Or taken to the Mavuradonha and fenced in.'

I thought this over for a while.

'Then why,' I finally asked, 'do we get all this bullshit about villagers loving elephants?'

Tendai gave me his you're-being-naïve-again look. I glanced at the list of expenses he'd handed me. T & S, and beer for the meetings, and goats and chickens and maize-meal. The GEF was providing sustainable livelihoods all right.

Mr Mhene's political and religious worlds were about to collide. It began with a rapid shrinking of attendance at any meeting called by – or even involving – him, possibly because local elections were coming up and throwing people out of sacred forests wasn't a vote-winning strategy. He lost his seat on the district council, got sacked from the Mavuradonha's management committee, and was cast into political darkness.

Having lost the political kingdom, he made a strenuous effort to assert himself as a traditional leader. Maybe naïvely, I continued to regard him as our wellspring of local knowledge. I received an ominous summons to attend a full-dress district council meeting. I flew up to Muzarabani, parked Z-WMP beside the cart-track and walked the mile or so to the untidy collection of concrete bunkers known as the council offices.

The meeting was made up almost entirely of newly elected councillors I'd never seen before. They accused me of a lot of nasty things including sabotage, spying and subversion.

This all came as something of a shock. However, when the meeting ended, Mr Ngandu, the council's large and genial chief executive officer, summoned me to his office.

'Don't worry,' he said cheerily, disposing of all these crimes with a dismissive wave.

'You can carry on with everything,' Mr Ngandu went on, 'But you mustn't talk to Mr Mhene. Nobody must talk to Mr Mhene.'

I promised not to talk to Mr Mhene. I wanted to get out of there and into Z-WMP before those councillors decided to call the fuzz. But when I got to the front porch, who should be on the doorstep but Mr Mhene, sitting on the low wall with his walking stick beside him.

'Aaaah, Mr Dick!' he exclaimed delightedly, rising to greet me.

That's my lot, I thought. The councillors were all coming out of the offices and there I was, shaking Mr Mhene's hand and being offered a pinch of snuff. But they all greeted him like a long-lost brother. Me too. We all had a nice little chat together.

And then Mr Mhene said his farewells and took me by the arm, and we ambled off down the road to the airstrip together, among the chickens and dust and donkey-carts, discussing the price of maize and fertiliser and the settlers in the forests, a couple of treacherous old anarchists and saboteurs together.

'It's Byzantine,' I said to Sal when I got home, 'or do I mean Machiavellian? Bizarre, anyway. I'll never understand African politics.' I concluded.

'I don't think many outsiders do,' Sal said. 'All best left up to them to sort their own lives out, maybe?' She paused and thought for a few seconds.

'Love, I think we need a break from all this,' she went on. 'Why don't we go down to the valley for a few days, wander around some of those places we've seen from the air, that sort of thing. Looked like lovely bits of wilderness.'

Sal was right, as usual. We were becoming insidiously distanced from the things that really motivated us. Dashing to Tashinga and thrashing through forests was all very well, but it left us with a sense of having merely glimpsed, rather than experienced, that overpoweringly compelling assault on the senses called 'wilderness.'

Some American writers have had a good go at formalising wilderness as a 'concept.' Things get difficult when you do this. Like a soap bubble, it bursts if you try to catch it; like an iridescent tigerfish, the colours fade as it dies.

'Why,' one of these writers asks, 'hasn't the wilderness concept spread more widely throughout the world?'

By which, of course, he means the American idea of wilderness. It has a lot to do with entrance gates, fines, prohibitions, portable TVs and Winnebagos, if some of the photographs are anything to go by. The idea had already spread quite well to a lot of our own parks, I thought.

However, Steve's bay, on the far side of the Ume, had suggested that there might still be a few places – mostly outside the national parks – that hadn't yet succumbed to the American wilderness ideal. Our excursions into the Zambezi Valley beyond the Mavuradonha had reinforced this suspicion. We fired up the old Land Rover and set off with bedding, fuel cans and food for a week.

By early afternoon we were winding down through the Mavuradonha and passing through the scattered settlements below. The old Landy grumbled and groaned as we lurched over the corrugations and through the potholes, but nothing fell off. Then the road narrowed to a track, and gradually improved as the fields and settlements were replaced by woodland and forest.

We began to see signs of elephant – a dried-out lump of dung here, a broken branch there. By early evening we were in – for us, anyway – terra incognita, somewhere in the long stretches of mopane woodland between the more far-flung patches of dry forest. We arrived at a sparkling pan, dotted with waterlilies and overhung by huge mahoganies and sausage-trees.

'Ow,' I said as I got out of the Land Rover and tried to straighten up. 'Should've brought the Toyota. My arms are falling off.'

'Nonsense,' Sal said firmly. 'Can't sleep on top of it.' The Landy has a roof-rack that accommodates a double mattress. Park it under a tree, sling a mosquito-net from a branch, and home's where you roll to a halt.

We strolled round the pan. Elephants had been there, and kudu and impala; and we thought we saw the faint remnants of a lion's pug-marks in the mud. They weren't there now, but that wasn't important: it was the comfortable knowledge that they were around that was.

The absence of threatening signboards, on the other hand, was immensely important. They're as common as impala in national parks. They're the first thing you see when you get there. 'WILD ANIMALS ARE DANGEROUS'. What, even that ducky little mopane-squirrel? 'DO NOT GET OUT OF YOUR CAR'. Not even if there's an orange-crazed elephant jumping up and down on it? Mana Pools is about the only park exempted from this rule, possibly for this reason. 'DO NOT DRIVE OFF THE ROAD', they go on, 'DO NOT PICK FLOWERS', 'DO NOT PLAY RADIOS', 'DO NOT FART'. Actually, the last one makes sense, if you're sitting immobile in your car with all the windows wound up in case a peanut-crazed mopane-squirrel comes bounding in and starts smashing up your picnic basket.

Sometimes they write 'Enjoy Yourself' as well, but it's usually in small letters at the bottom, and sounds faintly sarcastic, after all that intimidation.

My ancient hunter-gatherer genes began to assert themselves after a few thousand years of redundancy. I disentangled a fishing rod from the interior of the Land Rover – the damn thing had been sticking in my ear for a hundred miles, some things never change – and found a worm in our new, escape-proof Colditz Castle of a worm box. I cast it idly into the pan, caught a barbel and laid it at Sal's feet for her admiration and approval.

'Eeeeugh,' she said. 'Put it back.'

I'll admit barbel aren't superficially attractive. They've got flat heads with little piggy eyes, shovel-shaped snouts, long whiskers and a thick coating of exceptionally adhesive mucus. All the same, Sal disappoints me sometimes.

We had a brief but heated debate. No, I won't put it back. Yes, I am going to cook it for supper. It tastes better than it looks, trust me. Yes, of course I'll cut its head off. OK, OK, I'll do it somewhere else. Yes, I will wash the bloody chopping board afterwards.

I caught another barbel as it got dark and soon, reduced to anonymously headless fillets, they were sizzling away on the scottle. I turned them occasionally, illuminated by a small paraffin lamp that created a soft pool of light as the velvet Zambezi Valley night enfolded us. Bats wheeled across the sky, darting at moths; and nightjars swooped and called. Somewhere, far away across the pan, a hunting lion grunted. Idyllic.

A few minutes later one of the idyllic lions crept up behind us and blasted us with a full-on, quadraphonic Metro-Goldwyn-Meyer roar. The sound is impossible to describe, but earth and air vibrate as if being torn apart. Lions can do it – something to do with the bones in their throat – but other felines can't, thankfully. You couldn't live for long with a cat that shattered the kitchen windows whenever it wanted a saucer of milk.

'SHIT!' I exclaimed, in my usual constructive way when faced with imminent death. Like the Chizarira tree, the Land Rover's roof-rack is difficult enough to climb onto by day, let alone at night. It involves some tricky pitches, from bumper to bonnet to roof-rack. Opinions differ on who trod on whose head in the process – and on who kicked the scottle over as well – but we managed it in a microsecond. Perched hopefully out of lion's reach, we clutched each other and gibbered, reduced to man-as-potential-dinner and enveloped in a cloud of vaporised propane from the scottle below, which had gone out as it fell.

The lion roared again, further away, then became distantly idyllic once more. We climbed down. I rescued the barbel from the dust, rinsed them off, put them back on the scottle and ate them defiantly. Fried mud with garlic is one of life's underrated pleasures, I told Sal, but she opened a can of tuna instead.

And so on, for several more long, Arcadian gypsy days, punctuated by those occasional confrontations with elephants and lions that make Africa a heaven for conservationists in Land Rovers and a hell for the villagers on foot with whom, an occasional encounter reminded us, we were sharing it.

They've got words for impenetrable bush – *machesa* – and for woodlands – *sango* – but none for the idea of wilderness-as-entity. It's just there. Most of them wish it wasn't. At best, they'd like it to stay bottled up in places like Matusadona, Mana Pools and Mavuradonha.

We eventually decided to head homewards along a gravel road that passes through the back end of the Mana Pools National Park. To do this, we had to go through a parks department checkpoint.

Parks checkpoints are the Pearly Gates through which you enter certificated and properly-labelled wilderness, and the one at Mkanga Bridge was obviously built to make this clear. You can see it for miles. Gleaming corrugated-iron watertanks rise high above the surrounding woodlands.

Beneath the tanks lies an enormous housing estate, built by USAID for a vastly increased anti-poaching force that was going to save the Zambezi Valley rhinos. Unfortunately, the rhinos got killed first, then the housing estate got built. Then someone else said 'what the heck, we don't need the anti-poaching force any more.' The houses were broken-windowed and empty.

The St Peter who stood guard at this somewhat unpearly gate was a solitary game-scout in a shabby office adorned with mouldering memos from head office. He viewed Sal with suspicion, and me with distaste. I don't look my best after a week of gypsying in a Land Rover, and the odour of barbel slime is extraordinarily persistent. Sal, on the other hand, managed to look as if she'd been for a walk down the garden and back. She did the talking.

'Where is your permit?' he enquired. We haven't got one, Sal said, but we'd be quite willing to pay for one.

'Permits,' the scout announced, 'are only issued in Harare. You must get one in Harare.'

To get to Harare, Sal pointed out, we needed to drive along his road. He entered a quandary, and seemed set to remain inside it for an indefinite period. We helped him find the exit.

We would drive straight along the road, Sal promised, deviating neither left nor right, until we re-emerged from his domain. Nor would we get out of our vehicle, remove firewood, catch fish, drop litter, or play radios. We wouldn't, we assured him, enjoy ourselves in any manner whatsoever. Nor – a cardinal sin – would we sneak down the turn-off to Mana Pools without a booking. We knew how to behave in 'real wilderness'.

Thus reassured, the game-scout finally let us go. We drove meekly for fifty miles or so, glanced furtively behind us in case the game-scout was following, and shot off down to Mana Pools.

Their St Peter didn't seem to care about permits, only money. When they found out we were locals without US dollars, they assigned us to a site in between the toilet block and the incinerator.

We were harried by frilly Land Rovers and harassed by huge overland trucks full of wannabe Wall Street whizz-kids. There were beer bottles on riverbanks and plastic bags on the islands. Squads of guides with rifles akimbo and platoons of tourists behind them came marching down on us in the enchanted woodlands, looking as if they'd like to shoot us. They get cross when they stumble over people sitting around at ease under a tree, without a frilly Land Rover or a rifle to be seen. The tourists start wondering what they're paying all that money for.

When the occasional gap opened up between overland trucks, frilly Land Rovers and ranks of marching tourists, we could see brief glimpses of elephants posing for photographs and hanging around hopefully in case somebody had brought oranges. Sod it, I thought, the parks department mafia can buy the boots and backpacks for Mana's anti-poaching patrols from now on. The Zambezi Society can put its money elsewhere.

The 'elsewhere' I had in mind at the time was in the lovely, distant and unspoilt reaches of the Zambezi Valley we'd idled through before our illicit dash down to Mana Pools.

Maybe it's just as well this didn't happen. We'd probably have ended up by financing entrance-gates, water-tank towers, tar roads and tourist camps, and encouraging people to get there in Winnebagos and go game-viewing in frilly Land Rovers.

But then the third millennium dawned, with the promise of a new era, and that's exactly what we got, in Zimbabwe anyway. All the worlds of Zimbabwean society – black and white, farmers and politicians, spiritual and temporal – collided at once. There was a huge explosion, and the dust hasn't cleared yet.

Suddenly, the tourists all disappeared, from Mana Pools and everywhere else as well. Perhaps Muzarabani's had a lucky escape.

Chapter Ten

FLAMES, AND A
PHOENIX RISING

I circled over Chris and Dawn's farm, and wished I
hadn't. Tangled weeds grew where before there had
been neat lines of maize and tobacco between the rocky
kopjes. The swimming pool was half-full of muddy water.
The lawns had gone to seed, chickens scratched around
the empty garage and rusty roofing-sheets sagged from
the farmhouse verandah.

As for Chris and Dawn, they'd been evicted from their
farm by bands of armed thugs after Mugabe's government
declared war on white farmers. They'd hung around Harare
for a while, dazed and shocked, then gone to Mozambique.

We were taking the radio-collars off our Mavuradonha
elephants. They'd served their purpose. We knew how the
elephants moved from the Mavuradonha into Mozambique
and back. We'd mapped out our elephant movement corridor.
Unfortunately, the corridor was now being occupied by
thousands of workers who had also been evicted from the

farms by the invaders. Much of the bush we'd hoped to include in the corridors was being burnt and turned into maize fields.

A general election was imminent, and Muzarabani was a hot political potato. Neither the ex-commercial farmers nor the displaced farm workers were entirely convinced that recent events had worked to their benefit. White people running around in rural areas were suspected of anti-social activities ranging from encouraging political deviancy to preparing the ground for British commando airdrops.

We'd decided to carry on in spite of this. There was some urgency, because the elephant radio-collar batteries were due to go flat and then we'd never get the collars off because we wouldn't be able to find the elephants. We'd hired a helicopter flown by Doug Hensburg, an old and experienced friend. He and Richard Hoare were going to do the decollaring. Meanwhile, I was taking a look at some of the forests in Z-WMP with Rob Cunliffe, another botanist, in the back seat. Loki Osborne was driving around somewhere near Muzarabani village and the council offices.

Sal was acting as our collective radio ground station, parked in a lay-by halfway down the mountains. We'd taken the old Land Rover instead of the Hilux, for reasons I cannot now recall. She was perched on the roof-rack, passing the time by painting the view across the Zambezi Valley to Lake Cabora Bassa, when she heard several large trucks coming down the road behind her, accompanied by the sound of massed voices chanting political slogans. An electioneering team, she deduced, was on its way to Muzarabani to drum up support for its parliamentary candidate.

'This made me feel uneasy,' she said later. 'I was sitting on a truck full of subversive-looking radio equipment with a microphone in my hand. Somehow, I didn't think decollaring elephants would be a useful answer, if anyone asked.'

I knew what she meant, since I'd had similar thoughts in Z-WMP over Mozambique.

Sal stuffed the microphone into a pocket and tried to look like a harmless eccentric dabbling in watercolours. The trucks roared past her, with a lot of chanting and flag-waving, and carried on down into the Zambezi Valley.

Sal couldn't raise Doug, Loki or myself on the radio. Doug and Richard had landed beside a dirt road in the Zambezi Valley, and his ground team was refuelling the helicopter from Doug's pickup. Hunting rifles, dart guns and other assorted weaponry were casually propped against the truck. The electioneering trucks came hurtling round a bend and promptly ran into something that really did look like a mercenary army. They skidded to a stop, and a lot of nasty-looking people got out.

Questions were asked, mostly without pauses for reasoned answers. Ignatious, one of Loki's assistants, was helping the refuelling team. He said something about decollaring elephants, and got the answer about pulling the other one. One of the heavies grabbed him by the shirt and threatened to beat his head in.

'OK, go ahead,' Ignatious replied lightly. This disconcerted his attacker, who was more used to villagers screaming for mercy. Also, a small child accompanying Doug's ground team had climbed into the back of one of the trucks and was offering chocolate biscuits to the occupants. This seemed to defuse the situation a bit.

'Well, *famba*. Get out of Muzarabani,' a top heavy said, 'and don't come back.' Doug *famba'd* in his helicopter, showering the political bandwagons with dust and a barrage of small stones. The fuel truck shot off through the dustclouds before anyone could change their minds.

Rob Cunliffe and I were still obliviously pottering around in Z-WMP, looking at woodlands chopped down by refugee farm workers, when Sal finally managed to get through to us. Loki had run into the same bunch, albeit with less bother, since he didn't look like a mercenary army.

'But he says they were heading towards the airstrip,' she concluded.

I wondered if we should meander around in the air for a while, until things quietened down. Not only did we have a lot of subversive-looking radio-tracking equipment on board: we didn't stand a chance of passing ourselves off as dabblers in watercolours, as Sal had done. We didn't have any chocolate biscuits to hand out, either. They'd probably sling us in gaol if we landed, and set fire to Z-WMP into the bargain. I discussed the situation with Rob over Z-WMP's intercom.

'Trouble is,' he reminded me, 'my pickup's parked beside the airstrip. It's brand new. I'd quite like to get it out of there.'

I couldn't see the trucks and heavies when we got to the strip, but there again, I was below treetop height, hopping Z-WMP over fences and trying to avoid detection. Rob's truck was parked halfway down the strip, on the cross-track by the rusty iron pole. We stopped alongside it, and Rob jumped out of Z-WMP and into his truck.

I kept the engine running as Rob drove away. I couldn't see behind me from Z-WMP's cockpit, so I stood on the brakes and gunned the motor, kicking up a dense cloud of dust, squashed beercans and empty fertiliser-sacks in case the mob was coming up the airstrip. That ought to delay them for a moment or two, I thought. I watched Rob's truck until it disappeared into the hills. Then I took off again.

I stooged around the sky for a while. I couldn't see the trucks and heavies, but billows of flame and black smoke were rising from several of the scattered settlements. Then I flew to another airstrip, which I hoped lay outside the war-zone, and sat it out until Sal came to collect me.

We finally regrouped at the Mavuradonha campsite. During the evening we heard the trucks heading back up the road, the chorus of political slogans and songs swelling as it came. We held our breath.

'Already eaten all our bloody biscuits,' Doug observed. 'Suppose they'll want our dinner now.' Loki grinned, and waved a huge bunch of chillis. 'I'm ready for the buggers,' he said. But the trucks passed by, and the chanting faded.

In the morning we poked our heads out of the campsite like wary tortoises and ventured cautiously down to the police station near the council offices. Everything looked surreally normal. A couple of political deviationists were putting up new posters of their own election candidates to replace the ones torn down the day before.

The chief of police was profoundly apologetic. 'A misunderstanding,' he said. 'A minor disturbance.'

A few villagers had burnt their own houses down, it seemed, in spite of the efforts of some public-spirited political visitors to stop them. A lot more had beaten their own heads in with knobkerries, and been carted off to hospital. We tut-tutted at this strange behaviour.

'But you can carry on now,' he concluded. We decollared as many elephants as we could find, and scuttled back to Harare before more truckloads of public-spirited politicians arrived and tried to stop us setting fire to our own camp.

Things quietened down a bit in Muzarabani, after the elections, and Loki managed to do some more work on his chili-growing project. But more displaced farm workers arrived, and set about clearing fields wherever they could. And the Netherlands Embassy, which had stuck by us through all this, finally cancelled its Zimbabwean aid programmes along with most other donors.

I tried a few other sources of funding, but got the same answer: no ways. Not in Zimbabwe. We're making a political point. If wildlife suffers in the process – well, too bad.

The Mavuradonha Wilderness Area survived, but its income from tourism slumped even further. Its rolling woodlands and secluded valleys were turned over to the sport hunters. They couldn't find any elephants, down in the Zambezi Valley where the elephant movement corridors were supposed to be.

Conservation mega-projects are grandiose in concept, and stratospheric in their goals. Their budgets achieve escape velocity and go into high earth orbit. Some are conceived by multinational conservation agencies. Some are conceived by donor agencies like USAID or – in our own case – the Canadian government. They stake out immense slabs of Africa for rearrangement to their taste. They certainly aren't conceived by Mr Mhene or the villagers. They may get consulted half to death later, but only on the detail, not the grand design.

This replay of the Scramble for Africa is conducted through local surrogates to provide a semblance of legitimacy. People like Sal and myself don't count as local surrogates. However, we still had some knowledge that came in useful now and then. Some crumbs fell our way from the mega-project banqueting tables.

The Canadians particularly like things called wetlands. They'll hand out millions so long as wetlands are involved. They wanted to rearrange the Zambezi Delta to their liking, through their own local surrogate, the International Union for Conservation of Nature, or IUCN – an organisation that solicits membership fees from agencies like the Zambezi Society, then morphs into our biggest competitor for donor funds.

Even then, our involvement was puzzling. 'What,' I asked Sal, before we plunged into a three-day talk-fest organised by the Canadians, 'should we pitch for?'

'Endangered species,' Sal said, without hesitation. 'It's what we're best at.'

As we emerged after three days of scribbling profound, five-word thoughts on bits of coloured cardboard she said, 'So how the hell did we end up with biodiversity evaluation?'

Possibly because nobody except a few eccentrics like us was interested in endangered species any more, at least not for their own sakes. They were interested in 'maintaining ecosystem processes for human benefit'.

The snag is that to maintain an ecosystem process you need to know how it works. To do this, you need to know something about its biodiversity; the whole range of species, including mice, minnows and microbes, and what they do to actually make it work.

Biodiversity and ecosystem processes, therefore, are the conservation equivalent of the quantum physicist's search for a grand theory of absolutely everything. Rhinos, cheetahs and elephants are just some of its most visible manifestations. They are the *Andromeda Nebulae* of biodiversity. The microbes are the quarks.

It all gets a bit hazy from there on because, like the physicists, the biologists haven't even got close to identifying absolutely everything, let alone finding out how it all works. There's no guaranteed way of maintaining ecosystem processes except by leaving them strictly alone.

Anyway, IUCN said, don't you worry your pretty little heads about that. All we want you to do is to evaluate such bits of Zambezi Delta biodiversity as are relatively easily accessible.

Sal and I were in Z-WMP, following the Zambezi downstream to Marromeu, the small town that lies at the inland end of the Zambezi's Indian Ocean delta. Somewhere along the way we flew out of Zimbabwe, into Mozambique and into what – in retrospect – seem like the half-remembered fragments of dreams and nightmares.

Ahead of us, lost in the haze, was Cosmas Mutsandiwa, piloting a small Cessna with himself and Jonathan Timberlake, a botanist, on board. We needed two aircraft for the Zambezi Delta survey, and Cosmas – who had worked his way up to become a commercial pilot through sheer guts and determination – had volunteered to help.

Jonathan and I would do the actual survey in Z-WMP. However, the nearest aviation fuel was at Quelimane, seventy-odd miles up the coast. We would have wasted a lot of time and fuel if we'd had to fly Z-WMP up there every five minutes. Cosmas was our petrol-tanker. He'd periodically fly to Quelimane with a load of empty plastic jerry cans, fill them with aviation petrol, strap them into the passenger seats and bring them back to refuel Z-WMP.

Cosmas and the Cessna were our lifeline in other ways, too. The Zambezi Delta is wild and remote. He'd come and look for us if Z-WMP's engine blew up again. We, of course, would go and look for him, if the Cessna exploded on the way back from Quelimane with a couple of hundred litres of petrol in plastic cans on board. Not that there'd be much to find. His task on this trip was far more dangerous than mine.

Cosmas called me on the radio. 'I'm on the ground at Marromeu,' he said. 'Watch out for the pig.'

'Pig?' I asked, but he'd switched his radio off.

Marromeu loomed dimly through the haze. It lay beside the Zambezi, a neat little town of suburban villas and regularly patterned streets. Rows of railway wagons were parked in sidings close to a sugar factory. I could see the Cessna parked neatly on a smallish airstrip alongside another, much larger aircraft. Something seemed oddly – eerily – wrong.

I swung Z-WMP onto a final approach, noting that the middle of the runway threshhold was a strange place to put a small and abandoned control tower. As we got closer, the control tower slowly reinvented itself as a tank, gunbarrel pointing uselessly skywards and luxuriant weeds growing from a gaping hole where most of its turret had been blown off.

Just before we touched down, a smallish but very solid-looking pig tore out of the long grass flanking the airstrip and hurtled under the wheels. I hauled back on the stick. Z-WMP hiccuped over the pig, thumped back down onto the ground, and rolled to a halt alongside Cosmas and his Cessna.

He was looking thoughtfully at the large, twin-engined Ilyushin aircraft – or, more accurately, the mangled wreckage thereof – that occupied much of the available parking area. One wing sagged sadly to the ground, its nose and belly were crumpled, and the undercarriage was missing altogether.

'I wonder,' Cosmas said, 'if the pig did that.'

This seemed likely. We surmised that the pig had been trained by Mozambiquan rebels to throw itself into the undercarriage of any aircraft that tried to land, and it hadn't been told that Mozambique's civil war was over.

Someone was living in the wreckage. Torn and stained washing hung from the radio aerials. Several tiny children in loincloths, pot-bellied, with stick-like limbs, emerged and stared at us solemnly, then ran back inside, screaming.

Ramos, a tall, slight man, met us on the airstrip and identified himself as our guide and general factotum. Like many Mozambiquans, he'd had to become at least partly trilingual, learning Portuguese under the old colonial regime and some English as a general lingua franca, as well as his own native language.

He led us into Marromeu itself. The streets turned out to be baked mud interspersed with large stones and potholes that could swallow a bus and still have room for a couple of furniture vans. I suddenly realised what had looked wrong, as I'd circled before landing. There weren't any buses, furniture vans or even small cars for the potholes to swallow. Not a single one.

The streets were lined with derelict villas, their corrugated-iron roofs either blown off by mortar shells or stripped to build the shacks that lined every alleyway. The walls were pitted by machine gun bullets. We eventually came to a building which, possessing a roof, was in better repair than most. This was our guest house, Ramos announced.

He showed us to rooms in which bedrolls had been carefully laid out on the floor. The bedrolls smelt of generations of unwashed feet. A naked light bulb, dangling from a wire that snaked in through the window and up the wall, pulsed in sync with a generator that thumped away somewhere outside.

'Bugger this for a game of skittles,' I said, with a forced heartiness I wasn't feeling. I poured a couple of tots of the Scotch that Sal and I carry to ease the pain of long days in small aeroplanes.

'What I need,' Sal said, 'is a bath.'

We located a magnificent bathroom across the passageway. It had a huge enamelled bath with gilded taps, and a vast porcelain lavatory bowl. The bowl was covered in black grime, the cistern was empty and rusted solid, and nothing came out of the taps.

Sal went in search of enlightenment and found Ramos instead. He brought a twenty-litre oil drum filled with cold water which, Sal said, he had pumped from a well in the backyard. As the drains from the bath and toilet also seemed to discharge into the backyard, this was not encouraging.

Sal tried to rub the grime off the toilet pan with the remains of an ancient scrubbing brush she found in a cupboard. The brush had an instant nervous breakdown, after years of unemployment. She fashioned a makeshift toilet-seat cover out of plastic bags instead. This wasn't easy, there being no seat to fit it over. We allotted ourselves eight litres each for a shower and four for the loo, and joined Cosmas and Jonathan on the verandah, which had a nice view of the potholes in the street.

We had another whisky or two while waiting for supper to appear. It didn't. At half-past nine we sought Ramos.

'Supper? You want supper?' he asked, with an air of astonishment. Yes, we did.

'What you like? Chicken or bread? You got Mellican dollars?'

We chose chicken and bread, and sent him off with 20 US dollars. He came back an hour later with a loaf of bread tucked under his arm and a live chicken dangling by the legs from each hand. The chickens squawked and clucked agitatedly, as well they might.

'Now I cook,' Ramos announced. Sal, who'd had quixotic ideas about helping him in the kitchen, backed away from the imminent slaughter. An hour later, Ramos reappeared with what was left of the chickens after plucking, dismemberment and a savage roasting. We ate ravenously, eased the pain with some more whisky, and got to bed some time after midnight.

A WILD LIFE

I had been asleep for about five minutes when a cockerel exploded into what it believed to be song, outside our window. I was thinking about going outside and strangling it when I heard footsteps in the courtyard. Obviously someone else, Jonathan or Cosmas, maybe, was going to do it.

Instead of the sound a cockerel being murdered, centuries of Arab influence manifested themselves in the call to prayer of a muezzin with the strongest pair of lungs in Mozambique. It was accompanied by the cockerel. More appropriately timed – as a diversion over lunch, say – it could have been an eerily magnificent duet. The muezzin eventually wound down – no single pair of human lungs could maintain that volume for more than a few minutes – but the cockerel wound up, and kept going until sunrise.

In the morning, sunken-eyed, our hands shaking slightly, we set out to accomplish what we had come to do. Jonathan shoehorned himself into the back seat of the Super Cub, together with a satellite image on which he had marked features of interest. I had fed their locations into my GPS. We took off, flew over some long-abandoned fields, their outlines merging into the surrounding terrain, and thence back in time, into a primeval landscape.

Most of the delta seemed to be on fire. Infernos of blazing grassland spewed vast plumes of smoke that were flattened by the wind coming off the sea, far away to the east. Water spread across flooded grasslands between the fires, and snaked through channels choked with tall green, densely-packed stems of papyrus.

We flew through dark caverns of smoke, past storms of blazing grass. Charred stems of straw eddied into the cabin, borne on gusts of scorching air filled with dust and choking fumes. Once or twice we glimpsed a couple of elephant, a small group of buffalo, knee-deep in the swamps.

Jonathan settled down to the task of evaluating the delta's biodiversity. 'Flooded grasslands,' I heard him muttering over the intercom. 'Yes, that's what I thought it might be, from the satellite image. Ah, what's that now? Oh, more papyrus. Gosh, look at all those egrets! But what's that funny little patch of scrub, what's it doing here?'

A narrow river channel, choked with papyrus, suddenly broadened on both sides into an immense swamp. Lily-pads floated in occasional patches of clear water. Otherwise: nothing but an immensity of green reeds, 15 feet high and densely-packed, rippling in the wind. The edges of the swamp were lost in walls of smoke and haze, shot through with the red flickering of the fires.

It could have been taken from a picture book of the Jurassic. All it needed was a volcano or two and the snaking necks of diplodoci rearing from the reeds. Already slightly unnerved, I felt the first twinges of fear. We might survive a forced landing on the burning grasslands, if the engine exploded, and sit things out until Cosmas came looking for us. We might survive a plunge into the papyrus. But if we went down here, the swamp would swallow Z-WMP, and us along with it. There wouldn't be much for Cosmas to find, either.

'Interesting,' Jonathan said. I forced myself to concentrate on the job we'd come to do. 'Could be shoebills here,' he commented. Could be diplodoci here as well, I thought but didn't say. Now let's get out of here. After a few minutes the swamp narrowed again, to the relative safety of the burning grasslands.

By now I'd lost all sense of orientation, and followed the arrow on the GPS as we zigged and zagged through the smoke. I wasn't flying an aeroplane any more. I was playing a computer game, trying to make the right moves to avoid death by fire, drowning, or running out of fuel, and thus to amass enough points to go to the next level – a return to Marromeu, and another round with the pig.

We came to the sea which, being a fairly prominent landmark, enabled me to fix my position within a hundred miles or so. It stretched away eastwards into a fading jumble of breaking grey waves, threatening certain doom for anyone rash enough to venture over it. We turned back for Marromeu, up one of the Zambezi Delta's many channels. The pig came hurtling out of the grass from a new and unexpected direction, we swerved violently round it on one wheel, and drew up alongside the shattered Ilyushin.

Z-WMP's bright red and white livery was blackened by smoke, her air intakes clogged with charred grass stems. I was, I realised, trembling slightly. I calmed myself by cleaning the aircraft down and checking the tyre pressures, fuel and battery levels. The children living in the Ilyushin watched warily from its shattered windows. I tried to get them to come out and talk to me, but they ducked out of sight.

Later that afternoon we walked through the town to the Zambezi, through the empty, rutted streets and past the wrecked villas which, it slowly became obvious, were densely inhabited.

Haunted eyes, old and young, stared at us dully from the ruins, hunched over cooking-fires fuelled by bits of ruined plasterboard, broken doors, the remains of old furniture. Nobody greeted us. Nobody came out to offer us curios or fake currency. Nobody begged money from us. Tourism was unheard of in Marromeu. We were unheard of in Marromeu: aliens, half-seen through mists of time and space.

We came at last to the banks of the Zambezi, flowing strong and wide before it breaks up into the delta. There were no impala or even hippos, let alone elephants. Many had been killed during Mozambique's civil war. Those that survived had either headed for the safety of the delta's inaccessible channels and grasslands, or been killed for food by Marromeu's starving inhabitants.

Beside the river, the town's former engine of prosperity, a sugar factory, also lay in ruins: a huge, rusty, corrugated-iron structure punctured by bombs and bullets, with loose panels groaning eerily as they flapped in the wind. Outside, the neat lines of railway wagons had shrubs growing up through the buffers and couplings.

We turned back from the river as the sun dipped behind the long, flat horizon and came across a huge tree behind the sugar factory. It was covered with enormous fruits, like dark coconuts. Several of the coconuts suddenly dropped off the branches and flew away. They were fruit bats. This, we later discovered, was not only one of the biggest fruit bat roosts in southern Africa, but also an important 'range extension' for the species concerned, since they'd never been seen here before – not by biologists, anyway. This was of great interest to biodiversity conservation, but possibly not to the people of Marromeu.

As we walked back through the ruined town an ancient open truck, the only vehicle we'd seen, came clattering round a corner billowing black clouds of diesel smoke. Its driver concentrated on staying on what used to be a road while his conductor hung out of the cab and yelled 'BEIRA-BEIRA-BEIRA' at the top of his voice.

The truck shot off down an alleyway, swerving round shacks and market stalls fashioned from black PVC and scavenged corrugated-iron. It reappeared a couple of minutes later from a different direction, the conductor still bellowing, 'BEIRA-BEIRA-BEIRA!'

Beira's a small coastal town, a hundred miles or so to the south. Not many people wanted to go there, it seemed. The truck never left Marromeu, as far as we could tell. It spent its days careering round the town, the same two resigned, weary but eternally hopeful passengers in the back. Maybe careering around Marromeu in a truck that never goes anywhere is a way of staving off eventual madness.

And then, as the truck faded into silence, we became aware of the sound of children singing, borne on the evening breeze. Slowly, as we walked, it swelled until it filled the air. We came to the Roman Catholic cathedral – a roughly but gaudily painted concrete structure, apparently modelled on a small aircraft hangar. It stood above the neighbouring buildings solely by virtue of not having been flattened by high explosives.

The pure, sweet harmonies cascaded from the open cathedral doors and spread a golden aura across the surrounding rubble, incongruous, incredibly moving.

And from there we walked back through the silent streets; past the mocking water-tower, the bullet-holes rusting unrepaired; and through the gauntlet of haunted eyes staring, always staring, from the ruins...

Zimbabwe looked like Paradise when we went home. But we'd glimpsed a possible future.

As for the biodiversity: ours was only a reconnaissance trip. Jonathan went back with teams of biologists and sorted out the mice and minnows, but not the microbes. A flood of technical papers went off for peer review. One of them came back from Beijing, with a note from Professor Kloppers.

'The mention of shoebills seems purely speculative,' it said sternly, 'and I consider it highly unlikely that...'

Flames, and a Phoenix Rising

Three fat reports lie on our shelves. Of the US $250, 000 it cost to produce them, maybe a couple of hundred got spent on bread and chickens, and thus percolated down to the starving children of Marromeu. Maybe they all got some T & S later, from the stakeholder consultations.

Chris and Dawn gone to Mozambique. Rob Clifford in England, and Richard Hoare working in Tanzania. Mark Atkinson in America, and Mike Cock roaming Africa like a veterinary *Flying Dutchman*. So many good friends gone. At least they were alive.

Andy Searle, who'd bravely fought every move the parks mafia made to get rid of him, died in a mysterious helicopter crash. The accident report said he'd run out of fuel. I find this hard to believe. Andy was the finest bush-pilot I've ever known.

The country Sal and I thought we knew so well had turned into unpredictable, unknown territory. Our project portfolio dwindled as, one by one, our donors abandoned Zimbabwe and its wildlife to an uncertain fate. We found ourselves drifting, rudderless. We took refuge in the minutiae of office and home life.

'You know,' I said to Sal, as I surveyed our garden, 'I sometimes wonder about this fragile African wilderness bit.'

Perversely, our garden demonstrated an appalling ability to maintain its own biodiversity and ecosystem processes in spite of anything I did to it. Termite mounds sprang up overnight, in the middle of the lawn. Trees sent out clandestine root-suckers that popped up in the veggie garden. There were snakes in the shrubbery and lizards in the letter box. I wouldn't have been surprised to find a rhino in the rockery. The whole thing seemed determined to turn back into an acre of untamed Africa.

Granted, little things like gardening were being largely ignored. I was spending a lot of my time fixing up *Giselle*, the old wooden sailboat, which – subsequent to our discussion in the canoe at Msango Lodge – we'd decided we could afford. Apart from anything else, we could go and hide somewhere on Lake Kariba if Zimbabwe descended into civil war and bullets started coming through the windows. We could afford the boat, it turned out, because the Ecosystem Processes had been at work here too. She had dry rot in the deck and holes in the hull, and nearly sank the first time we put her in the water. But it was a kind of therapy. I could cover myself in glass fibre and glue, and enjoy the immediacy of finely honed chisel on wood and the sweetness of a well-fitted panel of plywood.

'For heaven's sakes, love, give the boat a break and mow the lawns instead,' Sal says. I do. Several hours later I present myself in the kitchen.

'Pfwaargh. What's that awful smell? Is it you?'

It's a fine semantic point. It's not me, strictly speaking. It's a top coat of doggy-doos over a primer of half-cured resin. Our dogs convert an ounce of biscuits into a ton of crap, which they hide in the tall grass. The mower has sprayed it over me from the knees down. However, the point doesn't seem worth arguing.

'I'll have a shower,' I say.

'Not in the bathroom, you won't,' Sal says. 'Go outside and hose it off when the water comes on again. If it does.'

A few tiny threads of reassuring familiarity remained. We flew Z-WMP to Tashinga with a sack of horse cubes for the baby rhinos. They weren't actually babies anymore. The weighing-machine creaked and groaned as they took their turn.

Flames, and a Phoenix Rising

Horse cubes were cheaper than vitamin supplements, glucose and milk powder. Our overseas members – who'd paid for most of our rhino work – were falling away, along with the big donors. They'd been told by the newspapers that there weren't any rhinos left in Zimbabwe, and not much of anything else either. Luckily, there was also Chisipite Junior School for Girls, in Harare.

Every year, for the past ten years, I've been invited to attend the school's Christmas end-of-term assembly. Two hundred girls, ranging from little five-year-old moppets to eleven-year-old seniors, sing hymns and recite prayers in Shona and English. Then the headmaster summons me to the lectern to give a short address on rhino conservation.

A game is being played: there are things I am not supposed to know. When I've finished, there is a dutiful scattering of applause. I make as if to return to my seat, but am detained by the headmaster. The head girl presents me with an envelope. I open it, prepared to feign surprise and delight.

I've never had to feign it yet. The cheque inside is always enough to sustain a herd of baby rhinos for a year. I read out the figure – with difficulty, these days, since it amounts to ever-increasing billions of local dollars. It converted to over £3,000, in December 2006. The girls earn it themselves, by holding discos, making biscuits, cleaning cars.

Afterwards, I try to shame the local embassies into providing a matching contribution. I get courteously dismissive replies. Saving rhinos 'does not conform to our current goals and objectives'.

Zeph comes with us as we follow the young rhinos and their handler into the bush. They've learnt how to use those funny little lips, now. They strip the leaves from the twigs with studied carelessness. Their horns aren't so nubby, either. They push and prod at each other to get at the more succulent branches.

'Need to start releasing them soon,' Zeph says.

'And then?' I say.

Zeph knows what I mean. 'Hope they stay where we can keep an eye on them,' he says. 'If they go up into the hills...'

We don't go on to Steve's camp this time – or to Fothergill Island, for that matter. They are closed for the duration. Nobody's coming to Zimbabwe. We don't have room for worm boxes anyway. We have to carry a can of petrol around with us instead, there being none at Kariba airfield and precious little anywhere else. I pour it into Z-WMP's tanks, and we fly home.

We drive the old Landy to Mana Pools and find that we've forgotten how to behave ourselves in real wilderness, now that we're spending so much time in Harare. I'm caught in the glare of Sal's flashlight as I stand stark naked in the middle of the Nyamepi camping-ground, holding a pepper spray aloft and watching a hyaena vanish into the bush with our cooler-box clamped in its jaws.

There's a shriek of laughter from a nearby campsite. 'Man, look at this,' someone calls. 'Mana Pools cabaret. Gonna dance for us, hey?'

'Bit skinny,' a female voice chuckles. 'Needs a good graze.'

This is the one thing I'm not likely to get. I locate the cooler-box in the morning. The hyaena's eaten all the meat and bacon. He's had a tentative chew at the pepperoni sausage, covered it in slobber, and spat it out.

'Should be alright if I wash it,' I say to Sal.

'All yours,' she says pointedly. 'Serves you right anyway. Why on earth did you leave the cooler-box out?'

Flames, and a Phoenix Rising

Me? What happened to collective responsibility? Happily, our few fellow campers are all dispossessed but still cheerfully generous farmers who understand these things. They have a whip round. Fillet steaks and whole chickens appear from portable deep freezes. We eat like lords for the rest of the week.

But most of the campsites are empty. All the tourists are across the river in Zambia, as we see after nightfall: the far bank of the Zambezi, once dark and mysterious, is lined with the lights of safari camps springing up like the termite mounds in our garden.

We stroll through the park-like acacia woodlands. They've thinned a little – the Mana floodplains are likely to turn to grasslands in a few decades – and the extermination of half of Mana's elephants is still a hot topic. Otherwise: they're much as they were, with herds of golden impala and pyjama'd zebra seen down long sunlit vistas; and the elephant bulls shaking the trees and rearing up on their hind legs to get at the apple-ring pods.

We walk to Chine Pool, and sit on my anthill. The fallen acacia at the tail of the pool has crumbled; but the fig is still there, strong and sturdy as ever, and so is the *jesse* bush on the far bank, growing back after several years of good rain. We wait, to see if the nyala come down.

'Isn't this where you got that pic of a galloping rhino that hangs in the office?'

'Yup. Silly old bugger. Thought he was charging me. Ninety degrees off course. Kept motoring on and into the bush.'

There's a refreshing absence of tourists. Nobody pushes in front of us in a frilly Land Rover and blocks our view when we find a pride of lions on their buffalo kill, on the way to Mcheni and the magic woodlands. The young males lie around on their backs like bored teenagers; a trio of cubs pounces on their mother, and gets swatted with a huge paw. Flies buzz round the buffalo's entrails, and vultures sit in the trees, waiting.

Nor are there phalanxes of tourists marching down on us in the enchanted Mcheni woodlands, with rifle-wielding guides giving us irritated stares for denting their macho images. There are mopane-squirrels giving us irritated stares instead, peering at us from behind the tree-trunks; and kudu browsing on the low, spreading branches of the stately mahoganies.

We sit on the lower slope of a great anthill and sip from our water-bottle.

'Old Rip's favourite,' I say. 'The rhino I used to follow around. This is where he used to sleep.'

Sal chuckles. 'All those pics you've got of a sausage in a bowl of chocolate porridge.'

'Not my best. Too light if I exposed for the rhino, too dark if I read it off the sunlit bits. Well, it was only an old Ferrania.'

Now I'm carrying a Canon Digital SLR. It's so automated that it regards me as a useless appendage. I sometimes think I should just tell it to go to Mana and take photos on its own.

'Be nice to have another go,' I say, wistfully. Fat chance. We can barely keep our Tashinga youngsters going, let alone start moving rhinos back into Mana.

In the evening we're sitting quietly, watching the sun set over the Zambian hills, when a magnificent old bull elephant comes ambling along the riverbank.

'Sit very still,' Sal says, echoing Dolf all those years ago. The elephant meanders up to the Landy and runs his trunk over the doors, fanning his ears idly while he reminisces about oranges and campervans. Then he turns and looms over us, awesomely huge. He picks up a stray acacia-pod from beneath Sal's chair and chews it, gazing at us from long-lashed, liquid eyes.

Flames, and a Phoenix Rising

Finally he wanders away. Twenty-odd years isn't long, for an elephant. Maybe he's the one that came up to us, when I first flew into Mana, and did the same thing. I'd like to think he is, never managed for being superfluous, never controlled for stealing oranges from Art and Martha.

There's only one problem in all this. There is no money to keep Mana – or Matusadona, or anywhere else – going. Absurdly, their future has been hung entirely on the income from tourists. This was all well and good during the tourism boom – and possibly how the parks department mafia acquired all those Rolexes – but the tourists have all gone.

Then, amazingly, things take a turn for the better: the parks department mafia goes. We can't quite believe it, until one of them turns up in my office begging for work. I'm tempted to laugh my socks off, call the police and turn him in as a suspected rhino-poacher, but you never know what people might do to you later, especially if they get a job with the police. I ask him very politely for his CV and burn it ritually as soon as he leaves.

Goodness knows what actually happened. Maybe so much cash had been diverted into luxury bubblecruisers, so much expertise wasted or thrown away, that it couldn't be ignored by even the most determinedly blind politician.

Whatever the reason, a new, user-friendly parks department arose phoenix-like from the ashes. The incoming management even sent us a letter of thanks for our subversive efforts of the past few years. Someone must have stumbled over a forgotten filing-cabinet full of our donation forms. If I was of a cynical turn of mind – which heaven forbid – I'd have said the answer lay at least partly in the discussion I had with the department's new director.

'We haven't got any money,' he said, despairingly. 'We need your help.'

Unfortunately, we didn't have very much money by then either, so we adopted the time-honoured principle of governments everywhere: make a lot of promises – about supporting rhinos in the Matusadona, in our case – and hope something turns up.

Zeph Mukatiwa had died. He'd been replaced at Tashinga by Eleckson Ndhlovu, a short, slight bundle of energy, enthusiasm and intellect. On our side, we'd employed Duncan Purchase, a tall, slight, slow-talking, carefully-phrased bundle of intellect, energy and enthusiasm. He and Nettie, his wife, went to live at Tashinga to supervise our rhino activities. I flew there for a meeting, looking for rhinos as I went.

'Didn't see many,' I said to Duncan as we settled down in Eleckson's office.

'Try looking out of the window,' Duncan said. I did. Two almost-grown rhinos were carefully stripping the leaves from the shrubs growing around the lawn. Beyond them, Lake Kariba sparkled in the sun.

'Ummm,' I said. 'Not going very wild yet, are they?'

'I think they will,' Duncan said. 'The others have.' One or two of the hand-reared rhinos had initially been so horrified by the absence of horse cubes in the bush that they'd tried to break back into their pens. They had been even more appalled to find there weren't any horse cubes there, either.

'And if they don't,' he added, 'I'll build a release boma further away and try again.'

'I wish you would,' Eleckson said. 'They're wrecking the garden. Tea, gentlemen?' A game-scout poured tea from a vast enamelled pot. 'Powdered milk only, I'm afraid,'

Eleckson went on. 'Anyway. Business. First and foremost, I'd like to know how many rhinos we've actually got in this park.'

'The department's head office says…' I began. Duncan frowned.

'Head office says all kinds of things, notably that there are sixty-two rhinos in the Matusadona, although how they work that out when nobody's been near the place for years is another story.'

I knew very well how they worked it out. The old business of known animals, plus five per cent, minus known deaths. Work it back over a decade or so, and Matusadona's got 62 rhinos. Easy.

'We know we've got at least eighteen down here on the lowlands,' Eleckson says. 'That leaves' – he did a quick sum – 'forty-four in the hills. Forty-four? We've seen a couple up there, when I've been able to get some men in, it's dreadful terrain, but forty-four? I find that hard to believe.'

So did Duncan and I.

'We need a full-scale operation,' Duncan said. 'Census and radio-collaring, all at once. Darting from a chopper, find them with light aircraft. Two light aircraft, preferably. Z-WMP and another Super Cub. Get the scouts out on the ground for a month beforehand.'

'Sounds good,' Eleckson said. 'When?'

'Hang on,' I said. 'Is your head office going to buy into this? Helicopters and aeroplanes flown by civilians, radio-collaring rhinos, buzzing all over the park for days on end?'

'Things have changed,' Eleckson said. 'The only problem is' – he went into calculator mode again – 'let's be optimistic, say forty rhinos altogether including the flatlands and the hills, a thousand dollars a rhino including aircraft, drugs and so forth, that's forty thousand or so US dollars. Which I haven't got.'

The swivelling eyeballs came to rest on guess who.

Nettie, who had hitherto been silent, spoke up before I could frame a response. She's a predator expert, with an Aberdeen zoology doctorate. 'What about the cheetahs? Shouldn't we try to get a handle on them too?'

'What, from helicopters and Super Cubs?'

'Good heavens, no. We'd need a separate exercise altogether. Ground transects, spoor counts, vehicles. Another twenty thou or so ought to do it.' Nettie doesn't go in for eyeball swivelling. She was looking straight at me.

I bounced the ball to Adrian Wilson, one of our UK members.

'I'll try,' he said, 'but it's not going to be easy. Zimbabwe...'

I began to bristle, and launched into what was becoming a familiar litany. 'Fucking crocodile tears. Everyone banging on about Zim's wildlife going to pot, nobody overseas raising a bloody finger to stop it. Self-fulfilling prophecy. The bastards want us to fail. Bloody politics. I...'

'Don't worry, I'll do my best,' Adrian interrupted. He badgered, wheedled and cajoled the money for the rhino exercise out of a reluctant British public.

Eleckson's scouts went up into the hills for a month, and still couldn't find more than two rhinos. This was worrying, and I thought seriously about calling the operation off. However, I'd got two aeroplanes, a helicopter and Doug Hensburg to fly it, fuel, a vet, darts, drugs and radio-collars all available at the same time, a feat that was becoming increasingly difficult.

It was a July evening, and bitterly cold in Harare. Sal and I sat beside a roaring fire. We were contemplating the next day's flight up to the warmth and sunshine of the Matusadona – and the start of the census operation – with immense pleasure. The telephone rang. It was Doug Hensburg.

'I'm not going to make it,' he said. 'I've just been eaten by a lion.'

Ha ha, very funny, Doug, I don't need winding up at this stage, it's been murder getting this lot together.

'Gotta go now,' he went on. 'They're wheeling me into the theatre.'

Well, hot damn. They were, too. Doug had serious lacerations and a nasty chest wound that later turned septic and gave all of us a worrying time before he finally recovered.

I called the exercise off. There's a big difference between taking part in aerial rhino operations, and having the responsibility of running them. They need careful co-ordination between helicopter and aeroplane; cool-headed calculation through the valleys and between the trees. Lives are at risk, and helicopter pilots of Doug's skill and experience are worth their weight in gold.

This, added to the game-scouts' meagre findings in the Matusadona hills, said: there isn't any more money where this came from. Don't risk it. Think of something else. Instead, Duncan located three experienced rhino trackers who'd become unemployed when their game ranch had been land-reformed into maize fields. He instructed them to go off and search every one of the Matusadona's thousand-odd square miles, which is about what it covers when you've evened out the lumps and bumps by footslogging over them.

They were still doing it when this book went to print, thanks to the help of two extraordinarily dedicated overseas conservation funders who believe saving wildlife transcends international political quarrels. One is Save the Rhino International, based in the UK and run by Dave Stirling and Cathy Dean. The other is called SAVE (Australia), which

A WILD LIFE

– in spite of its name – actually tries to save Zimbabwe and its wildlife.

Eleckson was right. There certainly aren't 44 rhinos in the Matusadona hills. There may be a couple, if we're lucky. There had almost certainly been a poaching revival during the dark days of the parks department mafia.

But he was right about the lowlands, too, down near the Kariba lake-shore. A good rhino population has survived here, and they're breeding. We've got our fingers crossed.

As for the cheetah: Fauna & Flora International stumped up with their customary generosity. Nettie Purchase got to work. It took another year of painstakingly recording cheetah spoor and sightings. Today there are at least 20 adults in the Matusadona, plus cubs, and juveniles in between. All are direct descendents of Blondie, Clive and Louise, Fred and Bonk and Bonk's Cubs, and of the others we'd released unnamed. Even of poor old VS, if he'd got to do his thing before he was snared. The new Matusadona cheetah population is well launched. And the cheetahs haven't eaten all the park's impala, either. As with the rhinos, we're keeping our fingers crossed.

But Duncan and Nettie were doing all the fieldwork, and I found myself chained to the desk again, signing cheques and fretting about staff costs, budgets and donors. I'd become even more disillusioned about the workshops and conferences that seemed increasingly to substitute real action. Our work with rhinos and cheetahs in the Matusadona may have been unfashionably focused on 'single species', but at least something got done, and at relatively little cost as well, which is more than can be said for a lot of the grandiose conservation mega-projects spawned by the workshops.

By 2006 I'd been leading the Zambezi Society for a quarter-century, as chair and then as director. Africa is plagued by leaders who don't know when to quit. I resolved not to imitate them. Duncan was displaying so much appalling energy, competence, motivation and youthful flexibility that I punished him by promoting him into my job and retreating to a safe seat on the society's committee.

This puts me in grave danger of turning into a rambling old fart, pontificating on how things ought to be done and then watching everyone going off and doing them differently, at half the cost and five times the efficiency.

The best thing I could do, I thought, was to get back in touch with the things that had inspired me to become a conservationist in the first place: the morning light filtering through the Mana woodlands; the elephants standing knee-deep in a Kariba inlet, pulling up tufts of submerged grass and slapping it on the water to get rid of the mud and grit; all the things Dolf had meant so long ago when he said: 'It's all so *lekker*, man. So beautiful.'

Maybe I'll put the fancy Canon Digital to work. Maybe I'll try to convey some of that beauty to others, and hopefully inspire them to help look after it. That seems a worthwhile ambition.

But I'm not going to the bush without Sal. I'll have to drag her away from the multi-billion-gig computer on which she's helping Duncan update the website.

'But he wants this done by...'

The computer goes 'Plink!', emits a brilliant white flash, and dies along with several brilliantly-conceived web pages.

'Bloody ZESA,' Sal exclaims. Maybe she won't have to be dragged. I think of reminding her about the cod number as well – no, that's better left unmentioned, make it the empty geyser and dry taps waiting for us at home – but I don't need to.

'Time we went into the bush again.' she says.

Chapter Eleven

THROUGH THE LOOKING-GLASS

After struggling to pass 11 articulated trucks crawling through the hills, now we're down on the flatlands with Kariba in sight and we're held up by a blasted elephant. He's plumb in the middle of the road and plodding slowly along the white line. Once again, we slow to walking-speed. My hand hovers over the horn.

'Don't you dare,' Sal says. 'Look at him. He's beautiful.'

'Beautiful be buggered,' I say. 'I want to get the boat in the water this afternoon, get the shopping done, get off early tomorrow.'

She looks at me. 'Why?'

Why? Why? Because…

The realisation that I'm not actually in a hurry hasn't yet dawned on me. We slow to a crawl, a few yards behind him. An admission here: we've retired the Landy and bought a Cruiser instead. Not a bubblecruiser, I add hastily; one of the older, no-frills jobs, seriously pre-owned and pre-scarred from past brushes with various bits of wild Africa.

Through the Looking-Glass

The elephant's tail swings slowly from side to side and – a strange habit, this – as soon as he hears us, he gives us his equivalent of the finger: three feet of well-used willy, dangling from his belly and bouncing along the tarmac.

Where's he going? To the bakery, that's where. The bakery lies a few hundred yards from the natural harbour where we keep *Giselle*, our lovely old sailboat. It's surrounded by a high wire fence, outside which several of these elephant bulls are lurking in the surrounding scrub.

They've got it all worked out. They usually let you in, because they know what you're up to. You're buying bread, and you've got to get out again. This saves them the fuss and bother likely to follow if they knock the bakery down to get at the bread.

Local people, too poor to afford vehicles, dash through occasional gaps in the elephants' defences. Getting out again, carrying several loaves, is like avoiding attack by a panzer unit. We, the fortunate, drive up to the gate in the wire fence; the guard opens it from inside, then closes it hurriedly behind us.

We go on to the local supermarket, another mile or so along the road. Our progress is interrupted by a whole herd of elephants who've dug up a water main and are drinking from the resulting pool. Maybe they think there's fluoride in it. Elephants die when their teeth give out.

Once again we are forced to a halt, since the herd is milling around all over the road. We are, I note, on the outskirts of one of Kariba's so-called 'high-density suburbs' – a lingering colonial euphemism for 'slum' – which is one of the last places you'd expect to find a thriving herd of elephants. We don't have to wait very long. A local inhabitant arrives in a battered Peugeot, clamps his hand onto his hooter and charges past through a melee of irritated elephants.

A WILD LIFE

Sal's tempted to deplore this irreverent behaviour but, as I point out, we don't have to live and work with elephants getting in the way. Nothing much gets done in Kariba anyway, because of the heat. Nothing at all would get done if everyone stopped to gawk admiringly at elephants.

Our general impression is that – far from being annihilated by Zimbabwean anarchy, as the world's press would have us believe (or, indeed, managed to death by the parks department) – elephants are doing rather well. They're fighting back. They're trying to retake Kariba. This impression is reinforced by a couple of conversations.

'Destroyed it,' one of the harbour's lady managers says tearfully, surveying the wreckage of her vegetable garden. Scraps of chewed cabbage leaves lie among shattered gum-poles and torn shadecloth.

'Wrenched it off in one go,' says an old acquaintance, surveying the remains of a new and obviously expensive electric gate. It lies, buckled and bent, besides a heap of rubble from a partly-demolished garden wall. 'Didn't come in and eat anything. Just did it. For the hell of it.' We tut-tut sympathetically, but chuckle secretly to ourselves.

Sometimes I wonder why we bother to go across to the Matusadona. Here, herds of impala graze on the far bank of the harbour. Terns and skimmers congregate on the sandbanks. One of Africa's biggest concentrations of marabou storks hangs around a nearby crocodile-farm. We've seen leopard on the road to the supermarket.

And the harbour's full of hippos. They are as blasé about human goings-on as the elephants, but less *bandito*-ish. They merely creep up alongside the boat at night and spray it with crap. They do this by wagging their tails vigorously. The momentum they can impart to a gallon of semi-solid shit is unbelievable, until you see it spattered up the hull and over the cabin, where it sticks like Superglue.

We scrub the hippo-crap off the boat, early in the morning. Although not what you would call a fancy gin-palace – *Giselle* cost us four hundred quid all in – she has got nice lines and new paintwork, neither of which are enhanced by brown clumps of half-digested grass. Finally we leave.

It's calm in the harbour, but this time I'm not deceived by this, as I was when I set out from Fothergill in Rob Fynn's powerboat all those years ago. The rising sun shines orange through the haze, and a fresh wind is kicking up a waste of white horses out on the lake. I hoist the mainsail and the smallest foresail we've got; and *Giselle* leaps ahead when we clear the promontories, heels to the wind and slices through the waves with a long-legged, easy canter.

I handle the sails while Sal helms, keeping a sharp lookout for the rusting, black-painted fishing-boats returning from a night's work, nets hanging from gantries and boxes of silvery sardine-like fish piled high on the decks. We soon leave them behind and find ourselves alone, our world confined to a few square miles of white-capped water bounded by the haze. Ahead of us, invisible as yet, lies the Matusadona.

The wind begins to slacken after an hour or two. I change to a bigger foresail, my feet locked round the foot of the mast as the bow rears high above the crests and plunges into the troughs, showering me with spray.

'Coffee-time,' Sal says, with the unwavering intent of a caffeine addict, as I scramble back to the cockpit.

I hope we have remembered the gas stove, which – on one memorable trip – we forgot. Or, as Sal insists, I forgot. The stove has never forgiven me for this. It connives with the lumpy swell to hurl the coffee-pot into the bottom of the cockpit.

The wind dies even further. I clamber back to the foredeck and hoist the gennaker – a big, brightly-coloured sail which, though it lacks the maliciousness of the gas stove, has mischievous tendencies of its own. I've got it halfway up when it suddenly twists itself into a tangle of wildly-flailing sailcloth. I shout instructions to Sal, but they are rendered unintelligible by the frenzied flapping of the sail.

'Ulred the Pope?' Sal shouts back. 'What do you mean?'

'Pull the red rope!'

She does. The gennaker fills with a thunderous crack and almost wrenches her arm out of its socket, the mast out of the boat and me over the side, then subsides into docility and sways meekly from the masthead. By this time, the Matusadona lowlands and their mountain backdrop are floating ethereally in the haze ahead.

And the wire-tailed swallows are with us – Lake Kariba's harbingers of imminent landfall. Lovably brash little birds, they dart and swoop through the rigging and between the sails, seemingly for the sheer fun of it. They perch on the end of the boom, swaying with the boat, eyeing us boldly before taking off with a muted *chip-chip* and darting round the sails again.

'Which way?' Sal asks.

Kanjedza? Bonde? Nyamuni? Kakongwe? It's not an easy call. All these tiny rivers have their own unique flavour – Kakongwe, tucked up beneath the mountains; Kanjedza with its wide grassland; Bonde with its lagoon and Nyamuni with its red cliffs. Each is as beautiful as the next. Each is home to hippos, crocodiles and elephants; each is visited by lions and kudu; each is haunted by the cries of fatheads and fish eagles. Each has its own storehouse of memories.

'Let's try the Nyamuni,' I suggest. It's one of the first rivers I ever explored, back in my days on Fothergill Island. There's a lovely little floodplain at its upper extremity, covered with grass and dotted with ilala palms.

The wind finally dies. We furl the sails and motor the last two or three miles across a lapis lazuli lake. Distant islands create *Fata Morgana* mirages, hanging-baskets of unruly vegetation suspended on the invisible line between sky and water.

'Watch out for the monster,' Sal says. There have been reports of strange sightings here, where the old bed of the Sanyati River runs a couple of hundred feet below the surface. We scoffed at them, until Sal and I saw an immense, greyish shape roll on the surface one flat-calm day, then disappear. It wasn't a crocodile. It wasn't a hippo either. Our best guess is a vundu – a large catfish, grown to giant dimensions down in the still, dark waters where the Sanyati once flowed. Or maybe someone actually did introduce a manatee or two.

The land reaches out to meet us on either side, and there are – as always – elephants grazing on the fringing grasslands, hippos snorting and huffing among the trees, and crocodiles slipping off the sandbanks as we pass.

We throttle back as we negotiate the steely-grey ramparts of standing trees. I stand on the foredeck looking for submerged stumps, which could pierce *Giselle's* plywood hull as if it were papier mâché. We don't want to sink in full sight of our goal.

'Try not to fall in again,' Sal says.

I knew that would come up. We were here a few months ago, in January, albeit not in *Giselle*: we'd hired a cruiseboat to celebrate Sal's birthday with her family. I'd taken the cruiseboat's tender to go fishing on my own, far out of sight.

I should have known better. The tender was another of those rafts-on-pontoons affairs, similar to the one on which I'd taken Gerald and Lee Durrell on their near-death experience on the Zambezi. It was also in the same tatty condition, due to the slump in Zimbabwean tourism. Even worse: as Sal couldn't see what I was doing, I was having a sneaky try at bream-fishing. Well, they do taste rather good. Not so oily as tigerfish, and not so many bones either.

After wasting a lot of worms on tiddlers I decided to try another spot. The outboard's starter-cord didn't actually break. The handle came off the cord, which recoiled into the depths of the engine with a triumphant 'Sproingg!' and took me half an hour to sort out. This was an awful warning, which I didn't heed. I moved the boat to a dead tree, more or less in the middle of the river. As we approached, I shifted the outboard into neutral and went forward to tie up.

Whereupon I slipped on a patch of worm crap mixed with glutinous black soil and fell off the raft into 20 feet of crocodile-infested water. When I surfaced, the raft was rapidly receding backwards, trailing its painter, the gear lever in neutral but the motor – it transpired – in reverse.

I halved the ten-metre freestyle record, grabbed the loose end of the painter and was towed away like live bait being trolled specially for crocodiles.

Outboard engines stop when they shouldn't, and don't stop when they should. I went on an unguided tour of the Nyamuni, thrashing around impotently on the end of the rope. The raft banged and bounced off several standin' deads, but it was several minutes before it hit something solid enough to stop it and I was able to clamber back on board.

'That was really stupid,' Sal had said then, and says again now. 'You could've been killed. This place is lousy with crocs. I hope it taught you to be more careful.' It did. It taught me to stick to tigerfishing and never, ever, mess around with worms again. Or rafts, come to think of it.

We thread our way between the dead trees towards the red, water-washed cliffs, find a pleasant spot beside them, and moor the boat. There's another school of hippo bobbing and snorting at us indignantly; behind them, the floodplain and its ilalas dotted with impala; then the bush, alive with the hum of insects and, behind the bush, the mountains.

Through the Looking-Glass

The heat from the land hits us as if someone's opened the door of a blast-furnace. We erect a canvas awning, and wait for eternal truths to write themselves in the sand.

Not that they get much of a chance to do so. The minutiae of self-sufficiency see to that, at first anyway. There are rituals to be gone through – the binding up of wounds, for instance, such as the barked and bleeding knuckles resulting from forgetting you need three feet of unoccupied space to pull an outboard motor starter-cord. Then there's the hunt for the gasbottle key, aka the stove's revenge.

During all this, unwelcome thoughts still pop into mind unrequested. Did we turn the stove off at home, and will they cut the phone off, even though the bill arrived a week after its due date? Our surroundings are irrelevant, at this stage: we might as well be moored in a canal beside a steelworks.

Gasbottle key located and knuckles bandaged, I finally get off the boat onto the warm red sand, scramble up the bank, and set about getting in touch with wild Africa again. I ponder a mopane tree. Its grey bark is rutted and runnelled, its branches twisted and broken by elephants, but it's a survivor. It has to be, down here, rooted in sandstone and scorched by unrelenting sun for nine months of the year. A mopane doesn't just give up and die when it's pushed over by elephants. It lies there, thinking things over for a year or so, then sprouts four or five new mopane-shrubs from its old trunk.

I finger its bright double leaves, break one off, rub it in my hands and smell the strong scent of turpentine: then I hang my arm over a branch, like a drunk with his good ole buddy.

'Well,' I say, 'howzit, mate? Been a long time. Truckin' on?'

'Did you say something?' Sal calls from the boat.

'Nope. Just talking to the trees.'

'Ah,' she says, as if it's the sort of thing she's come to

expect from me. She goes back to scanning the shoreline for birds.

'Black egret,' she says, pointing to a bird wading in the shallows, forming a canopy with its wings and darting at fish.

'Black heron,' I call back. Gotcha. Don't come the Kloppers with me, my girl, not in the Matusadona anyway. I didn't live on Fothergill all that time without learning a thing or two.

'Egret,' she repeats adamantly. 'They changed its genus since your day.'

They would have, wouldn't they? Dammit. And what's this 'my day' business? Matusadona Methuselah, that's me. I sit down under the mopane, scuff my toes in the sand and crackling dead leaves, catch the scent of elephant dung on the warm, eddying breeze.

Thinking of Fothergill... there, perched in a dead tree in the middle of the river, close to the floodplain and ilala palms, are the remnants of the tiny tree house Fynn built almost 30 years ago. Just a platform, really, a few square feet of rotting planks with an untidy thatched roof: somewhere to deposit clients who expressed a desire for peace and isolation.

Fynn and I deposited a young Englishman in the tree house by boat late one afternoon, with a sleeping bag, a flask of tea, a bottle of wine and a picnic hamper. He waved at us cheerily as we left, and we didn't give him another thought until we went to collect him the following morning.

By which time he had morphed into a gibbering wreck. As he scrambled down the rickety ladder and into the boat, he uttered fragmented phrases in which Fynn and I fancied we could detect words like 'irresponsibility' and 'sue'.

'What happened?' we'd asked fearfully. Had flocks of vultures descended like squadrons of Stukas and stolen his chicken sandwiches? Had he witnessed the fabled dance of the warrior hippopotami, with its blood-curdling beat of gnashing incisors, as they threatened to knock the tree house down and let the crocodiles gobble him up?

None of these things. He'd simply never been marooned at the mercy of an unknown, unpredictable, apparently menacing wilderness before. When Fynn and I chugged out of the Nyamuni we'd taken all his familiar reference points with us. No car to jump into. No telephone to call us with. Sensory deprivation. He'd become lost in a mental wilderness he never even knew existed. It takes time to get your bearings. Some never have the chance – or the inclination – to try.

I return to the boat, heave a fishing-line over the stern, and settle down to watch the impala on the floodplain on the other side of the lagoon. They graze peacefully, gleaming gold in the sunlight while the herd male prowls suspiciously around, ready to lock horns with challengers.

My contemplation is interrupted by Sal, who's temporarily run out of birds to watch.

'What I need,' she says, 'is a shower.' She pauses. 'And so do you.'

I'll be the judge of that, thank you. However, this means I now have to do battle with our bush shower, which is just as frustrating as the gurgling geysers of home. Its sole redeeming feature is that the angst happens in nicer surroundings.

It consists of a flimsy black plastic bag with a short pipe and shower-rose attached. If the instructions on its box are to be believed, all we have to do is fill it with water, hoist it up a tree to warm up in the sun, and enjoy a long and luxurious shower.

Dream on. The tiny hole at the bag's upper end is obviously designed to be filled from a tap. Look, guys, if there were taps all over the bush we wouldn't need to buy your stupid bloody shower, would we?

I lean over the side of the boat and hold the bag under water, but it collapses to a flat black wafer. A few bubbles come out, but no water goes in. In the end I fill it, little by little, with a very small jug. This takes ten minutes. I carry the shower up the bank, hoist it into a tree and leave Sal to get on with it.

She's stripped off and comprehensively covered with soap when, having returned to my reverie in *Giselle's* cockpit, I hear something going *sperLISH-sperLOSH-sperLISH-sperLOSH* in the river, and getting gradually closer. Its source is out of sight round a bend in the bank, but it sounds like a hippo learning to do the crawl.

The origin of the sound eventually appears. A man is riding a bicycle up the Nyamuni. It seems unlikely, the water being at least 12 feet deep, but I've no explanation other than the evidence of my eyes. I relay the information to Sal.

'Get your clothes on,' I hiss. 'There's a man on a bicycle riding up the river.'

Sal gives me the kind of look she reserves for morons, wilful children, and me. 'Pull the other one,' she says, and carries on soaping up.

Suit yourself. I go back to studying the man on the bicycle, who is drawing closer by the second. He's wearing a battered old sun hat, shirt and shorts, and is gazing happily about him. Finally he pedals into Sal's view.

'Eek,' she shrieks. 'Why didn't you warn me?' She makes an ineffective dash for the towel, which she had hung on a neighbouring tree a few yards away.

This attracts the attention of the man on the bicycle – which, I now see, is a home-made pedalo with the floats more or less submerged. The faintest hint of surprise flits across his features before he regains his composure and raises his hat. 'Good afternoon to you, madam,' he calls across the water. 'Splendid weather.'

The cyclist spends a little time over by the tree house, watching the school of hippo. Sal dresses hastily, a white rim of unrinsed soap glinting on her shoulders. He pedals back to us and comes alongside *Giselle*.

He's another dispossessed farmer. 'Carry it on my boat,' he says cheerfully, 'Moored up the Kanjedza. Ridden this thing over half of Kariba.'

Well, each to his own. It's probably better than paddling around the place on a raft made of bamboo and tractor-tyres. He departs. I have my own battle with the shower-bag, which it wins by running out of water while I'm still heavily soaped up.

By now the sun is kissing the tips of the mopanes, the heat slackening. Two young elephant bulls emerge onto the floodplain and, perversely, squabble over a small landlocked pool instead of drinking at the river. They lock tusks and push and shove at each other like wrestlers. The smaller of the two steadily loses ground; and the victor returns to the pool.

While he's drinking, the small bull comes up behind him, studies his opponent for a few seconds, then gooses him with a tusk. There's a squeal of outrage and another outbreak of sumo wrestling. After a minute or two they call it quits, drink companionably at the river instead of the pool and wander off together, back into the bush.

The water turns shot-silk, then indigo. I'm still adjusting to the sensory deprivation – no telephones, no traffic noise – and I feel curiously detached from my surroundings. I'm not back in touch with wild Africa yet.

'Sundowners?'

'Mmm,' Sal replies.

This isn't as easy as it sounds. The wine is in a cooler-box which is stowed beneath a large crate filled with tins and vegetables in *Giselle's* cabin. I try to shift the crate, which promptly becomes wedged between the bunks. There is a brief battle, which the crate wins by emptying a pile of potatoes, cabbages and tins of beans onto the cabin floor.

Ten minutes later I emerge to find the sun already down.

'I thought I heard a hyaena calling,' Sal says, 'but it was hard to tell, with all that ruckus going on.' I stifle the urge to say it was probably the sound of a man with his foot trapped between a cooler-box and an upturned plastic crate.

Sunrise is harsh and brittle, with none of the softness of the previous evening's sunset, most of which I managed to miss anyway. Flights of cormorants and ibises pass overhead, on their way to their daytime feeding-grounds. Otherwise, the shorelines are deserted. I do some tigerfishing, catch a barbel instead, and subsequently try to convince Sal that they are really quite good to eat if they are marinaded in lemon juice, well seasoned with garlic and haven't been trampled underfoot during a scramble for the top of a Land Rover.

'Throw the bloody thing back,' she says, 'before we get that slime all over the… oh, dammit, dreadful things, there's a cloth in the washing-up bowl.'

No there isn't, as I well know but haven't told her yet. It went overboard last night. Serves it right for hiding in the washing-up water. Serves her right for making me do the washing-up.

The heat begins to build. Crocodiles appear as if from nowhere and crawl up onto the warm sand. Meanwhile the hippos, which spent the night grazing along the shore, are back in the water. They doze.

The Matusadona's animals slowly begin to emerge from the bush. A parade of elephants comes and goes, grazing along the foreshore, drinking from the lake, sucking up water in their trunks and throwing it over their shoulders and onto their backs. Their babies play in the mud, and then chase the egrets around.

'Why is the Matusadona so special to me?' I muse aloud. 'Why not Mana?'

Mana's where it all began, of course, with Dolf and the dam. Mana is special, and we go there whenever we can, to wander the magic woodlands, sit beside the pools and wait for nyala, stroll along the Zambezi, and watch the elephants as they swim across to the islands.

Somehow, though, we always end up here. The irony isn't lost on me. Conservationists are supposed to be anti-dam, almost by definition.

Sal looks at me, slightly mischievously. 'Maybe you love the Matusadona so much because of all that racketing around you did up here, before I came along?'

In a way, I suppose. Halcyon years, when Rob Clifford was on Fothergill and Mark and Mike were saving rhinos; when I was up and down to the Matusadona in Z-WMP every few days, tracking rhinos, guarding cheetahs in the boma; when it seemed as if it would all go on for ever, before the parks mafia took over and the roof fell in.

But there's something more that draws me back to this place time after time. It's a continuity thing. The buffalo, for instance.

'Way back, in 1979, when I was on Fothergill...' I begin.

'... the old man said,' Sal puts in, smiling indulgently. 'Another trip down memory lane? Never mind. Go on.'

'... there were maybe a thousand buffalo in the Matusadona,' I continue. 'We often saw them in herds of, oh, up to couple of hundred or so, I guess.'

I'd often taken tourists to see these herds when I was living on Fothergill, once I'd learnt a little about guiding and a lot more about keeping Hansies under control and Kloppers in their places. It pays to be careful where buffalo are concerned. Usually, though, it's the lone buffalo bulls you have to worry about. Too damn cheeky, as Kenny had said when we'd stumbled over that old buffalo in the Tashinga *jesse*. And likely to cause a big bugger-up, as Jackson pointed out. The herds – mostly females and little brown calves – are more inquisitive than aggressive.

The females grazed; the calves sucked at their mother's udders, then scampered around mock-charging each other, sending up clouds of snow-white cattle egrets. From the herd arose a muted chorus of grunting and lowing, and the air would be filled with the scent of their dung, mingled with dry leaves, that I find so evocative.

It's often useful to let animals know you're there. A surprised buffalo is a dangerous buffalo, male or female – so I didn't worry too much about noise or concealment. When the heads began to lift from the grass and stare at us, we'd stop, watch and wait.

Slowly, they'd come towards us, a step at a time, gazing at us curiously, until we were half-surrounded by a crescent of densely packed buffalo. Once everyone had got their photos we'd back off, step by slow step; and the crescent slowly dissolved back into an amorphous black mass.

Occasionally, though, they'd spook and come thundering past us in a maelstrom of flying hooves, tossing horns, clouds of dust and dried dung, to the accompaniment of the tourists' clacking cameras.

'Yeah, yeah. Mr Macho Man,' Sal puts in. 'Bet that got the Sophies going.'

'Anyway, then the droughts struck, the lake dropped and the grass began extending over the shorelines,' I go on, hurriedly. We had that huge explosion of almost everything – impala, waterbuck, zebra, you name it, but buffalo in particular. In the end we had herds of two thousand buffalo, and those enormous lion prides as well.

Other strange things happened, too. We began seeing elephants – bulls, mostly – with some kind of paralysis of the lower trunk. It became inflamed, and hung limp, like a fat dead worm. A few died, but many adjusted. They could drink by wading into the lake, and they could still browse by using the upper part of their trunks.

'Nobody ever got to the bottom of that, did they?' Sal says.

No, they didn't. It caused a huge stir and even made it into the world press. We had people ringing us up from New York and London, asking what we were doing about it.

Theories flew like leaves in a summer whirlwind. It was lead from the bird-shot the safari camps fired at the elephants to get them out of the veggie gardens. It was minerals from rocks uncovered by the low lake. It was old munitions sunk at the end of the bush war and uncovered by the low lake. It was a selenium deficiency. It was a selenium oversupply. It was – and this is possibly nearest the truth – an exotic plant of some sort, growing on the lake-shore.

Then the lake filled again, after fifteen-odd years of unremitting drought. The lake-shore grasslands and exotic plants vanished; and the floppy-trunk elephants recovered.

The buffalo went into decline. Those that remained took to the hills in the south. The lions learnt to kill rhino calves, hippos and even crocodiles: and then they, too, declined. But our cheetahs began to increase.

And the elephants never went. There are some on the floodplain right now, grazing, drinking, throwing mud over their backs with a deft flick of the trunk, blissfully ignorant of the debate that's raged around them for all those years. All I can say is that the Matusadona doesn't look as if it's being hammered to death by too many elephants.

Then isolated reports of buffalo sightings began to come in again. In 2004, when Nettie Purchase was counting our cheetahs, Duncan and I had surveyed the Matusadona buffaloes in Z-WMP – this to help get a handle on the complex relationships between cheetahs, lions and prey species.

We took off from Tashinga and began a methodical search, brushing the hills with our wingtips in the south, then across the parched mopanes to the lake-shore in the north, making a wide, controlled turn and back again.

We saw elephant in plenty; small zebra groups; herds of impala; sable and kudu and the fat brown sausages of hippos in the bays, but not a single buffalo until – two-thirds of the way through:

'Hang on,' from Duncan, on the intercom. 'Can you circle?' A pause. Then, 'Down there. At the head of the creek.'

There was a herd of buffalo meandering slowly out of the mopanes. Duncan gets busy with his cattle-clicker. Finally: '… ninety-four, ninety-five, ninety-six. Best part of a hundred.'

The buffalo are coming back; and now Lake Kariba seems to be going down again. Will the whole cycle of long lake-shore grasslands, huge buffalo-herds and abundant lions repeat itself – or will it be something totally different, this time around?

That's why the Matusadona is so special. Mana Pools is a series of exquisite cameos. Matusadona is continuity, through a personal quarter-century. Knowing its moods, through the green of the rains and the sere beiges of the long dry months; through drought and good years; through the decline of the buffalo and their eventual reappearance; through the sadness of the rhino poaching and the happiness of knowing our cheetahs have survived.

It's also the only place I know where I can relax on my own sailboat, fishing rod in one hand, beer in the other, and watch elephants while Sal does the washing-up.

'What?' she exclaims. 'You lost the cloth, you can sort it out.'

The sun blasts down from an eggshell sky, sucks the colour out of the landscape, crushes it into submission. Grey trees rise from ruffled brown water. Brown backs of hippo, and crocodiles lying like driftwood on the floodplain's muddy margin. Dry brown grass, on red-brown sand; and grey mountains, behind. A strange landscape – sinister even, to the unaccustomed eye.

Crocodiles are one of the Nyamuni's – Kariba's – defining features. There is, on average, one mature crocodile for every two hundred yards of shoreline, which is an extraordinarily high density for a top predator of any description. It says a good deal about Kariba's abundance of fish and wildlife.

A fair-sized specimen is hauling out onto the floodplain. I draw Sal's attention to it. It noses up to the bank, then lies immobile for a minute or two before crawling out with a ponderously sinuous motion. The scales on its dark olive back glisten wetly: its greenish-amber eyes slowly close, but open at every tiny sound or movement. Unconcerned impala glance at it briefly, then go on grazing. 'They know it's not hunting, don't they?' Sal says.

We've watched a glutted male lion stroll right through a herd of impala before now, and out the other side. Again, the impala watched alertly, but unfazed. You know where you are with elephants and rhinos, and even with buffalo and lions. At least you can see them when they're pondering your right to life or otherwise, and get a good idea of what they're thinking, even if it's not particularly reassuring.

The crocodile you can see isn't thinking very much, except possibly about getting warm in the sun. It's the ones

311

you can't see that you've got to worry about. I've seen how they can move when they've a mind to. Once, at Mana, I surprised one basking on the edge of a shallow channel and watched it as it lunged into the water, then flattened its legs against its sides and reached – I would say – possibly 20 miles an hour underwater with a couple of sweeps of its tail.

I may have been towed around the Nyamuni like live bait by a berserk raft, but I've never had a major 'crocodile experience', for which I'm profoundly thankful. Not many people do, and survive. Crocodiles are one of the most efficient predators in nature.

Risk and reward. It's a favourite theme: one of the reasons, Sal and I have often remarked, why we're still in Zimbabwe. But there's a sense of an era ending in the country's wild places, too. I don't mean possible threats to wildlife, such as poaching, important as they are. I'm talking about the mental attitudes we'll probably import along with the tourists, when they start to come back.

Maybe we're the last to enjoy the kind of freedom we're enjoying now. You're happy to sit for days on end in the Matusadona, in a flimsy plywood sailboat surrounded by hippos? Suit yourself. You want to wander the banks, talking to trees and inhaling the heady aroma of elephant dung? That's fine. You want to fall off rafts into creeks full of crocodiles? Go ahead. It's your right to get yourself killed in your own way, however absurd.

Increasingly, though, everything's got to be safe. It started with that electric fence on Fothergill, to pre-empt the lawsuits. We're still allowed to wander around Mana Pools on our own, but I wonder how long it'll last. One or two tourists have got themselves killed.

And the wilderness is in danger of being turned into virtual reality, not only safe, but carefully packaged for people accustomed to instant gratification. Television tells them that the African wilderness is an endless parade of charging elephants, stampeding herds of antelopes, and lions dragging buffaloes down in clouds of dust.

I've seen a few stampeding antelopes in thirty-odd years, granted; but I've only witnessed one seriously charging elephant, and I've never seen a lion kill anything at all. Manufacturing all these spectacles for tourists on a three-day visit isn't going to be easy, but you can bet someone's going to try. It'll be safe, of course. They'll probably put the tourists in an air-conditioned bus with plate-glass windows. It'll be just like the telly.

But it isn't the seeing that's so important. It's the being in, with its heightened awareness, occasional hazards and constant mental rewards. Sal and I prefer to weigh up our own risks and be responsible for our own lives. Falling off rafts into crocodile-infested rivers pushes the envelope a bit, but that's not the point. It's my life.

Trivial concerns, maybe: but what will all the safe, virtual-reality people do when disaster cannot be averted by the click of a mouse-button or a TV remote? Climate change looms over us like a Matusadona thunderstorm, gathering strength for its swoop down from the hills to engulf us. Will the parks, the rhinos, the cheetahs survive at all, whatever we do? Will we survive?

Sometimes I have to fight a sense of futility and impotence in the face of overwhelming forces. Not long ago I came across a lost buffalo-calf – a tiny, browny-black, wide-eyed little thing, about the size of a smallish Labrador – while I was wandering around in the mopane woodlands behind the Mana floodplains.

For reasons I now find inexplicable, I knelt down and tried to make a sound like a buffalo-calf's mum, a sort of rising guttural 'MnwaAH!'

The calf pricked up its little ears and trotted towards me.

'MnwaAH,' I went again. The calf trotted closer, then stopped. I tried again.

'MnwAAH!'

The calf studied me carefully, then went from nought to 60 in about two seconds. It hit me amidships, knocked me flat on my back, tore on without breaking its stride and vanished into the mopanes.

That's what you get when you mess around too much with things you don't understand: climate, forests, oceans, or just little lost buffalo calves, which probably weren't lost at all.

The crocodile lies motionless on the sand. The fish eagles are duetting, high in a thermal, barely visible as tiny dots in the sky; closer to earth a grey and white pied kingfisher hovers over the water in a motionless whirring of wings, head down, looking for fish. It folds its wings, plummets 30 feet into the water like a champion high-diver, making barely a ripple: then emerges and flies away with a tiny fish in its beak.

I look at the crocodile again, and it acquires a strangely reassuring symbolism: the survivor. During our idyllic holiday in Muzarabani, just before the farm invasions turned everything upside-down, Sal and I had turned down a tiny track marked by a small pyramid of dead branches. The track didn't carry enough traffic to be corrugated, so it had become eroded instead.

We bumped and bounced the old Land Rover through water-worn gullies and down miniature cliffs; across riverbeds and through thickets where the track was barely discernible. It got fainter and fainter, until at last it petered out on the edge of a steep little river.

The riverbed was rippled by wavelets, cast in stone, that once plashed on the shores of an ancient lake where dinosaurs meandered in the shallows. Their footprints – big ones, little ones, babies – weaved in intricate patterns across the riverbed. Beside them lay piles of fresh elephant dung.

Through the Looking-Glass

In the Zambezi Valley, elephants and dinosaurs walk the same territory, separated by 200 million years. There was life here then; and there's life here now.

The dinosaurs disappeared in a turmoil of climatic upheaval, but some tiny mammals weathered the chaos. Many millions of years later, they evolved into elephants.

One of those tiny mammals also evolved into us humans, of course, which will probably turn out to be bad news for the elephants. But there were crocodiles as well as dinosaurs, 200 million years ago. They didn't become extinct. They've survived unchanged, through all those storms of time.

We'll go the way of the dinosaurs if we get it wrong. We'll probably take the elephants with us when we go, and most other things as well, but something else'll evolve in 50 million years or so. Maybe it'll have an asbestos exoskeleton, a metabolism based on carbon dioxide, and a silicon superbrain. Pity I couldn't leave a footprint in the sandstone riverbed for it to moralise over, before it screws up the planet and everything has to start all over again.

Everything, that is, except the crocodile. There he lies, on the Nyamuni sandbank, the survivor. He's probably good for another 200 million years.

The heat begins to go out of the sun. The last of the breeze dies, and the water falls calm. The big crocodile slips into the water; we see his craggy eyes and nostrils and an occasional hint of tail, cruising through the water, then he sinks without a ripple: gone hunting.

I am doing nothing very much, just watching the drowned trees turn to white-hot steel and fade to glowing orange, when something happens. I have come to call it the 'looking-glass effect' because, like Alice, I pass, totally involuntarily, through the looking-glass. ZESA and the gurgling geysers are forgotten, evaporating like fragments of fantastic dreams, as I enter a new reality. The previously flat, two-dimensional scene, of which I have been a detached observer, suddenly acquires a stunning depth and vibrancy. I am no longer looking at things. I am inside them and experiencing them.

I have a sense of mental expansion, of sending out fingers of thought which, like the figs on the red cliffs at my back, take root and draw nourishment from the interstices in which they find a foothold. Everything comes into sharp focus. It doesn't matter if the lagoon is crammed with elephants and impala, or temporarily but totally devoid of spectacular wildlife: there is a hum of activity about the place, of life going energetically about its business, doing what it must to survive and adapt.

And I am – at last – back in touch with the things that have inspired me since I embarked on these adventures, almost 30 years ago. That's why I come here as often as I can: to remind myself that the things I've done, and hope to do, are worthwhile, after all. And that sense of futility is, I realize, an impermissible selfishness.

Things go more easily, after that. The crate of food stays right-side-up, and the cooler-box yields up the Chateau Cardboard without a fight. This latter item undertakes a half-hearted rearguard action – the plastic tap, as ever, is buried in folds of silver bladder, stubbornly refuses to fit the slot provided and then squirts sideways into my lap instead of downwards into the glass – but it gives up in the end.

There's a sudden commotion in the bush, beyond the floodplain: a squealing and trumpeting of irritated elephants and a long, slow growl, deep in the trunk.

'Driving off a lion?' Sal says expectantly.

The Matusadona lions hunt elephant calves sometimes, and sometimes they succeed, but not often. Those matriarch elephants don't give them many chances. Besides, we haven't heard lions calling yet.

A grey shape appears on the edge of the bush, too low for elephant, not black enough for buffalo.

Rhino.

He raises his great head, and sniffs the air, ears twitching and oscillating like radar scanners. Then he slowly, measuredly, paces across the grass and down to the water. Another pause, to scent the air. A movement catches his short-sighted eye: an inquisitive impala. He takes several steps towards it, snorting and tossing his horns which, I note, have grown long and full. The impala retreats.

The rhino turns back to the water, sniffs again, and drinks. His back is streaked with the droppings of the oxpeckers. They fly up and at us, chittering, but the rhino ignores them.

We've probably met before. Mbizi? Madonna? Number Sixty-One? Another of the ten hand-reared rhinos, or of the 14 we'd caught in Chizarira? No idea, and it doesn't matter. He's there, and that's the thing.

He stands for a while when he's finished drinking, lost in what always looks like deep philosophical thought but is probably nothing more than wondering whether to have a wallow in the mud or get back at the mopane-shrubs. Finally he wanders back into the bush, ridiculous piggy-like tail flicking absently from side to side, and disappears.

The dikkops call, *TIEEU, TIEU, tieu, teu-teu-teu*, from the jumble of stones at the feet of the red cliffs. The water turns to indigo, then black; the last of the afterglow lingers in the western sky; and fades.

We relax quietly a while, revelling in the pleasure of simply being. At length – 'Chicken curry?'

'Mmm.' Heat and eat: we usually manage three or four pre-cooked meals before going on to the tins and salami. I light the candle-lamp and hang it from the boom. We don't have electrics on *Giselle*. The tiny yellow flame flickers in its glass bowl and swings gently as we move about the boat.

There's a fluttering sound from my wine glass. I hold it up to the light. As I thought: a mopane moth. Mopane moths are unredeemable alcoholics. It's clinging to the inside of the glass, head down, drinking avidly. I lift it out with a finger: it flies up, erratically, and is instantly nailed by a bat that comes swooping through the rigging. That's what mopane moths get when they mess around with things they don't understand.

We finish our supper, clear away the debris, and make our bed on *Giselle's* decks.

'Blow the candle out, love,' Sal says, 'we don't need it any more.' A billion stars blaze forth in the sky above. Orion marches overhead, and there's the Southern Cross, low on the horizon; and the Jewel Box, a sparkling king's ransom of emeralds and diamonds, reflected in the still water below.

The air is laden with the scent of tamarinds, leadwoods and raintrees, mingled with dry leaves and a hint of elephant dung. Nightjars flutter past like ragged black handkerchiefs, and there's a little Scops owl, calling in the woodlands.

Now we hear the distant lions, far away in the bush; and occasional plashings in the shallows as the crocodiles hunt the fat, slow-moving barbel. And as our eyes accustom themselves to the starlight, we see the dim silhouettes of elephants against the skyline, and of hippos grazing, with the slow *rrrip-rrrip-rrrip* of grass being torn from its moorings.

If we – mankind – can build a dam and make something as lovely as the Matusadona by accident, what couldn't we do if we tried?

Slowly, the bush falls silent. The velvet Zambezi Valley night enfolds us, and we drift into sleep.

www.summersdale.com